THE POWER AND THE STORY

ALSO BY EVAN CORNOG

Hats in the Ring: An Illustrated History of
American Presidential Campaigns (with Richard Whelan)

The Birth of Empire:
DeWitt Clinton and the American Experience, 1769–1828

THE
POWER
AND THE
STORY

HOW THE CRAFTED
PRESIDENTIAL NARRATIVE HAS
DETERMINED POLITICAL SUCCESS
FROM GEORGE WASHINGTON
TO GEORGE W. BUSH

EVAN CORNOG

THE PENGUIN PRESS

NEW YORK

2004

THE PENGUIN PRESS
a member of
Penguin Group (USA) Inc.
375 Hudson Street
New York, New York 10014

Excerpt from *Camelot,* by Alan Lerner and Frederick Loewe. © 1960, 1961
(Renewed) Alan Jay Lerner and Frederick Loewe. All rights administered
by Chappell & Co. All rights reserved. Used by permission.
Warner Bros. Publications Inc., Miami, FL 33014.

Library of Congress Cataloging-in-Publication Data

Cornog, Evan.
The power and the story : how the crafted presidential narrative has determined
political success from George Washington to George W. Bush / Evan Cornog.
p.   cm.
Includes bibliographical references and index.
ISBN 1-59420-022-X
1. Presidents—United States—History.   2. Political oratory—United States—
History.   3. Self-presentation—Political aspects.   I. Title.
JK511.C67 2004
973'.09'9—dc22   2004044462

This book is printed on acid-free paper. ♾

Printed in the United States of America
1   3   5   7   9   10   8   6   4   2

Designed by Stephanie Huntwork

For Lauren

CONTENTS

THE POWER AND THE STORY

INTRODUCTION

"I SHALL GO TO KOREA," SAID DWIGHT D. EISENHOWER ON OCTOBER 24, 1952, with the presidential election just eleven days away. The Korean War had been under way for more than two years and peace negotiations for more than a year when he made the statement. The Republican nominee's promise had impact because of Ike's stature as a military leader—the great architect of victory in Europe, the first commander of NATO. The statement invoked both past stories—about his wartime leadership and his skill as warrior and diplomatist—and the prospective story of the promised trip. It appealed to voters because Americans, weary of the war, believed that Ike's very presence in Korea would lead more quickly to peace. His Democratic opponent, Adlai Stevenson, had considered issuing such a statement himself but dismissed it as grandstanding. The truth is that such a promise from Stevenson would have meant far less than it did coming from Eisenhower. Ike's statement mobilized a powerful set of stories in aid of his candidacy and helped ensure his decisive victory in that year's race.[1]

The essence of American presidential leadership, and the secret of presidential success, is storytelling. From the earliest days of the American republic to the present, those seeking the nation's highest office have had to tell persuasive stories—about the nation, about its problems, and, most of all, about themselves—to those who have the power to elect them. Once a president is in office, the ability to tell the right story, and to change the story as necessary, is crucial to the success of his administration. And once a president has left office, through either defeat or retirement, he often spends his remaining years working to ensure that the story as he sees it is the one accepted by history. Without a good story, there is no power, and no glory.

From George Washington on, the success of every president has depended on his ability to build consensus for his narrative, and to persuade the press and the people to accept his story line. It is through such narratives that presidents capture the public imagination and build the support they need in order to govern. Such stories have meaning, they have lessons and morals. They connect a politician with both the issues of his time and with the hearts and minds of the voters. And a successful presidential life story connects with people as people, on a very human and emotional level, creating a link that makes voters care about what happens to a distant politician, just as we care what happens to a sympathetic character in a movie. These crafted narratives are the principal medium of exchange of our public life, the currency of American politics.

There are all kinds of presidential life stories, because there are all kinds of stories. The word "story" can refer to the course of a person's entire life or a single moment in that life, to factual narratives and fictitious ones, and can even suggest a lie (or a "tall story"). In the political arena stories may be advanced by a presidential candidate or by his opponent, or might first appear in a journalistic account such as a newspaper article. Presidential narratives can be lengthy and complex (as when expressed in a campaign biography) or quick and crude (Herbert Hoover caused the Great Depression). Stories can be promulgated through many media and can be told in a variety of forms, from straightforward exposition to the highly economical and emotionally charged form of a symbol (William Henry Harrison's log cabin, William McKinley's full dinner pail, the mug shot of Willie Horton).

Stories work and stories matter because they are fundamental to the way we understand the world. As children we hear stories that teach us where we came from, what our family duties are, how we fit into a larger society, what our place is in the cosmos. Religions explain the will of God principally through stories, not through laws and rules (although these, too, are important). Stories, we discover, have morals, lessons that we can incorporate into our understanding of life. The tale of Moses underlines the importance of ancestry, and that of David Copperfield helps us to navigate the hazards of youth. The example of Jane Austen's Elizabeth Bennet shows how to select a mate, and Henry James's Isabel Archer demonstrates how not to. Prince Hal's growth into Henry V is a guidebook for those who would wield power, and Lear's end provides a tragic lesson on the difficulties of relinquishing it. A president's life story is laid out against a background that contains all these struggles and countless others. By connecting his own story to these ready-made points of reference from literature and history, a presidential candidate can add depth and context to his own life story, magnifying his own stature in the process.

Stories not only help us comprehend the world, they help us remember what we have learned. Life itself is too complex to comprehend without being reduced to more manageable dimensions. Stories are the tools we all use to bring order to chaos. Stories are where facts gain meaning. We all instinctively appreciate the power of stories. Religion, literature, cinema, and advertising exploit this power, and so do politicians. Journalists, too, appreciate this power—indeed, for many it is the reward that compensates them for long workdays and poor pay.

Although the power of stories is present in politics around the world, it is particularly strong in the United States. As a nation, the

United States has always lacked the sort of linguistic or geographical rationale that helped create older nations. Its sense of nationhood, and of individual citizenship, was founded on a set of political ideals, ideals that are communicated through stories—stories about first settlement and religious freedom, stories about the struggle for independence and political freedom, stories about the overthrow of slavery and other forms of oppression that limited personal freedom. Also, because the Founding Fathers chose a presidential rather than a parliamentary system, the choice of the head of government has been subject to a national vote of the people rather than the choice of a leader by a political party in parliament. So candidates for the presidency had to find ways to make themselves appealing to large numbers of voters. They had to create and circulate stories that would attract the attention and engage the affections of the entire nation.

Over time, the kinds of stories that are politically acceptable, the ways those stories can be told, and the role and power of the press have changed. Presidential storytelling is more important than ever in today's media-driven political world, where presidential campaigns have come to be focused upon personality and the contest itself, rather than upon issues and ideology. But even though presidential life stories have come to be more and more carefully edited and presented, the core of the story has to be true or it will not work. The public can tolerate artifice—it's part of our daily media diet—but it cannot abide deception. The successful president is one who best understands the rules under which the game proceeds in his time and who advances his life story most effectively.

Politicians' life stories are played out on a stage that contains the same kinds of characters that populate great works of fiction and drama. These stories take advantage of the public fascination with the doings of the powerful, and of how presidential politics has helped to fashion our current cult of celebrity. Looking at presidential politics as a contest of narratives has a tremendous explanatory power—it explains why Ronald Reagan succeeded at being the "Teflon president," why the Monica Lewinsky affair did not shatter the Clinton presidency, and why a humble background helps some candidates (Lincoln, Truman) and a privileged one helps others (Madison, FDR, George W. Bush).

It also demonstrates the relative unimportance of truth. A good story trumps a true story almost any day, and so Washington's hacked cherry tree and William Henry Harrison's log cabin remain part of the national lore, though they never existed. The press, by showing conclusively that a story is false, can destroy its effectiveness. This is the source of the press's power. But candidates have learned to harness the power of narrative and have found ways to take their stories to the electorate without the intermediation of the press.

For all the campaign talk about résumés and experience, issues and qualifications, it is the battle of stories, not the debate on issues, that determines how Americans respond to a presidential contender. Candidates' stories can predispose the press to trouble a contender over every error or give him great indulgence, to anatomize his personal life or leave privacy intact, to probe motives or unquestioningly report actions. The play's the thing that advances the agenda of the king.

The presidential scholar Richard Neustadt argued that the essence of presidential power is the power to persuade. Rhetoric is the art of persuasion, and stories are the vessels of rhetoric. Presidential life stories are the most important tools of persuasion in American political life. Crucial to the success of any rhetorical strategy is the creation of a sense of identification between the protagonist and his audience. This can be done crudely—a candidate visiting Chicago mentions that he studied at a college there, or that his wife was born there—or more subtly, through how a candidate dresses, how he speaks, how he acts. Jimmy Carter tried to create a bond with the American people by carrying his own luggage and by wearing a cardigan to demonstrate that he was turning down the thermostat to save energy in the White

House, just as he was asking all Americans to do. It was not a very effective gambit, but it has become part of presidential lore. Long after a president is dead and buried, the stories he animated live on. They are incorporated over and over into new narratives of persuasion by the final arbiters of presidential careers, historians.

Historians and journalists are rhetoricians, too, and seek to establish a bond with their readers, to forge ways for the reader to identify with the writer—to see what he or she has seen, and then to trust the judgments arrived at and the conclusions reached. Of course, historians and journalists are supposed to be dedicated to the discovery of the truth, not to the dissemination of propaganda, and just because there are elements of persuasion embedded in historical and journalistic writing does not mean that their objective is false. After all, once a writer has discovered the truth as he or she sees it, it is natural to try to persuade others of the rightness of those views. As long as the evidence is not tampered with and the desire to tell a good story does not interfere with telling a true story, no harm is done. But the tug of narrative is strong, and many an untrue story survives simply because it is entertaining.

When writing stories about politics, journalists are subject to the suasion of politicians and their handlers. After the 1988 election, many in the press felt they had been manipulated by the well-choreographed activities of George H. W. Bush's campaign, hoodwinked by Lee Atwater and Roger Ailes, Bush's strategy and communications gurus. The press plays a vital role in determining the efficacy of different rhetorical strategies. It hardly matters, after all, whether a candidate and his team have devised a persuasive story line if nobody ever hears it. And it is largely the press that determines that. This is why much of the energy of a modern campaign, or of a presidential administration, is dedicated to ensuring that one's own stories make it into the press and that opposing narratives are relegated to the sidelines. The more effectively a politician can define the terms of a debate, the more likely his success. When Richard Nixon spoke of the "silent majority" in a 1969 address to the nation, he was explicitly contrasting the many Americans who did not protest with a vocal minority that appeared with regularity on the nightly news and in the morning papers. Nixon defined the situation in a way that delivered victory to himself— because those who were silent were anointed as the majority. The speech both used the press to deliver its message and undermined the press (whose practitioners were the ones, after all, devoting headlines to the protesters). The term "silent majority" successfully established itself in public discourse, doing its master's bidding faithfully.

But the very power of stories can also pose grave problems for candidates. Presidents become trapped in the stories they have told (or that have been told about them); the logic of the narrative eclipses other realities. Nobody stands outside this process. Stories shape not only our reactions to what presidents do but the courses of action presidents themselves decide to pursue. Franklin Roosevelt looked at the story of his distant cousin Teddy's rise to the presidency—from election to the New York State legislature to service as assistant secretary of the navy, then on to the governor's mansion in Albany and eventually the White House—and chose to pursue the same path. He managed to touch every base. George W. Bush's stance toward Iraq was shaped by his own relationship with his presidential father and his father's experience of making war on Saddam Hussein. How strong was his desire to rewrite the ending of his father's narrative? In recent years, some politicians seem to have lived their entire lives calculating how each choice they make might affect their ultimate electability— Bill Clinton and Al Gore come to mind.

For journalists (and voters), well-crafted or familiar narratives often provide convenient substitutes for thought. Rather than trying to understand the complex vectors of a new scandal, one may simply add "-gate" to a convenient word and all political chicanery is leveled, whether it involves a fundamental perversion of the Constitution or a petty exercise of patronage power. And the attention of both press and public can be diverted; too many times, the power of a gesture or a joke outweighs the power of truth.

Stories are not, of course, the whole story. It matters how much money a campaign has to spend—not least because it principally spends that money to disseminate its most important stories. It matters what a candidate's positions on the issues are, even if a campaign mostly stresses just a few issues that have tested well in surveys of likely voters. It matters whether the candidate is handsome or ugly, thin or fat, black or white. But it is the power of stories that determines how much these things matter.

The Power and the Story traces the history of presidential storytelling by following the trajectory of an archetypal career of a man of power. My intention is to explore the role of stories in the interplay of politicians, the press, and the public as a career evolves from the politician's first emergence as a public figure through his rise to national prominence, the presidential campaign, the exercise of power, reelection or defeat, and then his efforts to reinterpret and redefine the story until his death.

American politicians have been crafting narratives for more than two centuries. But the power of stories has been taken for granted, something recognized but not explained, acknowledged but not explored. This book attempts to explore and explain this central fact of American political life, ranging over the entire life span of the American presidency, and ending with an examination of the various stories that have shaped the career of President George W. Bush—including his own Ike-like journey to a war zone, the surprise trip to Baghdad for Thanksgiving 2003, which gave Bush a brief, but real, bump in popularity. Along the way, I hope to show how more than two centuries of practice have refined the level of presidential storytelling into a political art of the greatest sophistication and importance.

CHAPTER ONE

AMERICAN HEROES,
AMERICAN MYTHS

B ADLY BURNED IN THE FIRE THAT HAD RESULTED FROM THE RAM-
ming of his boat by a Japanese destroyer, Pat McMahon had been
in the water for four hours. The sea was warm, but McMahon was
afraid of sharks—he'd seen plenty of them in his patrols in these waters—and he was in great pain. He wore a kapok life jacket, the straps
of which were held in the clenched teeth of the officer who was tow-
ing him toward shore. After more than four hours of swimming, Lieutenant John F. Kennedy was spent, so tired he could hardly pull his
shipmate. As he finally reached the shore of Plum Pudding Island, he
collapsed with his feet still in the water and his face in the sand. Despite the burns on his hands and arms, McMahon tried to drag
Kennedy ashore, pleading with his commander to hide himself behind the bushes that would conceal them from any passing Japanese
patrol boats. Kennedy managed to crawl forward, and soon the rest of
his crew, who had followed in his wake as he towed McMahon, struggled ashore and took cover. A few minutes later, a Japanese patrol boat
did cruise by, but its crew failed to spot the exhausted American
sailors.[1]

In the pre-dawn hours of August 1, 1943, the Japanese destroyer *Amagiri* (Heavenly Mist) had rammed PT-109, the patrol torpedo boat Kennedy commanded in the Solomon Islands during the Second World War. Two members of Kennedy's crew had been crushed to death instantly, and the *Amagiri*'s prow had sliced through the boat only a few feet away from Kennedy's spot in the cockpit. The lieutenant gathered the surviving members of his crew on the still-floating prow of PT-109, but it was apparent that the hulk would either sink or, failing that, attract the attention of the Japanese. So Kennedy had decided to lead his men to Plum Pudding Island, a tiny speck a hundred yards long by seventy wide. JFK hastily chose it as the destination because it was both large enough to conceal his ten surviving men and small enough not to have a Japanese garrison stationed there.[2]

But relief from the immediate peril of drowning or capture by the Japanese did not end the plight of the crew. Kennedy soon decided that the island was too far away from the normal path of American PT boats in the area to be able to signal for rescue, so he led his men on another, shorter swim to the larger island of Naru (or, as Kennedy thought, Nauro). There they were fortunate to encounter two natives who were providing the allies with intelligence about Japanese activities. On the husk of a coconut Kennedy carved the message NAURO ISL NATIVE KNOWS POSIT HE CAN PILOT 11 ALIVE NEED SMALL BOAT KENNEDY and asked the natives to take it to their Allied contact. His message worked: rescuers were dispatched, and on August 8, a week after the sinking of PT-109, Kennedy and his crew returned to their base on Rendova Island in the Solomons.[3]

The story of Kennedy's heroism formed a crucial chapter of his biography when he ran for president in 1960. Survivors of the action appeared with Kennedy during the fall campaign, and then rode on a PT-109 float in the inaugural parade. Kennedy's story had become widely known long before the campaign, because he came from a prominent family (his father, the Boston businessman Joseph P.

Kennedy, had been chosen by President Franklin D. Roosevelt in 1937 to be ambassador to Great Britain).

After the rescue was complete the story appeared in papers such as the *Boston Herald* and the *New York Times,* and in 1944 John Hersey chronicled Kennedy's PT-109 exploits in *The New Yorker.* Hersey's piece opened casually, saying that Kennedy (identified as "the ex-Ambassador's son") "came through town the other day and told me the story of his survival in the South Pacific. I asked Kennedy if I might write the story down." Not surprisingly, his answer was yes. He urged Hersey to talk to his crew, which the reporter did. The resulting article portrayed Kennedy in heroic terms, describing his physical sufferings and making clear his leadership qualities. When his men despaired of ever being rescued, "Kennedy was still unwilling to admit that things were hopeless." It was a glowing portrait, a useful asset for a young man headed toward a career in politics.[4]

THE LEADING MAN ENTERS

The stories we like best contain heroes. Heroes' stories have many elements, but there is almost always a moment of emergence, an event that sets them apart from others and marks them as extraordinary—Hercules strangling the serpents in his crib, or Einstein revolutionizing the world of physics from his post in the Bern patent office. Such events establish a sort of origin myth for the protagonist, defining the person's character and marking him as a person to be watched. For a politician, such a story provides an invaluable head start over the competition, rendering him both admirable and memorable at the same time.

Having found their stories, such men advance in politics because they understand how to build on them, to burnish their existing reputations, presenting themselves to the world in a flattering light, and allowing that which is best about them to be seen. There's great power in this, because stories are fundamental to how we perceive the world. "Stories," after all, are what newspaper reporters write and television news broadcasts. And voters, awash in the complexity of current events, use stories as their means of boiling down complicated realities to simple choices. Our minds just naturally organize information in the form of stories, sorting the disparate data that reach our senses and constructing stories as a way to retain and make sense of it all. Out of the swirl of events and issues, we find good guys and bad guys, winners and losers, and make our choices accordingly.

American heroes such as George Washington, Andrew Jackson, Thomas Jefferson, Abraham Lincoln, and John F. Kennedy have had stories of emergence to set them apart. Their stories demonstrated enough appeal and staying power to become part of the national myth—not myths as stories that are fabulous or untrue, but rather as tales that embody popular ideas on social phenomena. Just as Greek myths taught their audience lessons about the importance of filial duty or the hazards of vanity, and the stories in the New Testament encourage acceptance of Christianity, American political myths portray the nation's history in ways that promote loyalty to the nation and reverence for its highest principles.

To work, stories need heroes, individuals whose experiences reveal truths about life, whose sufferings make us feel pain and sorrow, whose victories fill us with happiness and pride. Any person aspiring to be president of the United States must to some extent fulfill these narrative expectations. A person to whose fate we are indifferent, or even hostile, will scarcely inspire us to follow his lead. But the character who inspires trust and admiration will find it easier to capture the voters' interest and steer a nation through hard times.

For the presidential aspirant to have a chance, he must first be noticed. He requires a point of entry onto the national stage, an event that separates him from others and brings him to prominence. Such stories of emergence are not self-creating. They arise out of the way a person structures his life and circumstances, the way credit is given and taken, and the way the press plays the story. As the narrative develops, there are moments of risk. Those unwilling to take the risks or who muff their chances do not remain in the game.

To be sure, not all presidential contenders have dramatic moments of emergence. Few get the opportunity for heroism that Kennedy encountered, and fewer still take advantage of the opportunities they do receive. But when a man makes a grand first impression on the public stage, it helps mark him as a leader. It can also provide a vivid first chapter of a life that eventually seems to fit the role of president. A good origin myth takes a contender a long way. And over the long span of American politics, the most useful origin myths have been stories of military leadership and heroism in war.

MASTERS OF WAR

The tradition of the military hero as president was begun by Washington and revived by Jackson, and has dominated long stretches of electoral history. The military hero has the advantage of a role that goes back thousands of years. He follows in the steps of David and Joshua, Achilles and Hector, Caesar and Charlemagne, El Cid and Drake. With such a rich background, every gesture can be freighted with meaning, every incident has historically charged parallels. Such reference points create a compelling story and make the job of the press that much easier—the formula of the narrative is ready at hand, serving the convenience of reporters and attracting the attention of voters.

The North American frontier of the 1750s was a violent place, the point of intersection of four strong forces—the imperial designs of France and Britain, the expansionist aims of American colonists, and the self-interests of the Native American peoples of the region. Three major wars had already engulfed the frontier in the preceding half century. In the spring of 1754, the actions of a small force under the command of twenty-two-year-old Major George Washington, adjutant general of the Virginia militia, would help to ignite the last, and largest, of these imperial conflicts in North America.

Although most residents of the thirteen British colonies in North America lived within a hundred miles of the Atlantic, land speculators and other optimists foresaw a continuing push into the interior. Powerful Virginians were speculating in western lands (Washington himself had investments), and word that the French were making forays into these lands led to the organization of an expedition by Virginia's royal governor, Robert Dinwiddie (his actual title was lieutenant governor, the top post being a sinecure held in absentia by Lord Albemarle). The danger and misery of travel in the remote interior discouraged many would-be commanders. George Washington was young, fit, and ambitious, and his connections sufficiently good to get him a job few others wanted. A terrific horseman, Washington looked every inch the military leader, and his troops followed him deep into what is now Pennsylvania on a diplomatic mission to the French. In the fall of 1753 he set off, and after many hardships he reached the French position at Fort Le Boeuf. There the French commander politely rejected Dinwiddie's ultimatum that they leave, and Washington struggled home to report the unsatisfactory response. Dinwiddie ordered Washington to prepare an account of the encounter for publication. Washington wanted time to polish his prose, but Dinwiddie ordered it rushed into print. Published early in 1754 as *The Journal of Major George Washington,* the report created a stir in the colonies and in London, where the young major's readers included King George II himself.

Dinwiddie then dispatched Washington on another mission into the interior, this time with a broader mandate: Washington was to warn the French to leave, and if they persisted in defying Dinwiddie's wishes, he was to attack. An important part of any such military mission in those days was to ally with local Indians, who provided additional fighting men, knowledge of the terrain, and tactical guidance. Washington's allies on this trip were Mingo warriors under Tanaghrisson, the Half-King (as the British called him). The Half-King was a more experienced warrior than the young Washington, and although the Virginian was nominally in command, his stance toward the Half-King was more deferential than imperious. Washington depended on the Half-King for advice and support and had to be careful not to offend his ally.

It was an awkward position for any leader, and Washington was not equal to the challenge. His orders stated that when he located the French he was to order them out of British territory (as London saw it) and give fair warning before initiating hostilities. Washington's detachment spotted a French force under Joseph Coulon de Villiers de Jumonville. The Half-King, schooled in the harsh realities of frontier combat, persuaded his young ally to launch a surprise attack, rather than proceeding according to Dinwiddie's orders. On May 28, 1754, Washington's forces attacked Jumonville's small detachment, and the French quickly surrendered. Then the real horror began. The Half-King walked up to Jumonville and, brandishing his hatchet, hacked the Frenchman's skull open. He then plunged his hands into Jumonville's brains and washed them in his adversary's blood. The Half-King's warriors set out to massacre the surviving French, and were only prevented from completing the job when Washington's Virginians interposed their own bodies between the Mingoes and the French.[5]

The Half-King's actions were not just acts of senseless violence, according to the historian Fred Anderson, whose book *Crucible of War* offers the best account of the incident. Rather, the Half-King wished to antagonize the French to force a war in which Britain would have to support his efforts to control the Mingoes and claim certain disputed territories. He was manipulating Washington to advance his own geopolitical interests, and Washington could do nothing to prevent it.[6]

The French soon learned of the murder of Jumonville, and the slain officer's brother, Louis Coulon de Villiers, was sent to command a retributive expedition. The French caught up with Washington at an ill-conceived position the Virginian had staked out in a meadow surrounded by hills. Fort Necessity, as it was named, was an easy target for the French force, and the French spent a day firing down on the exposed Virginians from protected positions on the hillsides. Eventually they offered a deal to Washington—surrender, give back the prisoners captured in the attack in which Jumonville died, and the Americans would be permitted to go home, with their honor (and weapons) intact. Washington had to sign a document in French that included the admission—which Washington's translator mistranslated—that Jumonville had been "assassinated" in the earlier encounter. Washington signed, and this admission of culpability helped cloud the issue of which side had "started" what became the French and Indian War in America, and expanded into the global contest called the Seven Years War.

So, at the age of twenty-two, Washington was a national, even international, figure. His writings had been published on both sides of the Atlantic, and an action in which he had played a central role had ignited a vast war. As he walked away from the ill-chosen site of Fort Necessity, he was dejected and filled with the awareness of his own failure. The date was July 4, 1754, and as Francis Parkman observed in his nineteenth-century account of the incident, "He could not foresee that he was to make that day forever glorious to a new-born nation hailing him as its father."[7]

Washington's performance was hardly brilliant, but he showed courage and perseverance, and the prominence he had earned made him a leading military figure among the colonists and helped clear the path for his appointment as commander of the Continental Army two decades later. In that larger role, too, Washington sometimes made errors and lost battles, but he kept his army in the field against the superior forces of the British and persevered to victory.

Fame came early to Washington as it did to Jack Kennedy, but some men wait many years before bursting onto the national stage. Andrew Jackson was forty-seven years old when his transforming moment came. And, again, it was an act of war that brought him notice. In January 1815, Jackson led an American force to a stunning victory against the British in the Battle of New Orleans. The triumph was entirely unexpected. The previous year had seen a British invasion of Washington, D.C., and the burning of many of the most important buildings there (including the Capitol and the White House). Napoleon's abdication in April 1814 had freed British forces for service in the war against the United States, and a large force had been dispatched to take New Orleans, the vital port for all western trade in those pre-canal, pre-railroad days. With communications agonizingly slow, the cities of the Eastern Seaboard were forced to speculate on what was happening there, and the *New York Evening Post* told its readers that "if an attack has been made on New Orleans, the city has fallen" to the superior British forces. The *Post* ought to have been right—the British forces were superior and should have easily prevailed. And they probably would have, had not their commander, Sir Edward Pakenham, grown impatient with the speed of a flanking force and foolishly ordered a frontal assault on a well-fortified position Jackson had established. Pakenham courageously led the assault and was slain for his trouble. A British naval officer who observed the British Army's effort wrote, "There never was a more complete blunder."[8]

From the American point of view, the story was not about British blundering but about American heroism. Although the victory came two weeks after the treaty ending the War of 1812 was signed at Ghent, news of that accord was slow to reach the United States, and

Jackson's triumph was hugely important to American self-esteem. Regardless of the reason why, Jackson had crushed a battle-hardened British force that had been sent to America from its victories in the Napoleonic wars in Europe. Jackson's victory both showed the potential of American arms and allowed Americans to believe that they had won a war that was, at best, a draw.

Jackson's triumph was undimmed by its context—the lesson Americans wanted to learn was about the majesty of American might, not the folly of a British general—and his countrymen rushed to celebrate his feats. New Orleans, grateful to its deliverer (and thankful that victory had rendered moot Jackson's plan to torch the city rather than allow the British to conquer it intact), gave the Tennessee general and his troops a lavish celebration. Ever a city of sophistication, it naturally turned to the emblems of the ancient world to mark Jackson's triumph. Odes were read, Jackson was crowned with a laurel wreath, and beautiful young women of the city waved flags emblazoned with the names of the different states, all of which were said to owe their continuing independence to Jackson. As news made its way up the East Coast, parades were held, toasts were drunk, and large illuminations of Jackson and his troops—large paintings on translucent material that were lit from behind for impressive nighttime effect—were displayed in Philadelphia. Even the hero's wife, Rachel, was affected; she stopped referring to her husband as "Mr. Jackson" and started calling him "the General."[9]

In response to this adulation, and to the inquiries from the press about his background and character, Jackson asked a supporter named John Reid to write his biography. Reid died before he could get very far, and the book was completed by another Jackson partisan, John Henry Eaton. The Reid/Eaton account presents an energetic Andrew Jackson facing down the British forces and laments that had the national government not been so deficient in supplying the troops, Jackson's victory would have concluded with the wholesale capture of the British Army.

For the balance of Jackson's career, his fame as the vanquisher of the British at New Orleans proved his most valuable political asset. The image of Jackson as conqueror may have been colored with tints drawn from ancient Rome, but his story contained a distinctly American tone, with its emphasis on the untutored forces he commanded (against British regulars) and his frontier toughness, memorialized in the nickname "Old Hickory" bestowed upon him by his troops.

As the military hero became a political leader and presidential contender, Jackson and his followers developed this frontier theme. In 1822 a performer named Noah Ludlow performed a new tune, with lyrics by Samuel Woodworth, called "The Hunters of Kentucky," which recounted the battle:

> *But Jackson he was wide awake, and wasn't scared with trifles,*
> *For well he knew what aim we take with our Kentucky rifles;*
> *So he marched us down to "Cyprus Swamp"; the ground was*
>   *low and mucky;*
> *There stood "John Bull" in martial pomp,* but here was old
>   Kentucky.[10]

This theme would prove one of the most durable in American history, and frontier roots and experiences continued to pay electoral dividends long after the frontier was gone. John Kennedy himself, in accepting the Democratic nomination in 1960, spoke powerfully about the challenges of the "New Frontier" that his generation of Americans faced. But Old Hickory had staked his claim first.

Jackson's ascent to the White House showed how a presidential career could rest upon a single military victory. (In preparation for the 1824 and 1828 presidential races, Eaton modified the book from what had started out as a merely laudatory biography of the general into a worshipful one.) Other presidents followed the example. William Henry Harrison's success at the Battle of Tippecanoe (in 1811, against

Tecumseh's Shawnees and their allies) was largely responsible for his election in 1840, and Teddy Roosevelt's 1898 ride up "San Juan Hill" (actually Kettle Hill) at the head of the Rough Riders during the Spanish-American War established him as a national figure, leading to his nomination as vice president at the Republican Convention of 1900 (to the later regret of the Republican bosses). Many other politicians (including John F. Kennedy) tried to follow in Jackson's footsteps and looked to capitalize on isolated moments of military glory.

Washington, Jackson, and Kennedy all took care to present their stories to the public through intermediaries, all realizing that it was better to have others do the bragging for them. They all fashioned public personas that were in tune with the dominant themes of their origin myths and built on these personas as their careers advanced. Their own life stories in turn drew upon a larger context of heroes in history and fable, so Kennedy's story had its hints of Robinson Crusoe, and Jackson his Roman triumph. These elements possessed a force of their own, imposing their own logic and expectations upon the various audiences they reached. And each of their stories took its place in the larger myth of America, to be drawn upon, appropriated, and modified as later politicians saw fit.

But while acting the part of the battle-tested hero may be the best way to emerge as a political contender, it is not the only way. Others started on their way to the White House not by living their stories but by telling stories.

WORDSMITHS

Thomas Jefferson was just thirty-three years old when, in the spring of 1776, he was selected to draft the Declaration of Independence, an honor that arose in part from the success of his 1774 pamphlet, *A*

Summary View of the Rights of British America, a patriotic effort that denied Parliament's authority in the colonies. The Continental Congress assigned the drafting of the Declaration to a committee of five men, including John Adams and Benjamin Franklin. Adams, as a Massachusetts man, was an impolitic choice to produce a first draft— Massachusetts was the cradle of rebellion against the British, and Adams was seen as an ill-tempered radical by other delegates. Franklin was indisposed by an attack of gout; Jefferson was picked because of his literary gifts and because he was from Virginia, then the most populous and influential state. The Declaration itself in its final form was the product of many hands, and the historian Pauline Maier termed the genesis of the document "an act of group editing that has to be one of the great marvels of history." In Jefferson's later years, his recollection of the contributions of others seems to have faded while his sense of his own primacy grew, and when he began to think about his place in history, he listed the Declaration first among the accomplishments for which he wished to be remembered.[11]

But his career was to have many chapters after this glorious early one. While still in his thirties he was elected governor of Virginia, and although he was criticized for his inept handling of the British invasion of the state during his term in 1781, his career moved forward with alternating achievements in public office (as a member of the Continental Congress, for example, in 1784 he set forth the principles that were adopted three years later in the Northwest Ordinance, which helped set the pattern for the nation's westward expansion) and literary efforts (such as his *Notes on the State of Virginia*—first published, in France, in 1785—a pioneering work that combines history, natural history, and sociology). Jefferson's rhetoric was his greatest asset as a politician, and although the political mores of his era forbade active campaigning, the rhetoric of the Declaration—and its claim that "all men are created equal"—gave Jefferson heightened power in his political battles against the Federalist party. It shielded the slave-owning aristocrat against charges of elitism and helped inspire the have-nots to rally to the side of his party.

In the generation after Jefferson, a rising democratic tide did away with property qualifications for voting and expanded the electorate to include virtually all white males. But if voting rights became almost universal among white men, literacy did not, and the spoken word therefore rose in importance. Campaign rallies, debates, and other opportunities for political oratory increased, along with their importance in the electoral and governing process. With the rise of railroads, improved transportation also meant that a public official or candidate could speak to a large number of voters by riding swiftly from town to town. All of these changes provided new opportunities for a rising figure eager to gain national attention.

It was just such oratorical forums that brought Abraham Lincoln national notice in 1858, when he traveled around Illinois to debate Stephen A. Douglas, the North's leading Democratic politician, in the race for Douglas's seat in the U.S. Senate. A large fee that Lincoln had earned from a case in which he represented the Illinois Central Railroad (and which he had to sue to collect) gave him the financial security he needed to run against Douglas. Lincoln had little record as an orator before 1858, but all that changed on June 16, in Springfield, when the candidate delivered a speech to the Republican state convention that had nominated him. Lincoln and the Republicans had a problem: how to oppose slavery, particularly the spread of slavery into new territories, while avoiding abolitionism, which was still too radical for mainstream politics. If blacks were to be free, voters asked, Where would they live? How would slaveholders be compensated for their lost property? Would freed slaves be allowed to vote? Most disturbing of all: Would they be allowed to marry whites? Such questions put Republican candidates on the defensive.

In his speech, Lincoln shifted the ground of the debate. Whatever the problems of emancipation, the question had to be faced. Agitation on the subject was only growing more heated, Lincoln said, and "it will not cease, until a crisis shall have been reached, and passed."

He went on:

"A House divided against itself cannot stand."

I believe this government cannot endure, permanently half slave and half free. I do not expect the Union to be dissolved—I do not expect the house to fall—but I do expect it will cease to be divided.

It will become all one thing, or all the other.

Either the opponents of slavery, will arrest the further spread of it, and place it where the public mind shall rest in the belief that it is in course of ultimate extinction; or its advocates will push it forward, till it shall become alike lawful in all the States, old as well as new—North as well as South.[12]

When Lincoln had rehearsed the speech for some of his advisers, most had opposed it, but William Henry Herndon, his law partner, said, "Lincoln, deliver that speech as read and it will make you President." (Or so, at least, Herndon later reported, commenting, "At the time I hardly realized the force of my prophecy.") After the speech was delivered, Lincoln and his allies made sure it was carried in the newspapers, and in its correct form.[13]

The speech launched Lincoln's Senate campaign, but the core of that race was the set of seven Lincoln-Douglas debates held between August 21 and October 15. The first debate, in the town of Ottawa, attracted 15,000 spectators, who came in special trains from Chicago and other Illinois cities and towns. The crowd was even larger for a debate at Galesburg. Newspaper coverage of the debates was partisan, as was the custom in the papers of the day, but detailed and vivid. And everyone knew that the papers were as important as the large audiences present. In the debate at Freeport, Stephen Douglas was preparing to begin when a supporter said, "You can't speak yet, Hitt ain't here." Nothing could happen until the shorthand reporter from the *Chicago Tribune* had arrived.[14]

The debates themselves make strenuous reading today, filled as they are with labyrinthine arguments about federal laws and court rulings governing slavery. But for a public immersed in those issues, the debates were compelling reading, and editions of them were widely printed. It was a sign of Lincoln's success that more Republican printers were circulating the exchanges than Democratic ones. A pro-Douglas paper, the *Chicago Times,* tried its best to undercut Lincoln, on one occasion indulging itself in a lengthy comparison with an English rabble-rouser of the seventeenth century, Titus Oates. The labored likening seems to have been undertaken largely so that the paper could cite Thomas Babington Macauley's physical description of Oates—"his forehead low as that of a baboon, his purple cheeks, and his monstrous length of chin"—which the *Times* seemed to think was a clever jab at Lincoln. Lincoln's detractors liked to compare him to an ape, with an implied reference to the supposedly inferior African Americans he was allegedly favoring. That November, the Republicans polled more votes, but unfair legislative apportionment in the state (U.S. senators were elected by vote of the state legislatures until the ratification of the Seventeenth Amendment in 1913) gave the seat to Douglas. Still, the "House Divided" speech and the subsequent coverage of the Lincoln-Douglas debates had raised a hitherto obscure Illinois lawyer to the first rank of Republican politicians.[15]

Many other politicians rose to national prominence thanks to the power of words, sometimes their own, sometimes the words of others deployed in their service. An example of the latter is the Whig and Republican politician William Henry Seward, who served President Lincoln as his secretary of state, and whose career flourished under the care of his brilliant propagandist, Thurlow Weed. Among those who reached the national stage through their oratorical skills were Mario Cuomo, who electrified the 1984 Democratic National Convention with a passionate attack on Reaganism and a defense of party principles, and Hubert Humphrey, whose 1948 convention speech awakened the Democratic party to its responsibilities in the field of civil rights (and helped split the party into northern and southern wings that year).

Indeed, it is part of the logic of the wordsmith's route to (or near) the White House that his words must be deployed in aid of a cause—after all, one could hardly in good taste wax lyrical on the subject of one's own accomplishments. So Jefferson rose on the wings of his pen, which took as its adversary "all forms of tyranny over the minds of men," as he once grandiloquently put it. Lincoln merged the causes of opposition to slavery and love of the Union into an indivisible whole that led to his election, and then to civil war. William Jennings Bryan's oratory gave voice to the sufferings of those left behind by the transformations of the Industrial Revolution in America, and Ronald Reagan was the spokesman of people who felt alienated from the liberal state created by Franklin Roosevelt and expanded by his successors.

BUT THE STORIES enacted by military heroes and those intoned by the masters of the written or spoken word have something in common. In each instance, there is a daunting adversary, and in each case there are obstacles along the path to success. Where Kennedy faced the Japanese Navy, and Jackson the elite of the British Army, Humphrey did battle with the forces of racism within his own party, and Reagan took on an entire network of labor unions, interest groups, and entrenched politicians.

Whether the stories were acted or recited, they all shared the theme of overcoming adversity. It is a paradoxical truth that the very military exploits that establish a heroic reputation often contain rather unheroic, even embarrassing, elements. Kennedy's own adventures, heroic as they surely were, only unfolded after his PT boat was sliced in half by the *Amagiri*. PT boats were fast and maneuverable, so getting run over by a destroyer could be seen as a rather poor showing, in spite of the darkness of the night and the unfamiliarity of the waters. But Kennedy's subsequent achievement in leading the surviving crew members to Plum Pudding Island and eventually to safety has minimized that unfortunate aspect of the narrative. Washington, too, fumbled a bit, losing control of his Indian allies and choosing the indefensible Fort Necessity as his place to confront the French. But such hardships and blunders help make the stories credible and powerful. After all, a story of uninterrupted success is no story at all. One reason Al Gore was such an unsympathetic character is that his life held so little drama—he was elected to the House at age twenty-eight, to the Senate at thirty-six, and to the vice presidency at forty-four. The very fact that he seemed to be (and to feel himself to be) destined for the White House is probably one of the major reasons he did not make it. Americans are willing to accept a certain amount of dynastic succession, but not when it comes with the odor of aristocratic entitlement. Gore seemed at one point in his career to realize this, and he made the story of his son's near fatal car accident a Rubicon in his own personal development. Without such trials, how can the rest of the nation identify with the aspiring president? What would Teddy Roosevelt have been without his childhood illnesses, or Franklin Roosevelt without his polio? John Glenn, the astronaut who became a senator from Ohio, was an impressive man who had conquered tremendous challenges, but he prevailed so easily that it was hard to feel close to him, and voters did not flock to his campaign for the Democratic nomination in 1984. However fine Glenn the man was, his story lacked this vital element—his victories came too easily to make for a good story.

For in the end it is the stories, not the men, that the voters choose. After all, the candidates as persons are much too complex for us to come to understand, particularly given the structure of political campaigns, where everything that is revealed, and everything that is concealed, is done so for a purpose. To simplify matters, campaigns send forth stories to represent the candidates, and voters align themselves with the stories that most appeal to them. Finding the stories that will appeal to just over half the electorate is the art of politics.

MOST CANDIDATES do not emerge as dramatically onto the national stage as Washington, Jackson, Lincoln, or Kennedy. Those who do create life stories that become an integral part of their political identity, establishing a central character trait—heroism, constancy, toughness, eloquence—that becomes part of the person's public signature. They may be simple messages, but simple messages are the ones that stick in the memory.

Others, as we shall see, reach the public eye in more gradual ways. They all have their stories of emergence. But there is a story before these stories—in Hollywood parlance, a "backstory." It concerns ancestry and origins, childhood and youth. No aspect of a candidate's life story is more vital to the understanding of his character than the family saga from which he emerges.

CHAPTER TWO

FAMILIES MATTER

F EW VOTERS ARE WAR HEROES, CAPTIVATING ORATORS, OR WILY PAR-
liamentarians, but all voters have childhoods of their own. Stories
of a political figure's childhood and youth are easy to relate to, so candidates have used their childhood experiences to create personal narratives that pay political dividends. Presidential stories send their
roots deep into the warm earth of home and family, and up these
roots are drawn themes that nourish the presidential reputation and
explain the presidential character, or at least pretend to do so. Of
course, which parts of a story are told, and which are not, depends on
the aims of the candidate, the resources of his opponents, the dili-
gence, motives, and ethics of the press, and the curiosity of the public. Defining one's family story and getting it accepted are vital to the
upward path of the politician. Some politicians owe their careers to
their family stories—most notably, the sons and grandsons of presidents whose own careers were launched thanks to the advantages of a
family name. Others have risen from obscure origins and are rags-to-
riches figures who tell an American story of upward mobility and
meritocratic advance.

Just as psychologists examine patients' childhoods to find the keys to their characters, so journalists and voters look to a contender's youth for clues. And savvy aspirants for the presidency selectively draw on (and even construct) their youths to fashion useful stories for their later public lives. These stories are then integrated into the public character of the candidate, with attributes highlighted according to how well they match the nation's needs.

THE HATCHET AND THE AX

You know the story. Young George Washington was given a hatchet as a present. Playing with his new toy, he chopped down a cherry tree that was a favorite of his father's. When Washington Senior asked him whether he knew who had killed the tree, the future Father of His Country said, "I can't tell a lie, Pa; you know I can't tell a lie. I did cut it with my hatchet." This is almost certainly the most famous presidential childhood story, and it is almost certainly untrue. The story first appeared in the fifth edition of Mason Weems's biography of George Washington, which was published in 1806. Weems, an Episcopal clergyman and writer, attributed it to "an aged lady, who was a distant relative, and when a girl spent much of her time in the family." Weems was perhaps fonder of a good yarn than he was of truth, and one astute critic of his work, Massachusetts senator Henry Cabot Lodge—himself a prolific and serious historian, with a doctorate from Harvard—concluded, "To enter into any serious historical criticism of these stories would be to break a butterfly." Washington had been dead for seven years when the story appeared, so it had no effect on his political career. But it has cast its retrospective glow over that career and become a narrative archetype.[1]

Why is a story universally considered false the best-known anecdote of a presidential childhood? One reason lies in the circumstances of the story itself. The basic lesson that the tale conveys—that Washington was honest—is intensified by the fact that this event concerned a child. Young George, mastering his fear of being punished for his transgression, nonetheless holds firm to the truth. If one so powerless has the courage to tell the truth, surely no mendacity can be expected from him in the fullness of manhood. Yet the almost superhuman righteousness of the young hero is tempered by the fact that he has actually been bad—he did cut down the tree. The sin humanizes the virtue as much as the confession redeems the sin. And the confession did indeed redeem the sin, according to Parson Weems: Washington's father took his son in his arms and exclaimed, "Such an act of heroism in my son is worth more than a thousand trees, though blossomed with silver, and their fruits of purest gold."[2]

The story prevails because it demonstrates something we believe to be true of Washington's character. And it expresses something that Americans very much want, even need, to be true. The integrity of young George Washington helps to confirm the legitimacy of the American Revolution, of the Constitution over whose drafting he presided, and of the government he was the first to lead. If George Washington had been a liar, America would be a less noble place.

Such stories of childhood experiences foreshadowing the leader-to-be became a staple of presidential lore. Daniel Webster, whose candidacy in 1836 came about in part because of his reputation as a constitutional lawyer, told of having purchased, when he was eight years old, a small pocket handkerchief with the Constitution of the United States printed on it. He recalled sitting under an elm tree and reading it over: "From this I first learned either that there was a constitution, or that there were thirteen states. I remember to have read it, and have known more or less of it ever since." A similarly portentous story concerns Ulysses S. Grant's first encounter with a gun. While Grant was still a toddler, his father, to satisfy the curiosity of a neighbor, held a pistol while his son pulled the trigger. When the gun fired, the boy was ecstatic, and cried out, "Fick it again! Fick it again!" A martial spirit was born.[3]

The Grant story, so far as we know, is true. Weems's cherry tree yarn was almost certainly false. Yet both have had their effect on the American political imagination. It matters, of course, whether such stories are true or false. And it is the sometimes unsettling role of the press (and of historians) to expose false stories of youthful heroics and the like. But the hunger for such stories is real, and where there is demand someone will furnish a supply.

Part of Abraham Lincoln's life story is that one of the books he perused when he was first learning how to read was another life of Washington, written by David Ramsay and published in 1807. In William M. Thayer's 1863 biography of Lincoln, *The Pioneer Boy and How He Became President,* Ramsay's book becomes the raw material for a Weemsish story about Abe Lincoln. As Thayer tells it, young Abe learned that a neighbor, Josiah Crawford, owned a copy of Ramsay's life of Washington and humbly asked if he might borrow the book. Aware of Lincoln's reputation as a reader, Crawford happily complied, enjoining Lincoln to take good care of the book. Lincoln accidentally damaged the book, went penitently to Crawford to offer restitution, and then uncomplainingly performed the arduous chores (far out of proportion to the value of the book) that Crawford required of him. Thayer's story, of course, did not achieve the circulation that Weems reaped with the story of Washington and the cherry tree, but his book did sell 26,000 copies in the two years after it was published.[4]

Thayer's story was one of the building blocks of the Lincoln legend. Lincoln's youth was tirelessly mined by propagandists for the Union cause and the Republican party for childhood anecdotes that would charm voters and offer positive examples for future generations. As a youth and young man, Lincoln regularly cleared land for farming by chopping down trees, and then cut the wood into logs for cabins, firewood, and rails for split-rail fences. Lincoln's frontier origins became a classic narrative of American politics.

As the United States had turned increasingly democratic in principles in the early nineteenth century, the supposed ideal background of its leaders changed. Washington's ascent to the leadership of the Continental Army, and then to the presidency, would have been unimaginable without the relatively high social standing of his family and relations in Virginia. Humble birth, in his time, was not a political plus. An entire bookshelf of political theory pronounced that wealth and social standing were necessary qualifications for political office, because only a person from such a background would have the necessary independence of fortune and mind to resist corrupting influences.

But that world dissolved in the rising tide of democracy, and origins as modest as Lincoln's became a political advantage. The democratic surge made more and more presidential electors subject to a direct vote of the people, rather than allowing them to be chosen by state legislatures. With a broader electoral franchise, it became important for candidates to appear more like the people who were electing them. Lincoln's followers emphasized his hardy country roots and tried to make that aspect of his past the core of his political persona. His work as a humble "rail-splitter" was cheered by parading supporters in the 1860 presidential campaign, who sometimes marched down urban avenues in a zigzag pattern, a visual homage to the herringbone path taken by the split-rail fences of the midwestern frontier. Back east, the elites did not always appreciate such frontier symbolism. The *New York Times,* in a sarcastic editorial on June 9, 1860, observed, "It is true that in the days of his youth Mr. Lincoln was guilty of splitting rails, but as he did it simply with the intent of obtaining an honest livelihood, it is neither to his disadvantage or otherwise." Horace Greeley's steadfastly Republican *New York Tribune* replied that the "title of 'Rail-splitter,' given to Mr. Lincoln is merely an emphatic way of stating that he rose from the class of men stigmatized by slave-holding Senators as the 'mud-sills' of society." The *Tribune* went on to observe that if Lincoln had enough talent to rise from such humble beginnings to be a candidate for the presidency, "there *must* be talent and capacity enough in him to qualify him for the discharge of the duties of that office." On June 12 the *Times* responded to this argument by saying that it was doubtful that anyone would consider Lincoln's origins as sufficient to qualify him "for the Professorship of Surgery in a University," or that "Commodore Vanderbilt would give him a place [as an engineer] on one of his steamers, even at rail-splitting wages." That fall, the voters decided that while his past as a rail-splitter might not come first in his list of qualifications for the presidency, it certainly was no hindrance.[5]

But long before Lincoln, the story of American upward mobility was established as part of the national story, and no one did more to define that story than Benjamin Franklin. In his time, and for most of American history, Franklin has been in the first rank of American popular heroes. His inventions and scientific investigations won for him the approval of educated Europeans of his own era—a rare and significant accomplishment and one treasured by his fellow Americans, who, however disdainful they may have been of the flaws of European society, desperately wanted to be considered important by the older, more accomplished civilizations across the Atlantic.

Franklin spent most of his youth working, first as an apprentice to his father, a tallow chandler and soap boiler, and then to his brother, a printer. His rigorous process of self-education was founded upon the borrowing of books from neighbors. In his marvelous *Autobiography,* Franklin describes how he taught himself to write by, for example, noting the chief ideas in an essay of Addison's, then coming back to his notes some time later and trying to write a similar essay. The young apprentice would then compare his composition with Addison's original and look for where he fell short.[6]

Self-instruction is the constant theme of the work as it covers the author's youth and young manhood. The author improves his swimming technique by reading a book on the subject (and later, in England, earns money as a swimming instructor). He reads a book on vegetarianism and for a time embraces that doctrine strenuously, as he also embraces temperance. The man who emerges from Franklin's narrative is prosperous, healthy, intellectually curious, and highly complacent. The *Autobiography* was not, however, published in Franklin's lifetime, and was not intended to secure immediate political advantage (although Franklin, like other Founding Fathers, often wrote with an eye toward his historical reputation). But Franklin's example was an inspiration to young American boys of the nineteenth century, and his story of tenacity rewarded with wealth and fame remains central to our political culture, having been adopted, mimicked, or appropriated by political figures from Lincoln to Lyndon Johnson, from Huey Long to Ross Perot.

It was Andrew Jackson who first made clear the advantages of a disadvantaged childhood in a race for the presidency. Jackson's father died before Andrew was born, and his mother died when he was just into his teens, and it is as an orphan that the Hero of New Orleans earned his credits for being a self-made man. His family had been reasonably well off, but his youth brought a number of trials even beyond the deaths of his parents. He had a speech impediment—an involuntary slobbering—that caused other children to mock him. Jackson would fight those who did so, and his bellicose temperament owed much to these childhood conflicts. After enlisting in the army at age thirteen as a messenger, he was captured by the British in 1781. A British officer ordered the young rebel to clean his boots, but Jackson refused. The event is described in the Reid and Eaton biography of Old Hickory: "Incensed at his refusal, the officer aimed a blow at his head with a drawn sword, which would, very probably, have terminated his existence, had he not parried its effects by throwing up his left hand, on which he received a severe wound." A childhood patriot and orphan who had risen to become the nation's greatest living military hero was a life story bound for the Oval Office.[7]

Humble origins proved a valuable resource even to politicians without them. In the epochal 1840 campaign, the year when campaign rallies and ballyhoo truly came of age, the Whig party took the errant remark of a Democratic editor at a Baltimore newspaper concerning the Whig nominee, William Henry Harrison, and turned it into campaign gold. The editor had snidely suggested that Harrison, a former general with little previous political experience or ambition, would gladly eschew the race if he were given $2,000 a year, a jug of hard cider, and a log cabin to which to retire. The alert Whigs turned the log cabin into a symbol of Harrison's supposedly humble roots and portrayed the ex-general (who had grown up in comfort on the family's plantation in Virginia, and whose father was a signer of the Declaration of Independence) as a simple man of the people. (Daniel Webster later lamented wryly that by the time of his birth his family had moved from their log cabin into a frame house, thereby harming his electoral chances.) If the formula had worked so well for Harrison in 1840, there was every reason for the followers of the former Whig Abe Lincoln to employ the same techniques in 1860. In Lincoln's case, at least, the story of humble origins was true.

The seeming electoral potency of childhood hardship in the nineteenth century reflected the nature of the frontier economy and the growing electoral power of the trans-Appalachian west. Even more, it represented the triumph of Jeffersonian ideals in the form of Jacksonian democracy. Observing America in the 1830s, Alexis de Tocqueville judged that the democratic forces had taken "exclusive control of affairs. . . . Nowadays one may say that the wealthy classes in the United States are almost entirely outside politics and that wealth, so far from being an advantage there, is a real cause of disfavor and an obstacle to gaining power." The era Tocqueville was observing was, however, the time when democratic ideals were most ascendant in the country, and in other periods wealth has proved small hindrance to gaining the White House.[8]

SILVER SPOONS

Not every candidate can be fortunate enough to be born poor, of course. Some must struggle to overcome the terrible obstacle of a privileged youth. Carl Sandburg paints a vivid portrait of the night of Lincoln's birth, with the infant handed to his mother as she slept in their dirt-floored log cabin, warmed against the frigid February air by coarse bearskins. In contrast, Thomas Jefferson's earliest memory was of being carried on a pillow by a slave. Yet his background, too, had political utility.[9]

Jefferson's aristocratic origins were not an obstacle to his political career for several reasons. First, his presidency came at the very beginning of the democratizing trend of the nineteenth century, when his wealthy upbringing and large estates were still seen as more likely to support his claim to power than to undermine it. Second, since Jefferson was himself the great proponent of that democratization—author of the astonishing claim that "all men are created equal"—he made a bad target (and his opponents, the Federalists, were in fact the great defenders of property and inherited privileges). The fact that Jefferson's principles and his economic and class interests were seemingly at odds made it appear that his principles were exceptionally strong. Third, his political opponents were aristocratic in temperament, if not in wealth, and so hardly likely to use Jefferson's own comfortable circumstances against him.

Misfortune, too, can free a well-born candidate from the political liabilities associated with aristocratic lineage. Theodore Roosevelt was raised in the best New York society of the mid-nineteenth century, but his frailty as a child deprived his life of ease. So severe were his asthma attacks that his father would sometimes order his horses to be harnessed to the family rig and then drive young Teddy through the streets of New York at breakneck speed to force air into his diseased lungs. When the still frail boy was twelve years old, his strapping father told him, "You must *make* your body," and Teddy complied, undertaking a rigorous program of exercise that finally strengthened him. It was the story of that self-creation, and not of the surrounding privilege, that defined Teddy Roosevelt's childhood. And it was effective because this was the version of his youth that Roosevelt himself believed.[10]

Of course, one key to mining a childhood for good electoral anecdotes is to be selective. Consider, for example, the upbringing of Franklin Roosevelt, Teddy's distant cousin. The only child of a wealthy couple, FDR was educated at home until the age of fourteen and was doted on unceasingly. While FDR was a student at Harvard, his father died and his mother promptly moved to Boston to be near Franklin. Yet all this attention did not smother FDR; rather he seemed to obtain a kind of inner confidence from it. While others might have found all this parental pampering suffocating, Roosevelt seemingly found it nurturing and comforting, so much so that he tried to provide similar protections for an entire nation through New Deal programs like Social Security.

Some of Roosevelt's contemporaries were baffled by the sources of Roosevelt's tenacious ambition. Comparing the sheltered childhood of FDR with the scrappy urban roots of Alfred E. Smith, or the harsh circumstances that produced contemporary foreign dictators like Stalin, Hitler, and Mussolini, people wondered how this patrician acquired such resolve. Behind this question lies the assumption that a privileged background is truly a shortcoming, a practical as well as moral deficiency. Such an assumption is profoundly democratic and would have baffled a person of standing in the eighteenth century, when a pampered childhood meant having the time and resources to acquire a serious education.[11]

In our time, the appearance of a privileged background remains a political handicap and must be countered with other stories. The terms of the discussion have changed, however. In the Age of Jackson, Americans were comfortable talking about class, and about rank and privilege. In the supposedly "classless" society of the present era, talk of class and privilege is easily branded as unsavory radicalism, almost un-American. Now religious, ethnic, or racial background, not class, is the touchstone of brotherhood with the common man. John F. Kennedy's defense of his Roman Catholic background in the 1960 race, or Mario Cuomo's waxing sentimental about the mortadella in the Italian grocery store of his youth, or Joe Lieberman in a yarmulke is the modern equivalent of the log-cabin birthplace. A WASPy, private-school, Ivy League background has become an obstacle to be overcome, like Teddy Roosevelt's asthma. The first President Bush went to great lengths in his campaign to identify himself as a Texan. By donning cowboy boots and munching pork rinds, he succeeded somewhat in escaping his origins as the Yale-educated son of a Republican senator from Connecticut. His presidential son (Andover, Yale) and his son's opponent in 2000, Al Gore (St. Albans, Harvard), both to a significant degree children of the Washington Beltway, each embraced the southern states that elected them to high office and stressed their regional origins in their campaign rhetoric.

But the most elaborate and conscious attempt to define a candidate's past was the one undertaken by Bill Clinton's campaign at the 1992 Democratic National Convention. Although Clinton had a hardscrabble childhood, research by his campaign revealed that many voters thought of him as a child of privilege, owing to his educational experience—college at Georgetown, a Rhodes Scholarship to Oxford, and law school at Yale. Clinton's media advisers Harry Thomason and Linda Bloodworth-Thomason, experienced producers of sitcoms, countered this perception with a thirteen-minute documentary on Clinton's life, shown at the convention. *The Man from Hope,* as the film has come to be known, portrayed Clinton's childhood in highly dramatic—and highly effective—ways. The film opens with an establishing shot of the train station in the town of Hope, Arkansas, where Clinton was born. Next the candidate is heard describing how he was born in Hope "three months after my father died."[12]

The hinge of the story is the account of Clinton's confrontation with his alcoholic stepfather, who beat Clinton's mother. The candidate starts to tell the story, but his account is interrupted by his mother, who finishes the tale. Young Bill Clinton faced down his stepfather—"Don't you ever, ever lay your hand on my mother again"—and this confrontation became the symbol of his courage and independence. In place of the Ivy-educated son of privilege there stands revealed a resolute young man who puts himself on the line to protect his mother. Ending the film, he laments that he "never heard the sound of my father's voice or felt his hand around mine," but affirms that "I still believe in a place called Hope."[13]

The Clinton campaign had made no secret of its plan to highlight the candidate's childhood at the convention. In a July 12, 1992, article published just before the start of the gathering, the *St. Louis Post-Dispatch's* Bill Lambrecht wrote that television viewers "will learn of Clinton's modest roots; about growing up first in his grandparents' country store and later in a home dominated by a violent stepfather." Clinton's convention speech reworked the same material—indeed, the *Boston Globe's* Martin F. Nolan thought the film "upstaged many of the emotional moments in Clinton's message"—and ended with the same affirmative phrase as the film.[14]

The techniques of the Clinton campaign were far more sophisticated than those of William Henry Harrison's day, or Teddy Roosevelt's. Informal campaign advisers have been replaced by free-agent professional staffs, and test-marketed television ad campaigns have replaced torchlight parades and marching bands. Armies of pollsters test every possible variant of a candidate's message, from what he should think to what words he should choose to say it. But the power of the family story, and its manifest political usefulness, remain unchanged.

LEGACIES OF LEADERSHIP

One of the easiest, most natural, and oldest ways of catching the nation's attention is to be born into a prominent family. True, the newborn can hardly claim credit for his good fortune, yet the future benefits of a privileged bassinet are not to be lightly dismissed.

After all, at the time the United States was founded, hereditary monarchy was the world's prevalent form of government, and the harsh consequences of unclear or contested passage of power were laid out in cautionary texts such as Shakespeare's history plays and in the names of eighteenth-century European conflicts such as the War of the Spanish Succession and the War of the Austrian Succession. Indeed, at the Federal Convention in Philadelphia that drafted the United States Constitution in 1787, the possibilities (and threat) of dynastic succession were discussed (and had George Washington had a son the discussion might have been more pointed). So powerful was the logic of monarchy and primogeniture that worried republicans pointed out the fragility of the anti-aristocratic and anti-monarchical provisions of the Constitution. One anxious critic even suggested that the constitutional provision against titles of nobility was insidious, because if the Constitution had the power to block such titles, it could also be amended to allow them.

Yet for all these fears, influential fathers still hoped for sons who could build upon their successes. The very pamphleteer who warned against the possibility of titles of nobility in the Constitution, DeWitt Clinton, was himself the son of a Revolutionary War general and the nephew of the first governor of New York State, and later won the same office for himself. (His uncle, George Clinton, also served as vice president under Thomas Jefferson and then James Madison, against whom DeWitt Clinton ran for president in 1812.)

That sons should follow fathers (or uncles) into politics should hardly be surprising, given how frequently children follow the career paths of their parents. And in democratic politics it is particularly advantageous to have a famous father, since to be popular with voters one must first be known to them. John Quincy Adams and George W. Bush were the sons of presidents, and Benjamin Harrison was a presidential grandson. For the scions, the mere fact of having had a famous father or grandfather provided a helpful sense of legitimacy to aspirations that might have been nonexistent without the success of their forebears. Surprisingly, in American presidential politics it does not seem to matter much whether the presidential forebear was a success in office—John Adams and George H. W. Bush were voted out of office after a single term, while poor William Henry Harrison died a month after his inauguration.

These presidential heirs did not just inherit the office, though; they had to earn their own reputations. The most distinguished of them was John Quincy Adams. By the time of the 1824 election, he had compiled a remarkable record of public service, having represented America in diplomatic posts in the Netherlands, Prussia, Russia, and Britain, served as a United States senator, and then been appointed secretary of state by James Monroe. But the disputed election that brought him into office—Andrew Jackson had the most electoral votes, but support from Henry Clay brought Adams victory when the presidency was decided in the House of Representatives—fatally undermined the younger Adams's legitimacy as president. Throughout his term and in the 1828 campaign, his enemies lambasted Adams with accusations of corruption (because he had turned around and appointed Clay secretary of state) and incompetence. Among the charges were that he was "aristocratic" (that eminent family background had its downside) and that he had been educated abroad. An editorial in the *United States Telegraph* on May 4, 1827, summarized Adams's monarchical tendencies, rooting them in his family. His father had been "poisoned with monarchy and aristocracy during his embassy in London" after the Revolution, and JQA was tainted by association. What further proof was needed than the fact that "at the tender age of eleven, he was sent to *Eton,* in England, to be educated among the children of the British nobility and aristocracy." Adams had an extraordinary childhood, and he labored constantly to prove worthy of the advantages he had enjoyed. Yet this tireless striver was accused of idle and luxurious ways—the purchase of a billiard table for the White House was considered a telling proof.[15]

Benjamin Harrison was the grandson, not the son, of a president, and so the world's scrutiny was less intense during his youth. A diligent if unbrilliant soldier in the Civil War, he worked hard at the practice of law and rose to prominence in Indiana, where he made his home. In 1876 Harrison was persuaded to run for governor after the Republican nominee was forced to abandon the race because of allegations of financial improprieties. Running against a Democrat, James Douglas Williams, whose plebeian credentials were embodied in his nickname, "Blue Jeans," Harrison was caricatured as "Kid-glove" Harrison, and his formal manner was offered as evidence of his haughty superiority. Harrison lost that race. But in 1880 he was elected to the United States Senate, and his famous name and honest reputation helped him win both the Republican presidential nomination and the election in 1888 (although Grover Cleveland outpolled him in popular votes). His grandfather, William Henry Harrison, had won election as president in 1840 in the famous "Log Cabin and Hard Cider" campaign, masquerading as a humble son of the soil, so perhaps there was some poetic justice in the younger Harrison's having to struggle with a reputation for patrician coldness.

The shortest gap between presidents of the same family is the eight years that separated the departure of George H. W. Bush from office and the inauguration of George W. Bush, whose dynastic ascent will be discussed later. Just having a presidential forebear is not enough, of course, to secure for his political descendant election, or even nomination. Senator Robert Taft of Ohio, the son of President William Howard Taft, was such a staunch proponent of his party's bedrock principles that he was called "Mr. Republican," but his party denied him the presidential nomination in 1940, 1948, and 1952. And fathers and grandfathers are not the only source of presidential bloodlines. Sometimes the family name can prove useful even to a distant cousin, as it did to Teddy Roosevelt's relation Franklin. A successful brother can also prove useful, as both the Kennedy and Bush families have found. And today, as the possibility of electing a female president no longer seems impossibly remote, having married a president-to-be is proving a boost to the aspirations of Senator Hillary Rodham Clinton.

THE OTHER FAMILY

Nearly as important as the candidate's birth family is the one he forms by marriage. That partnership is often seen as a major indicator of his fitness to govern. The Constitution requires that the president be a native-born American at least thirty-five years of age who has been resident in the United States for fourteen years. But the public requires that he have a happy marriage with reasonably well-behaved children. There have been rare exceptions—Madison and Polk were childless, and neither Washington nor Jackson had children of their own—but not in modern times. Only one president, James Buchanan, never married.

If family life has always been one measure of fitness for office, it has become a more vital consideration since the advent of broadcasting and the growth of mass media. In the days before televised nominating conventions it was no great matter to forgo the now required photo of the candidates and their spouses before the cheering throngs. Clearly, too, women's gaining the right to vote raised the importance of presidential families. If campaign rhetoric is about creating an identification between a candidate and the voters, the advent of female voters meant that it was helpful to have a woman with whom these new voters could identify.

But even when not subject to press scrutiny, the wives of presidents and presidential hopefuls had, of course, been crucial parts of their husbands' lives long before public attention fastened on them. No woman was more fully a partner in her husband's life—in all its phases—than Abigail Adams. From the time of their marriage until Adams became president, and ever after, her support, counsel, and friendship were central to his success.

Domestic support also took more active forms. The political career of John C. Frémont (the first presidential nominee of the Republican party, in 1856) would have been unthinkable without the crucial alliance he formed with Jessie Benton, daughter of the powerful Missouri senator Thomas Hart Benton. It began as a love match—they fell for each other when she was just sixteen. When a displeased Senator Benton found out, he arranged for Frémont to be sent away on a journey of exploration up the Des Moines River. However, Frémont soon returned with his love for Jessie (and hers for him) undimmed, and the two secretly married. At last persuaded that his new son-in-law was a permanent fixture, the senator bestowed his patronage upon Frémont. Jessie's support was even more important. She was a much abler politician than Frémont, and her skill as a writer helped him to publish popular accounts of his explorations in the Rockies. These dramatic narratives spurred westward expansion and helped Frémont win the Republican nomination.

Not all wives were political assets. William Henry Seward's wife,

Frances, was pathologically attached to her childhood home, and her neurosis clouded Seward's life. Similarly troubled was the man who defeated Seward for the 1860 Republican nomination, Abraham Lincoln. Mary Todd Lincoln was from a wealthy southern family. Beset with mental illness (later in life she was temporarily institutionalized), she added significantly to the pressures President Lincoln was under in the White House.

Such stories remained largely out of the public world in the nineteenth century. But in the twentieth century, with the arrival of radio and TV, the equation slowly changed. The change was most apparent during presidential races and, with victory, in the growing public duties and responsibilities of the First Lady. But a new culture of celebrity, and new opportunities for women, made some wives an important part of the earlier chapters of some presidential life stories.

The marriage of Eleanor and Franklin Roosevelt was big news when it occurred in 1905. Her uncle Teddy, then president, was among those in attendance, doing his best to dominate the proceedings. Early in her life Eleanor involved herself in charitable causes such as settlement house work, and as Franklin's career advanced she became an active figure in politics in New York. She chaired the finance committee of the state Democratic party's women's division from 1924 to 1928, and campaigned actively for her husband in his gubernatorial races in 1928 and 1930.

Similarly high-profile nuptials united Jacqueline Bouvier and John F. Kennedy in 1953, although the Massachusetts senator's new wife was more comfortable in salons and soirees than she was in settlement houses or political meetings. But her beauty and celebrity attracted press notice, and her social graces helped secure a reputation for Kennedy as a sophisticated, cultivated man, a reputation he found politically useful. The darker family stories lying behind this façade—Jackie's father was too drunk on her wedding day to give her away at the ceremony—remained outside the realm of acceptable public discourse.

Kennedy's family was rich, but his running mate, Lyndon Johnson, had seen his father lose everything through bad investments in Texas. So Johnson secured his financial future by marrying a wealthy, painfully shy young woman named Claudia Alta Taylor, who had been nicknamed Lady Bird by a nanny. LBJ had bragged in college that he would marry a rich woman, and he made good on his boast. As Johnson ascended the political ladder, Lady Bird was a faithful and uncomplaining assistant, in spite of his rude abuse of her and his regular denigration of her appearance. She also helped by being the "president" of the Austin radio station that furnished most of their income, although it was Johnson himself who oversaw the station's operations.

Wives with glamorous careers made good copy, and the public response to Betty Ford's career as a dancer, including her studies with Martha Graham, and Nancy Reagan's movie career (as Nancy Davis) showed that the electorate was not overly threatened by wives with careers—as long as they were in properly feminine roles. It was acceptable for the political spouse to have a cause, such as Tipper Gore's crusade against profanity and abusive language in rock music, as long as the cause also conformed to popular expectations about women's roles. But more aggressive careerism in a spouse could prove politically damaging to her spouse, as Hillary Rodham Clinton would show during the health-care-reform debate during the first Clinton administration.

Political wives in the postwar era were expected to be prim, proper, and marginal: a few good works, photo opportunities with women and children, and back to the private quarters. But reticence was never part of Hillary's story. The Clintons' first meeting, in the Yale Law School library, came about when she walked over to Bill, who had been eyeing her, and said, "If you are going to keep looking at me and I'm going to keep looking back, we might as well be introduced. I'm Hillary Rodham." She then asked Clinton his name, and according to him, "Well, I couldn't remember my name." When Clinton became governor of Arkansas, his wife made it clear that she intended to pursue her career as a lawyer, a move applauded by some, denigrated by more. Her White House career would prove even more controversial.[16]

For many years, divorce was a political poison pill. As late as the 1960s it could cripple a candidate, as it did with Nelson Rockefeller in his quest for the 1964 Republican nomination. (Rockefeller also had to overcome the handicap of coming from one of the wealthiest families in the nation's history, a family hardly shy about displaying that wealth.) An early Gallup poll showed Rockefeller as the front runner for the 1964 Republican nomination, ahead 43 to 26 percent, but after his divorce and remarriage he was behind 35 to 30 percent.[17]

Only twelve years later Ronald Reagan's divorce did not prove an issue in his first presidential race. After the 1960s, a society in which divorce was becoming endemic had removed it from the list of politically fatal actions. Americans hunger for the presidential family to shine as an exemplar of "family values," yet with time the values represented have changed.

THE MARVEL in these family stories is their persistence in the face of all kinds of evidence against them. It is not just that some stories are false, as in the case of little George and the cherry tree, but that there appears to be so little correlation between the beliefs embedded in these stories and the actual performance of presidents in the White House.

Where, for example, is the evidence that a president from a wealthy background is necessarily the champion of his own class? Thomas Jefferson and Franklin Roosevelt were two of the most well-born presidents in American history, but they were also two of the most passionate champions of the rights and aspirations of the common man. Others who were born to modest circumstances—Henry Clay, a frequent candidate for the White House, and Ronald Reagan—were steadfast allies of wealth and privilege.

By all accounts, Jimmy and Rosalynn Carter have an exemplary, loving marriage. Yet few would consider his presidency to be a high-water mark in the history of the office. Lincoln and FDR had troubled domestic lives but performed brilliantly in the White House.

When the facts of a situation contradict the thrust of the governing narrative, the narrative often prevails. Despite the lack of evidence to show that either has any bearing on presidential performance, divorce and, to a lesser extent, wealth are public disadvantages for White House aspirants. Caught up in the flow of narrative, and oblivious of the countervailing evidence, voters buy into the story of the happy family that we all wish were true of our own, and thrill to the rags-to-riches story that affirms so much about American society that is admirable, while giving hope to our own economic dreams.

Political stories are simpler than real life. The childhood roots of adult character are complex and elusive, and the actual dynamics of a marriage are too elaborate, and too private, to be processed into slogans and sound bites. Aware that voters and journalists want simple, pleasing stories, campaigns gladly produce them.

CHAPTER THREE

FINDING A STORY, CHOOSING A CHARACTER

THE HEROES DESCRIBED IN CHAPTER 1 FOUND POWERFUL, SIMPLE stories that brought them national attention. Yet even those characters who emerge upon the national stage dramatically, and at an early age, must follow a long path before running for president. After the heroics of PT-109, John Kennedy launched a political career, serving first in the House of Representatives and then winning election to the Senate. Jefferson's path after the Declaration of Independence wound through state office in Virginia, diplomatic service, the cabinet, and the vice presidency. Kennedy and Jefferson were blessed by careers built upon their heroic stories as war hero and author of independence. Most presidential contenders have had to struggle to find—and sometimes to create—the stories that worked for them.

CHARACTER AND CHARACTERS

The critical part of finding one's presidential life story is figuring out what character to play. People are moved by stories, but they require characters to connect with those stories. In literature, the same sorts of characters recur constantly—the prodigal son, the damsel in distress, the hero, the saint, the villain. Such stock characters also dominate American presidential politics. A presidential hopeful is a collection of characters, each vying for supremacy, and each spotlighted or cast in shadow as circumstances dictate. These characters are themselves part of a larger collection of stock characters whose historical or literary manifestations are known to us all. The most common stock character is the professional sort—soldier, politician, businessman—and such persons have often run for president. Other stock characters are defined not by their professions but by aspects of their personalities. Some of these are as old as myth: the trickster, the drunkard, the idiot. Others are of more recent coinage: the wonk, the used-car salesman, the preppy. All have a real resonance, and they become a sort of shorthand for characterizing those in the political world.

Because stock characters economically convey an entire catalog of attributes, journalists and voters rely on this shorthand to quickly comprehend the personality of a candidate. Politicians have both public and private lives, but what we know about politicians is constrained by the stories they choose to tell and those that are unearthed by enterprising reporters or opponents' negative-research teams. In literature, by contrast, the novelist or the playwright allows us to see into a character's mind. When a politician is presented as a stock character—whether by himself, his advisers, his opponents, or the press— he gains an extra dimensionality because we can apply what we know about other characters of the same type to the particular person we are considering. Andrew Jackson becomes a triumphant Roman general, Calvin Coolidge a tight-lipped Yankee, and the Richard Nixon of the Checkers speech can be understood as a modern version of Dickens's unctuous Uriah Heep.

But it is not enough for the candidate to embody a character the public can understand—it should also be one the public will like and respect. By establishing a character that others find attractive and inspiring, a politician can greatly advance his cause. That character cannot be chosen at random—it must fit the politician's experiences and match his personality. To work, the character also has to suit the needs and issues of the time. A military background, for example, is more useful politically when the nation is facing or fighting a war, but the kind of military man the nation finds attractive differs with the circumstances.

THE MILITARY LEADER

Military heroes have been around for thousands of years, in both life and literature, so there is a vast array of models to choose from. Consider the varieties found in the *Iliad,* the source of many heroic paradigms. We see the hero of great physical strength, Ajax; the devious and clever warlord, Odysseus; the courageous, loving, and heroic warrior, Hector; and the driven, single-minded partisan of wrath, Achilles. Such examples come readily to hand. So when, following the American victory in the Revolutionary War, George Washington left the army and returned to his farm in Virginia, Americans cited the classical example of the Roman general Cincinnatus. In 458 B.C. he was made dictator to rescue Rome from a military crisis and then, when victory was won, ceded power and went back to his farm. To a nation wary of monarchical power, Washington's aversion to self-aggrandizement was proof of his heroic virtue and furnished exactly the sort of military hero most appealing to the republican sensibilities of the times. That the story of Cincinnatus is as much legend as fact was of little moment, since in this process narratives of fact and fiction commingle, each drawing power from the other. What was fact was Washington's thrusting aside of power.

Other times have called for other kinds of heroes. Andrew Jackson was a frontier soldier, a great popular general for a new, more democratic age. But he was also imperious and quick to anger. Opponents highlighted this negative side of his personality and suggested that Jackson might love power more than he loved the people. Remember the story of Julius Caesar, they warned. Caesar's betrayal of the Roman republic was part of the mental landscape that Jackson's detractors sketched while lamenting Old Hickory's excessive use of force to discipline mutineers and to punish presumed spies. Was Jackson a second George Washington, as his followers said, or was he a potential dictator, the home-bred Caesar who would subvert the American republic? Jackson's opponents also cited Cromwell and Napoleon as examples of military betrayers of republican ideals. The narratives contend, taking on a power of their own. The verdict is handed down by voters, journalists, and historians.

Characters drawn from world history and fable populate the catalog of American military characters. And it wasn't long before American politicians started to draw on military legends of a uniquely American provenance. George Washington himself soon became the nation's leading stock character. When William Henry Harrison came along in the 1840 election, his campaign literature referred to him as the "Washington of the West." During the Mexican War, General Winfield Scott (called "Old Fuss and Feathers" by his men, for his spit-and-polish European-style approach to military decorum) did all he could to prevent his rival for the Whig party nomination in 1848, Zachary Taylor ("Old Rough and Ready"), from winning notable victories. But Taylor did win a significant battle early in 1847, at Buena Vista, and his Whig partisans proclaimed him "an American Cincinnatus"—and thus another Washington. Taylor got the nomination; can anyone be surprised that Old Rough and Ready prevailed over Old Fuss and Feathers? As Winfield Scott's fate suggests, the nation had embraced the popular style of leadership personified by Jackson, Harrison, and Taylor.

The cataclysm of the Civil War boosted even higher the electoral importance of a military background. Indeed, after the Civil War having military service on one's résumé became vital. Every Republican president from the 1868 election to the end of the century had served in the Grand Army of the Republic. These Republican presidents had varied military records. Grant, the first elected post–Civil War president, was the principal general of the Union Army, the architect of the North's military victory. His modest roots were certainly appealing, but more important was his determination as Union commander, his unwavering pursuit of victory despite the great cost in human life it exacted.

But as the postwar years passed, it became the fact of service, not its distinction, that was essential. William McKinley, first elected to the White House in 1896, was the last in this string of Civil War veterans. McKinley served in the Union Army but rose only to the brevet rank of major. He was not an important military figure, and nobody would seriously argue that McKinley's army service qualified him to be president. But as late as 1896 such service was an invaluable political attribute. During the 1896 presidential race, a Civil War veterans' convention in Chicago called on voters to support McKinley, embracing the Republican with the words "Major McKinley is a comrade tried and trusted."[1]

Fortunately for one ambitious man in search of the proper character to play, a new war came along at the right time. In 1898 Teddy Roosevelt gave the role of military hero a new twist, deliberately seeking combat as a way to advance his political career. As the war with Spain broke out, Roosevelt decided that he must command troops in battle. He wanted to avoid being branded one of what he termed the "armchair and parlor jingoes," and, as he explained to the *New York*

Sun, "I have always intended to act up to my preachings if occasion arose." So act he did. He put together the Rough Riders, a well-connected and photogenic group of men who were assembled in part because their individual stories were so fascinating. "We had a number of first-class young fellows from the East, most of them from colleges like Harvard, Yale, and Princeton; but the great majority of the men were southwesterners," Roosevelt later wrote. "They were accustomed to the use of firearms, accustomed to taking care of themselves in the open; they were intelligent and self-reliant; they possessed hardihood and endurance and physical prowess; and, above all, they had the fighting edge, the cool and resolute fighting temper." Above all, they made great newspaper copy. And Roosevelt knew that being the leader of such a colorful group augmented his own prominence. Recognizing a great story when he saw one, Richard Harding Davis, the celebrity journalist of the era, followed the Rough Riders into action in Cuba. When Roosevelt seized military glory in the Battle of San Juan Hill, Davis was there to record and publicize the moment. Roosevelt's move vaulted him toward the White House. The newly minted hero was elected governor of New York late that year, and just two years later he was McKinley's vice presidential running mate. Military hero was a role that Roosevelt chose, but it was also one that fit him. Other American politicians have worn the trappings of the military man much less comfortably. Neither Richard Nixon nor Lyndon Johnson had particularly inspiring military records—though Johnson in particular tried to portray his service in glowing colors.[2]

There are also those in recent years whose avoidance of military service became part of their personas. The stock character of the draft dodger was applied to Bill Clinton and Dan Quayle, among others. The Bush-Quayle campaign's attempts to denigrate Bill Clinton's avoidance of the draft were undercut by Quayle's own use of a National Guard assignment to avoid service in Vietnam, a technique sometimes employed by children of influential parents. In September

1992, Quayle was attacking Clinton one day for "how he avoided military service," the next day Quayle was defending his use of family influence to get into the Guard—"no rules were broken, no regulations broken"—and acknowledging that he knew that there was much less chance of seeing combat as a National Guardsman than as a soldier in the army. The issue presented particularly tough problems for Clinton because the two men he ran against—George H. W. Bush in 1992 and Bob Dole in 1996—were both decorated heroes of the Second World War, card-carrying members of the Greatest Generation.[3]

THE BUSINESSMAN

Another career path that has generated presidential candidates is the world of business. Businessmen have had a certain cachet in the United States since at least the middle of the nineteenth century. As the rewards of business grew with the expansion of corporations later in the century, businessmen became respected in a way they hadn't been in earlier aristocratic cultures, in which having to earn a living was frowned upon. And so it developed that being a businessman could prove a useful accomplishment in politics, while business failure became a political liability.

The first president to embody this new dynamic was Ulysses S. Grant. Grant had been a soldier before the Civil War but resigned his commission in 1854 to go into business. Stints as a farmer and as a real estate entrepreneur didn't work out, and Grant pursued other vocations, including working for the family tannery. When war broke out in April 1861, Grant went back into the army. The national tragedy of the Civil War was Grant's salvation, and his leadership of the Union Army landed him the presidency. But his ascent was not without difficulties. His opponents tormented Grant with reminders of his business failures, while his supporters gamely tried to reverse the field by portraying General Grant as a humble workingman. In 1868, when Grant was running for president, enthusiastic Republicans formed "tanner's clubs" to celebrate his man-of-the-people résumé, but Grant himself took no pride in his descent from army officer to "common man." His long and fascinating memoir devotes just two paragraphs to his six years of business tribulations.[4]

Grant was not the only president mocked for business reverses. Harry Truman faced his own defeats early in life, including the failure of his haberdashery business in Kansas City. There is, *pace* Arthur Miller, little tragic dimension to a failed haberdashery. That failure dogged Truman throughout his political career, providing a convenient dig for political opponents, a vaguely comic blemish (perhaps it's the word "haberdashery") of a sorry, quotidian nature. In the 1948 race, a supporter of Henry Wallace, the Progressive party candidate, held up a placard at the party's convention saying "Missouri Wants Wallace in the White House and Truman in the Haberdashery." Republicans, too, treated Truman's business failure as evidence of his unfitness for the presidency. But Truman's presidential career came after the travails of the Great Depression, so the business failure of the Democratic president did not appear a terribly troubling fact to the voters of 1948, many of whom remembered their own economic setbacks of the previous two decades.[5]

Just as business failure is not necessarily an obstacle to political success, so a good record in business is no guarantee of a fortunate political career. One of the most successful businessmen ever to be president was Herbert Hoover. His success in the mining business led him into public service when President Woodrow Wilson tapped him during the First World War to handle war relief and then in 1917 named him chair of the federal Food Administration Board. Hoover won great praise for bringing relief to much of Europe after the war—in 1919, John Maynard Keynes wrote of the effort Hoover headed, "Never was a nobler work of disinterested goodwill carried through with more tenacity and sincerity and skill, and with less thanks either asked or given." Hoover became secretary of commerce in the Harding administration and successfully encouraged a probusiness attitude in the boom years of the 1920s. Unfortunately for Hoover, the Great Depression began just seven months into his first term, and all that had seemed positive about being associated with the world of American business turned poisonous.[6]

Hoover's legacy discredited the role of businessman in presidential politics for decades. The businessman has not been the most successful model, partly because successful businessmen rarely choose to enter electoral politics. But there are also fundamental differences between politics and business. Politics is not a command structure; it's much more one of consensus. A person who is used to being a CEO of a private corporation often lacks the political skills to deal, as president, with Congress and other power groups.

In recent years, with the decline and then the disappearance of the Soviet Union and the seeming triumph of competitive capitalism as the model for economic organization, the role of the businessman has again found traction in American politics, and businessmen-politicians have emerged from the shadow of Hoover.

Jimmy Carter is one example. In 1976 Carter, the ex-governor of Georgia, had a variety of potential life stories to highlight, and he chose wisely. Success in politics depends to a significant degree on highlighting the right aspect of one's story to match the mood of one's time, or the character of one's audience. After Watergate, the profession of politics was held in very low esteem; it was thus important for Carter to emphasize other aspects of his past that would link him to better-regarded stock characters. He bragged about being a peanut farmer, a nuclear physicist, "a lover of Bob Dylan's songs," and a variety of other things in addition to having been Georgia's governor, which was, after all, his most logical qualification for the job of president. Being a peanut farmer—an agrarian businessman—tied Carter to the land and to the ethic of hard work associated with agricultural success. To make sure the press got the point, he put his campaign headquarters in Plains, Georgia, his birthplace.[7]

Jimmy Carter had moved from business to politics and built a political career in Georgia before running for president. Ross Perot, however, decided to seek the top office without any intermediate steps. In 1992, with the federal budget distended by enormous deficits, being a businessman seemed a real plus. And there was more to Perot's life story: thanks to his involvement in the Iranian hostage crisis of the late seventies and early eighties, Perot could even lay claim to a sliver of military glory. He arranged the daring rescue of his own employees from Iran, a success that gave him a political profile that fit with being a "can-do businessman": it showed that he could apply his business skills—organization, risk taking—to a terribly difficult international problem. Perot had other personas as well, notably the pedant and the prima donna, which vied with the businessman for first place in news reports and in the public's perception of him. Not surprisingly, he preferred to emphasize his business acumen as a qualification for the presidency; his opponents and the press drew attention to the less flattering roles. But the stock character he chose to play—indeed, the character he was—made his critics' work easier, since Perot's imperiousness and aversion to criticism are the unfortunate flip side of the captain-of-industry character type.

PLAYING THE POLITICIAN

With rare exceptions, men who achieved prominence as soldiers or businessmen had to serve an apprenticeship in government before winning nomination to the presidency. Washington himself represented Virginia in the First and Second Continental Congresses, Jackson was a senator, Grant was secretary of war under President Andrew

Johnson, and Hoover was secretary of commerce. True, Wendell Willkie went straight from a business and law career to the 1940 Republican nomination, and Dwight Eisenhower's government service was confined to military positions before he headed the 1952 Republican ticket, but most presidential hopefuls have had to serve at least some time in appointive or (more commonly) elective political office.

Books and movies rarely portray politicians as heroes. Perhaps that is inevitable: politicians compromise and are compromised, and compromise is rarely the stuff of heroism. Consider the career of Henry Clay. Of humble origins—although not quite as humble as he liked to make out—Clay was spotted by a Virginia lawyer as a promising lad when he was fourteen, and made a law clerk. Clay soon attracted the attention of Chancellor George Wythe, the Old Dominion's most eminent spotter of legal talent (he had also taught the young Thomas Jefferson and future chief justice John Marshall). After passing the bar in Virginia, Clay moved to the city of Lexington in the bustling new state of Kentucky, where he soon became a prominent attorney. He entered politics and was twice elected to the United States Senate. But preferring to hold office in the House—"I conform to the sentiments I have invariably felt," he informed the *Lexington Gazette,* "in favor of a station of an immediate representative of the people"—Henry Clay ran for the lower chamber in 1810 and was victorious. A leader of the young, brash "war hawks" who favored an aggressive stance toward England, Clay was elected Speaker of the House in 1811 on his first day as a representative, when he was just thirty-four. From that day until his death in 1852 he was one of Congress's most admired leaders. Called, with respect, the "Great Compromiser," he was perhaps the most gifted American political maneuverer of the first half of the nineteenth century.[8]

But Clay always wanted more. Five times he sought the presidency, and each time he was thwarted. More comfortable in the cloakrooms of the Capitol than on the stump, Clay was always considered what we would call today "inside the Beltway," more alert to the wishes and prejudices of those in political or economic power than he was to the moods of the American people. John Quincy Adams, in whose cabinet he served, saw him clearly: "In politics, as in private life, Clay is essentially a gamester." It was not a role that led to the Oval Office.[9]

Some gifted politicians who, unlike Clay, did reach the White House have paid a price in reputation for the very political skills that helped them make it to the top. Lyndon Johnson passed landmark civil rights legislation and created a set of Great Society reforms— Medicare, environmental laws, employment programs, urban initiatives—that brought about fundamental transformations in American life. His actions helped advance the civil rights movement and the women's rights movement. But the image of Lyndon Johnson as the arm-twisting politician, the man who stuffed the ballot box, robbed him of grandeur.

Richard Nixon is often cited as the American president who most thoroughly embodies the negative traits of politicians. Interestingly, Nixon emerged into public view in the very different persona of an investigator. The foundation of Nixon's career was his relentless pursuit of Alger Hiss, the well-connected diplomat whom Nixon accused of spying for the Soviet Union. Nixon took masterful advantage of the publicity opportunities available to him. He made a dramatic return to the United States via seaplane from a Caribbean cruise after the discovery of the famous "pumpkin papers," which seemed to clinch the case against Hiss (these papers were microfilmed State Department documents from the 1930s, some in Hiss's handwriting, that the informant Whittaker Chambers led investigators to, concealed in a pumpkin patch). Hiss's conviction in 1950 virtually ensured Nixon's election to the Senate from California that year. Two years later, Dwight Eisenhower chose him as his running mate, and Nixon was on his way to the White House.

BORN TO RUN

One of the most venerable figures in American politics is that of the reluctant candidate. The genuine reticence that George Washington demonstrated toward becoming president became an expected aspect of candidacy throughout the nineteenth century, as ambitious men averred their humble willingness to accept the great station being offered by a too generous party convention. This choreographed ritual was jettisoned in the twentieth century, as naked ambition was allowed to fly its colors unhindered. In recent years, a breed of politician has developed that seems to have hungered for the office of president from earliest youth. Exhibit A in this regard is the photo of young Bill Clinton shaking hands with his idol, President Kennedy, when Clinton visited the White House in 1963 as a delegate to Boys Nation. Clinton credited the meeting with inspiring him to pursue a life in public service. But the boy in the photo taken that day, firmly grasping the president's hand and making forceful eye contact, certainly looked as if the idea of running for president had already occurred to him. And so a new character enters the play of presidential politics, the permanent candidate.

Clinton's vice president, Al Gore, also seemed to be running for the presidency from an early age. Gore's father had been a U.S. senator whose own presidential dreams were doomed by his vigorous opposition to the Vietnam War. Gore's decision to enlist in the army following his graduation from Harvard in 1969 seemed calculated to avoid his father's error and to ensure his future political viability— there were not many classmates following in his footsteps, and young Al was not even a backer of the war. Cynical though it may have been, the tactic worked. So swift was Gore's political rise that he made his first serious run at the presidency in 1988, the year he turned forty.

Such early ambition is not confined to baby boomers. In 1940, a wealthy Texas oilman had offered to cut the young Congressman Lyndon Johnson in on some of the profits from the business. The proposed arrangement was legitimate enough to avoid any criminal charge but would definitely tie Johnson to the oil industry. Johnson, though struggling for money and ever mindful of his father's poverty, turned the deal down on the grounds that it would kill him politically. Links to the oil business would be no problem in Texas, of course. Only in a race for national office could such an arrangement hurt Johnson. Although he was only in his second term in the House of Representatives, LBJ was already planning far into his political future.[10]

And such early ambitions are no longer limited to candidates—today they extend to their handlers as well. When Karl Rove, the mastermind of George W. Bush's 2000 campaign, was asked when he started to plan the race for the White House, he answered December 25, 1950—the day he was born. One suspects that such precocious politicos will only become more common in the future.[11]

NAME-CALLING

Any emerging politician has to contend with the labels that opponents and the press apply to him. Richard Nixon was considered the definitive American political trickster—Tricky Dick, he was called—but many political figures are saddled with reputations that center on their slipperiness rather than their accomplishments or their visions. After Nixon, Bill Clinton was tagged with the unfortunate nickname "Slick Willie." As the presidential hopeful nears contention, he must also deal with those who would apply negative labels to him.

The preppy label, for example, suggests a set of class ideas and antagonisms, above which some people have risen, in which others have become mired. Neither Franklin Roosevelt nor John F. Kennedy was faulted for having attended private schools, yet George H. W. Bush was branded a preppy and never fully escaped the child-of-privilege categorization. In the 1980 race, his opponent John Anderson called Bush "Ronald Reagan in a Brooks Brothers suit." After Bush defeated Reagan in that year's Republican primary in Pennsylvania, the *New York Times* noted that Bush "has shed his preppy, pep-rally chatter about 'Big Mo' (momentum)." But he never shed the label itself. Bush had, like Kennedy, been a war hero: one of the youngest pilots in the navy, shot down over the Pacific. And yet for him the preppy label stuck, while Kennedy's Choate experience had done him no harm.[12]

Why is one prep-school graduate saddled with a pejorative label and another given a free pass? Who decides which stock characters adhere to a candidate? Political leaders and their handlers may stress the character attributes that seem most politically potent, trying to avoid the negative labels that opponents or the press try to affix. But the matter does not rest in their hands alone. Bush and his aides certainly tried to defang the preppy stereotype. But they failed. Why? Perhaps the preppy label stuck because there was no stronger alternative theme, such as Kennedy's Catholicism (and better war story) or Roosevelt's polio. And perhaps it stuck simply because the stereotype seemed to fit George H. W. Bush in a way that it did not fit Kennedy or Roosevelt. Bush himself asked a media specialist why the Roosevelts, Kennedy, and Taft had not been branded elitists, yet he was, and was told vaguely that it had to do with "perceptions." For many voters, the notion that Bush was a preppy—not merely a graduate of a private school, but the embodiment of associated attitudes and traits—simply made sense. Ultimately, the label stuck because it fit, and there was no stronger story to push it aside.

There is a certain rough justice in the way that labels do or don't stick. Dan Quayle was quickly pegged as a nincompoop and managed numerous times to confirm the impression—in part, because the press began looking for confirmation. But it is also possible for a negative stock character to become part of a politician's persona without doing great damage. Much was made of Ronald Reagan's rather limited familiarity with complex national and global issues. But Reagan managed to convince enough people that his lack of detailed knowledge was not a handicap but an asset, and that it left him free to exercise the simple set of beliefs that guided his decisions. The fact that his predecessor, Jimmy Carter, often got bogged down in arcana lent credence to the idea. Similarly, Bill Clinton, who was notorious for his womanizing, persuaded people that this attribute, while hardly appealing, was at least not germane to his duties in office.

WHY STOCK CHARACTERS WORK, AND FOR WHOM

Reagan's Teflon shield and Clinton's status as the "comeback kid" reflected both the characters they played and the skill with which they played them. Perhaps the greatest testament to their political genius is that they turned the labels given them by the media into strengths. Journalists, after all, are the most important transmitters of stock characters and character traits. Presidents may choose to play certain characters, but others are chosen for them, and the press helps determine which ones will prevail in the public mind. Stock figures provide a useful shorthand for both journalists and the public. Say "warrior" or "preacher," "whiner" or "stoic," and your audience instantly has its bearings. Any lying president is Richard Nixon; any successful general is a potential George Washington.

Yet such convenient handles ignore the constant changes that take place in the real relations of power. The Nicaraguan contras were not the modern-day equivalents of the Founding Fathers, much as their North American supporters tried to suggest that they were. And the

Clintons' Travelgate—a minor brouhaha about patronage in the White House travel office—was not Watergate. Differences of degree and in kind get lost in the shortcuts of the stock character and the familiar story. The great power of the stories sweeps all before it. As a campaign progresses, a candidate's attempt to deal with the complexity of an issue is regularly going to be defeated by the power of the presiding story.

Characters are themselves a shorthand, not only for the candidate but for entire stories. William Manchester entitled his biography of Douglas MacArthur *American Caesar* because he knew that the title suggested so many ideas: Caesar was both a great military leader and a tyrant, the crucial figure in Rome's transition from republic to empire. Adding "American" evokes America's struggle between its republican ideals and its imperial ambitions. The title brilliantly summarizes a constellation of ideas in a mere two words.

Caesar at least was a real historical figure, although the image of Caesar most Americans summon up doubtless owes more to Shakespeare than it does to actual history. In the world of narrative, the boundaries of fact and fiction are permeable, and in politics the intermingling of fact and fiction is a common process. Calvin Coolidge became a national figure as a result of the Boston police strike of 1919. When the police struck and rioting and looting started, Coolidge, then governor of Massachusetts, called out the state militia and quelled the disturbance. His decisive action was praised by members of both parties, including President Woodrow Wilson. As the legendary newspaperman William Allen White later observed, "It was a great day for the simple mind of democracy when a fairy tale— featuring a real Jack the Giant Killer—came true." It didn't matter that Coolidge was being likened to a fictional character—this was high praise. As Richard Nixon prepared to launch the invasion of Cambodia in 1970, he grew more persuaded of the correctness of his decision through repeated viewings of the film *Patton* and took to lecturing aides in the cadences of George C. Scott, the actor who portrayed Patton. Thus a dramatized rendering of military history on film helped influence the actual course of history. The power of story-telling had dissolved the boundaries of fact and fiction, with horrific consequences.[13]

Characters have to fit their times, and new roles sometimes emerge. Perhaps the most important role to emerge in recent American politics is that of the celebrity as politician. The world of television has placed an ever higher premium on the ability to speak well, to play to the camera, to evoke emotions. George Murphy, a former film actor elected U.S. senator from California in 1964, was the first prominent actor in national politics. Ronald Reagan was the pinnacle of this trend, and Arnold Schwarzenegger has further cemented California's reputation as the home of celebrity politics. In any case, the role of actor-politician has become commonplace, and it suggests that perhaps the most important role for any politician to play is that of the successful man or woman. The idea is that success—as a quarter-back, wrestler, rock star, action hero, or businessman—somehow translates into suitability for public office. If celebrity translates into electability but not, with rare exceptions, into fitness for office, what will be the price paid by American political life, and how long will it take voters to reach the conclusion that they must stress other criteria? When George C. Scott's portrayal of Patton starts to shape American policy, the interaction of illusion and reality has become a seamless circle, and the line between truth and fiction has become less impor-tant politically than the line between good acting and bad.

CHAPTER FOUR

FASHIONING THE STORY

To win, a presidential aspirant has to fashion his story and character to suit the context of his times. That context includes a whirling flock of issues, foreign and domestic, on which the candidate is expected to take stands. More important, he must connect these issues to his own life story to persuade voters that he has a personal stake in the issues. Much of this process will be carefully scripted by the candidate himself, his advertising consultants, press secretaries, and speechwriters. From Jefferson's tame editor Philip Freneau and the Whig propagandist Thurlow Weed to George Stephanopoulos and Karl Rove, professional story-spinners have helped presidential candidates fashion their stories and identified the best methods of spreading their message.

This task can be simple or hard. It is relatively easy for a war hero to connect with the voters when the nation is on the brink of war. The real challenge is fashioning a story and striking a chord with the voters when the candidate's background is less obviously relevant. There are two ways to do this: through careful editing of the candidate's life story to make it fit the times or by linking the candidate's identity to a pressing issue, so that man and cause become identical.

On occasion, candidates who lacked a compelling life story have managed to identify themselves so closely with a dominant issue of their time that the story of that issue became their story. Ronald Reagan pulled off this feat. Reagan's journey from liberalism to conservatism between the New Deal era and the 1960s embodied a larger change of heart in American politics that came to a head in the late 1970s and early 1980s, and Reagan established himself as both the leader and the personification of that change. He successfully merged his story with that of the cause he championed. Without his personal conversion experience, Reagan's life story would have been far less effective.

The campaign biography has from the early days of the republic provided a direct way for a campaign to fashion the candidate's life story. Most of these biographies have been knocked out by party hacks, but a few were produced by real writers. Both Nathaniel Hawthorne and William Dean Howells wrote campaign biographies, of Franklin Pierce and Rutherford B. Hayes, respectively. In recent decades, campaign autobiographies have multiplied, crafted with the aid of ghostwriters and timed for publication so as to advance the candidate's story in the most effective way possible. Voters seem not to care much if the book was ghosted rather than written by the candidate, and in fact the real audience for the books is usually not the public but the press, as it is hoped that reporters will incorporate stories from the books into their campaign coverage.

The candidate must also cope with the fact that each of the major issues he confronts has its own set of contending stories, often stocked with analogies drawn from past experience. A candidate's stories have to mesh with the narrative requirements and assumptions of the dominant issue-related stories of his time, or his career will founder. With issues, as with people, the simplest stories are the ones that tend to stick, and our perception of the present is shaped by stories from the past. Thus in the wake of Munich 1938, negotiation is easily branded "appeasement," and after 1941 any sudden strike against the United States becomes a second Pearl Harbor. The debate over the most divisive domestic issue in the nation's history, slavery, was carried on using a variety of explanatory narratives, drawn from the Bible, from earlier history, and even from Harriet Beecher Stowe's *Uncle Tom's Cabin*.

This period of fashioning a set of stories to meet the particular circumstances of an election year is crucial for a candidate. To succeed, the candidate must understand his many audiences and appreciate the power of stories to move hearts and minds. When all the candidate's stories are properly aligned, he is ready to run for president.

CANDIDATES

It is not enough simply to invent a good story—one has to live it. The positions a candidate takes on issues and the offices he has held limit the choice of acceptable stories. By selecting the right roles early in his career, a candidate can construct a narrative that seems to lead inexorably to the White House, or at least to nomination. Calvin Coolidge the foe of anarchy and Thomas E. Dewey the crime-busting prosecutor displayed this sort of acumen. By far the most efficient way to become a nominee for president is to have been nominated for vice president. Twenty men who have served as president or led a major-party ticket were first offered to the voters as vice presidential nominees (twenty-one if you count Henry Wallace, the Progressive party nominee in the divided 1948 election). Eight of these succeeded to the presidency upon the death of the incumbent, of whom four later ran for president (all four—Teddy Roosevelt, Coolidge, Truman, and Lyndon Johnson—won their races). Others have held the second spots on losing tickets only to return as the top pick and go on to victory (as Franklin Roosevelt, the losing number two in the 1920 race, did in

1932) or defeat (as Bob Dole, Gerald Ford's running mate in 1976, did in 1996). Since the presidency is the sort of job for which no résumé is truly adequate, no prior experience sufficient, having been a vice presidential nominee at least testifies that the candidate was once found worthy of national trust. And if one is qualified to be next in line, it logically follows that one is fit to hold the office.

Another way of reaching the top of the ticket is to demonstrate leadership in a series of important governmental assignments. In the nation's youth the secretary of state's office was viewed as the waiting room for future presidents. Jefferson, Madison, Monroe, and John Quincy Adams all held the post before becoming president, and later Martin Van Buren and James Buchanan also served as the nation's chief diplomatist. (The job has also served as a consolation prize for former contenders—Daniel Webster, Lewis Cass, James G. Blaine, William Jennings Bryan, and Charles Evans Hughes all held the office after having been presidential nominees.)

But as politics moved away from the elite groups that exercised so much control in the days of the early republic and moved to a more popular basis, the actual qualifications of a person for the office of president faded in importance next to his electability. A story of demonstrated competence and responsibility still helped, but it also had its downside; actual power meant the risk of making unpopular decisions, of putting the national interest ahead of momentary popularity. It is hard to picture a former secretary of state emerging as a presidential candidate today; the realities of international diplomacy do not mesh well with domestic politics. A diplomatic mission to mollify or bully some fractious dictator may prove successful, but the ceremonial photo of the secretary of state shaking hands with the war criminal seldom ages well. Diplomacy has ceased to be a stepping-stone to ultimate power, and this has had consequences for the sophistication of American foreign policy. Capable politicians avoid diplomatic service as toxic to an electoral career, and elected leaders seldom have real acquaintance with international affairs.

In recent decades, two offices—governor and senator—have been the traditional launch pads for most serious presidential hopefuls. Each has its pluses and minuses. Senators work in Washington, where they naturally develop ties to the leading fund-raisers and media consultants whose allegiance is now taken as a useful measure of the viability of a campaign. Senators also have the chance to take notable public stands on national issues, yet are largely free of responsibility for negative outcomes because they are merely legislators. Governors, however, can brand their senatorial rivals as having been corrupted from too much time inside the Beltway. Senators also have trouble proving they can actually run something. Governors can prove that, but their executive records also provide ample material for the press and for their opponents' "opposition research" teams. In the 1988 campaign, for example, the failure of Massachusetts governor Michael Dukakis to protect Boston Harbor adequately against water pollution provided the Republicans with a damaging set of images with which to charge Dukakis with neglect of the environment.

Although American politics is often said to be profoundly nonideological, a number of candidates have claimed nomination for president as the avatars of particular movements or ideas. Thomas Jefferson did it first. He and his supporters portrayed his election as a necessary brake on a dangerous drift toward monarchism in the Federalist administrations of George Washington and John Adams. Andrew Jackson, too, was presented to voters as the spirit of his age, the embodiment of greater democracy and of frontier hostility to the eastern establishment. In 1856 and 1860 John C. Frémont and Abraham Lincoln were tribunes of the antislavery movement (as ex-President Martin Van Buren had been in 1848 as candidate of the Free Soil party). The newspaper editor Horace Greeley was the Democratic and Liberal

Republican nominee in 1872, an impolitic champion of the short-lived Liberal Republican movement for smaller, more honest government. Two decades later, William Jennings Bryan was the national voice of agrarian unrest, and he returned within four years as the embodiment of anti-imperialism. (Bryan's career owed nearly as much to his adaptability as to his eloquence.) In 1912 Theodore Roosevelt and Woodrow Wilson fought for leadership of the Progressive movement. Modern conservatism was born in the Barry Goldwater campaign of 1964 and revived in the Reagan campaigns of 1976 and 1980, when it finally triumphed. All of these candidates had other life stories swirling about them—Teddy Roosevelt the war hero, Bryan the orator, Wilson the professor, Reagan the Hollywood star—but each owed much of his influence to the force of the ideology he championed. It helped, too, that their causes had vivid enemies. No story line is older than that of the struggle of good versus evil, and monarchists, slave owners, robber barons, and godless Communists all served as powerful bogeymen, driving voters into the arms of their sworn opponents.

Ideologues need a conduit for their ideas to reach the voters, and each of these candidates was either the director or the beneficiary of a propaganda machine. Jefferson oversaw the editorial efforts of his party while furnishing some of the most important documents himself. In 1791 Jefferson secured the aid of Philip Freneau, who had matriculated at Princeton with James Madison, to launch a Jeffersonian paper in Philadelphia. Freneau was given a post as translator in the State Department—of which Jefferson was then secretary—and by late October he was printing the *National Gazette,* a paper that ceaselessly lashed the Washington administration and in particular Treasury Secretary Alexander Hamilton. The unleashing of Freneau contributed greatly to the hardening of partisan lines during the new nation's first decade. Other editors would follow Freneau in helping to usher the Federalist party into extinction.

Throughout the subsequent two centuries partisan members of the press told their stories in print. The many editors of the abolitionist and antislavery movement advanced their candidates and fiercely argued the case for their side. Greeley and Bryan ran their own papers, and in 1904 William Randolph Hearst tried to use his newspapers to raise himself to the Democratic nomination. Ronald Reagan's influence was felt more through television and radio—his political career was launched by a television speech he gave in support of Goldwater near the end of the 1964 race, and in the mid-1970s he regularly delivered political commentary on the radio.

The media have helped candidates to prominence in less direct and more serendipitous ways. Coverage of Herbert Hoover's remarkable efforts to bring relief to Europe after the First World War helped make him an international hero, and led to his appointment to Harding's cabinet. The tabloid-ready exploits of Thomas Dewey, the rackets-busting federal prosecutor in New York, led to three terms as governor of the state and two Republican nominations for president. And as the press became more aware of its hero-making possibilities, it tried ever harder to uncover the promising leaders of tomorrow. In the spring of 1971 *Time* proclaimed Jimmy Carter, the new governor of Georgia, an exemplar of the new, postsegregation South, helping to launch his national career. Even trivial media appearances have helped careers along: both Wendell Willkie and John Glenn received early prominence as contestants on broadcast game shows (Willkie on *Information Please,* Glenn on both *I've Got a Secret* and *Name That Tune*).

CAMPAIGN BIOGRAPHIES

The most straightforward way to get your story out is to publish it yourself, or to persuade someone to write it for you. Nathaniel Hawthorne, in the preface to *The Life of Franklin Pierce,* the campaign biography he wrote about his Bowdoin College classmate, admitted that Pierce had been frequently written about, but that he was usually "misrepresented by indiscriminate abuse, on the one hand, and by aimless praise, on the other." Setting matters right, Hawthorne blended these approaches and bathed Pierce in indiscriminate praise.[1]

Hawthorne's book contained most of the standard elements of a campaign biography. He covered the candidate's family background. Franklin's father, Benjamin, was a Revolutionary War soldier. Indeed, Benjamin Pierce was just eighteen, and at work in the fields, when word came of the British attack on Lexington and Concord: "He immediately loosened the ox chain, left the plough in the furrow, took his uncle's gun and equipments, and set forth towards the scene of action. From that day, for more than seven years, he never saw his native place." The father's exemplary service in the Revolution gave his son "a stronger sense, than most of us can attain, of the value of that Union which these old heroes had risked so much to consolidate." Young Franklin was "a beautiful boy, with blue eyes, light, curling hair, and a sweet expression of face. The traits presented of him indicate moral symmetry, kindliness, and a delicate texture of sentiment, rather than marked prominences of character." Hawthorne credited Pierce as possessing both "a strong endowment of religious feeling" and the "native qualities of a born soldier" (Pierce had served in the Mexican War), who calmly reacted to a nearby concussion from an enemy shell by saying, "That was a lucky miss!"[2]

Concerning Pierce's political career, Hawthorne emphasized his behind-the-scenes influence and excused the candidate's lack of rhetorical gifts. On the vital issue of slavery, Hawthorne invoked the shades of the Revolution and wrote that Pierce had chosen the "great and sacred reality" of the Union over "the mistiness of a philanthropic theory." Finally, he stressed that Pierce was a reluctant candidate, whose greatest wish was "to retire from public life."[3]

Negative campaign biographies have a long past, too. Alexander Hamilton helped to destroy the career of his Federalist rival, John

Adams, by writing a savage private account of the Adams administration, which Aaron Burr succeeded in acquiring and disseminating during the 1800 campaign. (The episode contributed to the Burr-Hamilton duel four years later.) In 1836 *The Life of Martin Van Buren* appeared, supposedly from the pen of Davy Crockett, though the real author was likely a Georgia politician named Augustin S. Clayton. The subtitle was *Heir-Apparent to the "Government" and the Appointed Successor of General Andrew Jackson,* and the vituperative text includes such libels as "He is laced up in corsets, such as women in a town wear, and, if possible, tighter than the best of them. It would be difficult to say, from his personal appearance, whether he was man or woman, but for his large red and gray whiskers."[4]

Hawthorne set a high literary standard for the campaign biography, although the book makes dull reading today. (One's expectations of Davy Crockett, or Augustin Clayton, are lower, so the disappointment is less.) Writers noted or obscure continued to pump out quadrennial volumes of praise or condemnation. Rutherford B. Hayes was particularly fortunate in his literary backers: Mark Twain stumped for him and his campaign biography was written by William Dean Howells.

Howells's *Sketch of the Life and Character of Rutherford B. Hayes* is actually a charming effort, blending frank admiration for the candidate with a sensibility far more thoughtful and balanced than the average campaign puffery. Some of it was clearly written with a particular political goal—his emphasis on the Ohioan Hayes's New England roots was surely intended to secure votes in the Northeast—but much of it was considerably more subtle. Howells commented on Hayes's literary tastes—a fondness for Hawthorne and Emerson—and described his innovative use of an insanity defense early in his legal career while defending a woman accused of murder (she was eventually committed to an insane asylum). Howells detailed Hayes's service as an officer in the Union Army—he was under fire for a total of perhaps a hundred days and was wounded four times—and then laboriously linked the candidate's war wounds to his presidential aspirations. Howells noted that one of Hayes's war wounds made it hard for him to climb stairs, but predicted that this would "not prevent his ascent of the Capitol steps" on Inauguration Day.[5]

The tradition of political biography gathered steam in the twentieth century. One of the better examples is *Up from the City Streets*, published in 1927 to celebrate the life and career of Alfred E. Smith, then governor of New York and the Democratic nominee for president the following year. The authors, Norman Hapgood and Henry Moskowitz, recognized that Smith's urban, Irish Catholic roots were the greatest obstacle to his election, so they met the problem head-on: "He is the first of our national heroes to be born amidst din and squalor. His story suggests that in the future our vast cities may do better by humanity than we have feared. It is possible that . . . their sons may show not less energy, persistence, and initiative than have come heretofore from the silences and the long labor of the ax and plow." And, in case the ax reference was too obscure, a few pages later they surmised that the talk Smith heard as a boy "was probably less philosophic than the talk Lincoln heard in the streets of Springfield, Illinois." They related his religious education—carefully noting for their Prohibition-era audience that "No drop of liquor ever appeared on church premises"—and described his early labors as a newsboy and at the Fulton Fish Market and then his reforming career in state politics. "The world is always learning from examples," the authors concluded. "Smith's story should be a bracing influence."[6]

Onward flowed the stream of campaign biographies, including such briskly titled efforts as *This Man Landon* and *This Is Humphrey*. Frederick Palmer's *This Man Landon*, published in 1936 to advance the hopeless presidential cause of Kansas's Republican governor, Alfred M. Landon, hit the same sorts of themes Hawthorne had sounded, but also invoked the great founders of the Republican party: "Lincoln from the Illinois frontier of his day, Grant clerking in a country store—we know that the man for a national emergency is where we find him." In Landon's case, they found him in the state capital, Topeka. Palmer stressed the simple frugality of Landon and his administration, and stated that "the New Deal in its general plan and as practiced is wholly repugnant to him."[7]

By Landon's time the tradition of the reluctant candidate had nearly expired, and in recent decades it has become common for the candidate himself to write—or at least put his name on—a campaign autobiography or manifesto. Four years after Landon's defeat, Thomas Dewey, then district attorney of New York County, was angling for the Republican nomination, and published *The Case Against the New Deal* to bolster his case. Dewey's essays critiqued New Deal programs while attacking Franklin Roosevelt as a practitioner of "charming super-salesmanship and political hypnotism" who "conceives himself to be the master, not the servant, of the American people." Dewey failed to win the nomination in 1940, but the Republicans did make him their standard-bearer in the following two contests.[8]

Campaign autobiographies and other books by candidates with a literary bent had been around before Dewey—William Howard Taft published *Present Day Problems* to help him in the 1908 campaign, and Louisiana's Huey P. Long published the cheery tract *Every Man a King* before his career was cut short by assassination in 1935. But in recent decades, the pace has quickened. Works like Richard Nixon's *Six Crises*, Barry Goldwater's *The Conscience of a Conservative*, and Jimmy Carter's *Why Not the Best?* have spread the candidate's desired narrative in advance of a campaign.

Six Crises was published in 1962. At the time, Nixon was campaigning for governor of California, trying to revive his career after losing to John Kennedy in the 1960 race—the sixth of the crises in the book. Nixon related the key moments of his career, as he saw them. He stated early on that he had not intended to write such a book, but changed his mind at the urging of friends. Moreover, he had a conversation with Kennedy in early 1961 during which the new president advised Nixon that it was a good thing for a politician to write a book, since "it tends to elevate him in popular esteem" (especially if one wins a Pulitzer Prize, as Kennedy did in 1957 for *Profiles in Courage*). Nixon claimed that writing the book proved to be his seventh crisis, but he later proved such a prolific writer that the claim is hard to take seriously.[9]

Nixon knew that he was part of a narrative tradition. He wrote of the "Great American Legend" of presidential candidates. "A mother takes a child on her knee. She senses by looking into his eyes that there is something truly extraordinary about him. She says to herself and perhaps even to him, 'You, son, are going to be President some day.' From that time on, he is tapped for greatness. He talks before he walks. He reads a thousand words a minute. He is bored by school because he is so much smarter than his teachers. He prepares himself for leadership by taking courses in public speaking and political science. He drives ever upward, calculating every step of the way until he reaches his and—less importantly—the nation's destiny by becoming President of the United States." This, one senses, is more Nixon's view of how the world saw John Kennedy than it is an accurate reflection of the real presidential legend.[10]

Nixon's account of his roots does contain the requisite humble childhood. As a boy, he longed to be a railroad engineer so he could see the world beyond Whittier, California. He worked hard in school because "I knew that I could not go on to college and to law school unless I was able to earn scholarships." And he revealed some political advice he'd gotten from New York's twice-defeated presidential contender, Thomas Dewey. After Dewey heard a good Nixon speech in 1952, he told the rising GOP star: "Make me a promise: don't get fat; don't lose your zeal. And you can be President some day."[11]

Two years after Nixon left the White House in disgrace, Jimmy Carter was elected president. In 1975, Carter had published *Why Not the Best?,* in which he lyrically described his childhood on an American farm in the 1930s and '40s, including a round of chores that seems drawn from a prior century (such as learning the rudiments of blacksmithing). Ben Franklin would have recognized, and extolled, the spirit the book expressed. Carter presented his life—decent, humble, hardworking—as an example of what the life of the nation could be like. His story was everyman's story, and in 1976 it helped carry him to a narrow win over Gerald Ford.

These campaign tomes, and many others, have presented the candidate's own version of his life story. Each attempted to define the terms of the coming debate. Such books are both expressions of a candidate's personality and testing grounds for issues and stories that will be deployed in the coming race. However colloquial or relaxed they may sound, today's campaign autobiographies are carefully deployed weapons of electoral war.

ISSUES AND THEIR STORIES

Presidential life stories are the backbone of a campaign, but as a race progresses other stories have to be integrated into or balanced with that central text. Whatever national issues are foremost must be subjected to narrative treatment. A current issue or event is often interpreted and explained in terms drawn from earlier days. Lincoln explains the Civil War in terms of the American Revolution (in the Gettysburg Address); feminists draw parallels between the women's movement and the civil rights movement; war with Iraq is likened to Vietnam by its opponents (the "quagmire") or seen as an anti-Munich by its supporters (the dangers of appeasing dictators, the rightness of confronting evil). Both character stories and issues narratives play key roles in shaping the outcome of elections and the course of a presidential administration. They are the shorthand that reporters and citizens use to portray and comprehend complex events. But if the past has the power to explain the present, as historians believe, these stories of the past also have the power to mislead, because no great historical personage appears twice—whatever Hegel and Marx may say—and no historical situation repeats itself exactly.

Today's pundits insist that presidential campaigns should revolve around the issues facing the country. They're not wrong. Yet an eagerness to run on the issues can spring from questionable motives. "Let's talk about the issues!" is a common cry from someone whose past is filled with controversy. What does it matter, such a candidate hopefully implies, if I cheated on my wife, accepted a kickback, or lied about my war record, when we face a looming crisis in the Middle East? On Wall Street? In our schools? Eventually campaigns do have to address issues. But the way those issues are addressed is often determined not by their importance to society but by the attractiveness and simplicity of the stories that are brought up on either side to exemplify them. Surely it mattered little to the nation that Michael Dukakis, while governor of Massachusetts, had vetoed a bill requiring that schoolchildren recite the Pledge of Allegiance in classrooms on the grounds that it was unconstitutional. Yet the legal argument was too complex for sound bites, and Dukakis's opponents portrayed the veto as evidence of his supposedly unpatriotic views.

Issues matter more in bad times than in good. The sectional crisis of the 1850s, the economic crisis of the 1930s, and the domestic and international crises of the 1960s all prompted more issue-oriented campaigns. But in calmer times, the issues, although important, are often less discussed than questions of character.

In politics, how an issue is framed—how its story is told—matters more than the accuracy of an argument either side puts forward concerning it. The framing of a story can and does take place over years, with each new iteration building upon the preceding ones, advancing, modifying, sometimes undermining the master narrative. Consider the first major contested election in American history, the election of 1800. It resulted in the first peaceful transfer of national power from one party to another, an election so important that it became known as the Revolution of 1800. The campaign pitted the incumbent John Adams against his own vice president, Thomas Jefferson. As the campaign went forward, the struggle between the men was seen as a clash between two ideas of government. The stories that each side told, drawn from the political debates of the previous half century, made the choice seem much starker than it really was. But it was the stories that defined the choice.

John Adams's partisans portrayed Jefferson as a dangerous radical. The Revolution in the United States had taken place twenty-five years earlier and was now almost universally accepted. But during the 1800 election another revolution, the one in France a decade earlier, was on many people's minds. The overthrown king, Louis XVI, had provided vital military support to the American rebels, and he was therefore popular in the new nation. Portraits of him and his wife, Marie Antoinette, had hung in places of honor in the first U.S. Capitol, in New York. But both royals had been executed in 1793, and the French state seemed to have declared religion itself an enemy. Jefferson sympathized with the French revolutionaries, whose anticlerical excesses did not disturb him nearly so much as they did others. Naval engagements related to France's war with Great Britain had drawn American vessels into the hostilities, and by the late 1790s the United States and France were enmeshed in the so-called Quasi War, a low-grade naval conflict. In this heated atmosphere, Federalists saw a Jefferson presidency as potentially treasonous. They viewed Jefferson's fondness for France and hostility to Great Britain as morally suspect and harmful to the economy and security of the United States.

For their part, members of Jefferson's Republican party looked at the Adams regime and saw excessive nostalgia for Great Britain and an unhealthy enthusiasm for the concentration of power in the federal

government—particularly the executive branch—that smacked of monarchical leanings. Certainly the rhetoric of the campaigns blasted away
any nuances of these harsh views. Real differences between the two
sides were exaggerated and presented as parts of larger, cartoonish stories. The Republicans cast themselves as the colonists and the Federalists as the British in a replay of the American Revolution. Adams
was a penny-ante George III, but Jefferson would secure the blessings
of liberty for the nation. The Federalists, on the other hand, cast the
Republicans as French revolutionaries. The party of Jefferson was the
party of regicide, anticlericalism, and rampant violence.

In one 1800 handbill intended for the citizens of Philadelphia, the
Republican party laid out differences between "Things as They Have
Been" under the Federalists and "Things as They Will Be" under the
Republicans. The first item on the Federal side: "The principles and
patriots of the *Revolution* condemned and stigmatized." But under a
Republican regime: "The principles of the *Revolution* restored; its patriots honored and beloved." The second item: "*Republicanism*, a badge
for persecution, and federalism a mask for monarchy." Under the Republican regime, "*Republicanism* proved to mean something, and federalism found to mean nothing."[12]

The Adams administration had provided some basis for such charges.
Two years earlier Adams had signed into law the Alien and Sedition
Acts, which authorized harsh measures against those opposed to the
Federalist agenda. And the Quasi War had pushed the Adams administration closer to Britain. But the Federalists had fears of their own.
In an address to the voters of Delaware in September 1800, a pamphleteer who signed himself "A Christian Federalist" waxed hysterical
about the Republicans, asking, "Will you pause, Fellow-Citizens, and
inquire what produced these afflicting and wonderful events in France,
and will you then ask do causes exist in this country capable of producing the same effect? In France, it was the suffering men of false and
wicked principles to get into power, *men who taught that there was no*

God—no Savior—no future rewards and punishments, but that death was an eternal sleep." The Federalists here took some of Jefferson's most interesting and appealing habits of mind, his being so quintessentially a man of the Enlightenment, and chose to recognize only a sinister side—one that was regicidal, anarchistic, and hostile to religion. Jefferson won, suggesting that fears of the old imperial oppressor, England, were stronger than any concerns over godlessness.[13]

The election of 1800 was the first in American history to be contested on the grounds of "liberal versus conservative." The line of attack used against John Adams has lived on in many different forms. It suffused the electoral campaign of 1828 between John Quincy Adams and Andrew Jackson. As president, the younger Adams seemed to share many political ideas with his father and the extinct Federalist party, from which he had separated himself in 1809 and which had essentially expired by 1815. When the two men faced each other in 1828, Andrew Jackson's Democratic Republican party hurled the accusation that at a gathering of Adams supporters in Massachusetts, one of his partisans rose and toasted "the political regeneration" of some old ideas: "Those who fell with the first Adams rise with the second." The Jackson literature enumerated all sorts of old Federalists who had been appointed to federal offices. Adams's side was also accused of having been in league with the participants in the Hartford Convention of 1814. At that meeting Federalist delegates from New England had discussed secession from the union in order to maintain good relations with England. When word got out, their discussion of secession was understandably viewed as treasonous. So charges of ties to England, federalism, and even quasi-monarchical sentiments rose again. The real issues of 1828 were set aside as the animosities of prior decades trotted out to do battle.[14]

STORIES OF SLAVERY

Revolutionary ideals retained great force in nineteenth-century America. Yet many Americans remained blind to the way slavery betrayed those ideals, or they allowed their self-interest to trump their consciences. Slavery—and the public debate over it—shows how an issue can be portrayed as a variety of different issues, appropriating a variety of different preexisting narratives, depending on the political agenda and rhetorical gifts of the side fashioning the portrayal.

No argument in American history has had such profound consequences as the one over slavery. It transcended the personality of any single candidate. And it was no diversion—it was the central question in American life. The problems surrounding slavery seemed dauntingly complex to many Americans, who knew how deeply embedded the institution was in the political economy of the South. How could it be rooted out? What would happen to the freed slaves? What would a postslavery America look like? The issues being debated inflamed people's passions, and the arguments involved emotion at least as much as intellect.

The case against slavery was made through constitutional argument, political diatribe, and personal testimony. The two great propagandists of abolitionism were William Lloyd Garrison and Frederick Douglass. Garrison wrote impassioned but carefully argued essays attacking the United States Constitution for its provisions protecting slavery. His arguments were lucid, consistent, and devastating, but many found them unpatriotic because of their attack on the national charter. It didn't help that Garrison's writing was anchored in logic and brimming with legalisms, eschewing illustrative anecdotes, sympathetic characters, and affecting stories. For all of his passion, Garrison was not always the most effective advocate of abolitionism.

Douglass, on the other hand, had a remarkable personal story to tell. His greatest written work was the story of his own life, in which he wrote of his oppression as a slave, his resistance, and his escape to the North. His is one of the great personal narratives of American history. But to antislavery Americans it was also understood to represent a potentially universal narrative about emancipation. And because Douglass was such a compelling figure—eloquent, brave, humane— he made this universal emancipation a powerful and appealing vision. In the *Narrative of the Life of Frederick Douglass,* the reader found all the justifications of slavery rendered loathsome and void in the face of Douglass's own humanity. No system that enslaved such a man, the book conveyed, could be just. Where Garrison's arguments lay on the surface for all to see, Douglass's were embedded in the very essence of his narrative, and of his being.

Still, the abolitionists were a radical fringe group in antebellum America, even at the time of the 1860 election. In most of the country, politicians seeking major-party support had to tread gingerly around the issue of abolition. For those opposed to slavery, the most politic argument was not about its fundamental injustice to the slaves but rather about how it betrayed the principles of the American Revolution. Slavery, the argument went, sapped the very willpower of the southern slaveholders. The luxury of slavery lulled them into lives of indolence and frivolity that threatened American democracy itself, because it was an article of faith that only a virtuous citizenry could ensure the continued health of a republic. This sounded an old Puritanical theme from the time of the American Revolution about the value of hard work. Those who opposed slavery employed various themes that resonated with the story of the Revolution. The Republican platform in 1856 proclaimed that slavery was at odds with the Declaration of Independence's statement that "all men are created equal." Douglass and Garrison also cited the Declaration in their writings, and in general the opponents of slavery claimed that it undermined the republican institutions the Revolution had been fought to win.

Proslavery propagandists, too, had useful authorities to invoke and stories to put their cause in the best light. They pointed to the Bible, saying that it sanctified slavery. In a country that was deeply religious, biblical references were understood by nearly all Americans and honored by most. The Bible was thus a tremendously powerful ally, as when one southern minister invoked it in support of slavery: "Had not the Jews practiced slavery under the watchful care of Jehovah? Did not the Ten Commandments mention 'servants' thrice? . . . Did not the Apostle Paul urge the fugitive Onesimus to return to his master?"[15]

The literal truth of Bible stories was a matter too controversial to debate in the 1850s. But other literary works also played a role in the national debate over slavery. By far the most influential of these was Harriet Beecher Stowe's *Uncle Tom's Cabin,* serialized beginning in 1851 and published in 1852 to remarkable success. The stoic heroism of Uncle Tom and the wanton cruelty of Simon Legree proved powerful narrative allies for the antislavery cause. When Stowe visited Lincoln in the White House in 1862, the president is said to have remarked, "So you're the little woman who wrote the book that made this great war!" Lincoln exaggerated, but his point was clear: fictional stories can sometimes be more powerful than factual ones in shaping public opinion.[16]

Not that factual stories weren't mobilized in the debate over slavery. The plight of workers in the ever expanding world of industrial capitalism was becoming a powerful issue. In the mid-nineteenth century the United States witnessed the development of an urban industrial working class. George Fitzhugh, an effective southern propagandist, attempted to seize this story line and use it in favor of slavery. In his book *Cannibals All,* Fitzhugh asserted that "slavery is the natural and normal condition of society. The situation of the north is abnormal and anomalous." He argued that to give men "equality of rights, is but giving license to the strong to oppress the weak" because "capital exercises a more perfect compulsion over free laborers than human masters over slaves; for free laborers must at all times work or starve, and slaves are supported whether they work or not." Fitzhugh ended by proclaiming slavery "the oldest, the best, the most common form of Socialism" and "the natural and normal condition of the laboring men, white or black." It was a radical argument, a sign that for some the values of the American Revolution no longer seemed relevant. In essence, Fitzhugh took the entire legacy of the Revolution and of its slave-owning tribune, Thomas Jefferson, and cast it aside. One could not cherish both slavery and the Enlightenment, Fitzhugh concluded, so let's discard the Enlightenment. Fitzhugh was much quoted; and there were clearly some in the North, such as the laborers who rioted against the draft in New York City in July 1863, who were receptive to Fitzhugh's anticapitalist rhetoric.[17]

FAMILIAR STORIES

Of course, Fitzhugh was far from the only social critic to discern a set of useful stories in the development of the industrial workforce. The politics of American capitalism was a new story, but it soon became a classic one. The existing supply of stock stories is always being replenished and edited. To examples drawn from the Bible, the ancient world, and Shakespeare are added new tropes drawn from history. Historical analogies go out of fashion and return, depending on circumstances.

In 1873 Mark Twain and his neighbor Charles Dudley Warner published a novel entitled *The Gilded Age*. The phrase was intended by Twain and Warner to draw attention to the difference between the authenticity of the Grecian golden age and the cheap imitation "Gilded Age" of the late nineteenth century. In the wake of recent corporate scandals that story line has returned. A *New York Times* article in December 1999, for example, shortly before the air started leaking out of the dot-com bubble, chronicled the conspicuous consumption (private planes, limos, pampered pets) of technology millionaires and asked, "Is it a new Gilded Age, with many thousands of robber barons, instead of just a few dozen?" The vast differences between the economic and political circumstances of the two eras, between the types of issues and the types of corporate crimes that were committed, can evaporate in the simplicity of the phrase "Gilded Age." The Gilded Age itself has become retrospectively gilt with an aura of luxury and wealth without retaining Twain's original concept of a thin coating of gold over a core of base metal.[18]

The story of the traitor is one of the oldest narratives of literature and history. Americans fused mythological and religious images of the traitor with their own real-life betrayers. Revolutionary-era prints depicted Benedict Arnold with horns and a pitchfork, a satanic servant of the British monarchy. To label someone a Benedict Arnold has conveyed the greatest censure ever since. Joseph McCarthy, the red-baiting Wisconsin senator, certainly understood the power of fear and the force of an accusation of treachery. In the early 1950s, his attempts to root out traitors in the government dominated domestic politics and shaped American foreign policy.

Few were immune to the contagion of fear. As a war hero, Dwight Eisenhower seemed unlikely to be associated with traitorous conduct. But McCarthy's search for traitors quickly expanded from the State Department, his initial hunting ground, to the United States Army. By 1952, McCarthy had set his sights on former army chief of staff George C. Marshall, the chief architect of American military policy in the Second World War and the mentor of Dwight Eisenhower.

Eisenhower meekly defended Marshall but would criticize McCarthy only obliquely, saying that he had "no patience with anyone who can find in [Marshall's] record of service for this country anything to criticize." The realities of presidential campaigning complicated the situation. In September 1952, Eisenhower was scheduled to campaign in Indiana with Bill Jenner, a local politician who had called Marshall "a front man for traitors." Observing Jenner and Eisenhower stumping together, the columnist Murray Kempton wrote, "The luncheon was ended, and Eisenhower walked off the platform, stopping for a minute to catch his breath and raising his right hand to lean on a friendly shoulder. He reached for Bill Jenner's shoulder, then saw who it was, and let his hand drop. Let it be said for Dwight Eisenhower that he did the thing he did not utterly without shame."[19]

Betrayal begets more betrayal. Joseph McCarthy told of traitors in the State Department and in the army, including George Marshall, and Dwight Eisenhower betrayed his friendship with Marshall. Such was the power of the story line McCarthy had animated that even Ike had to bow to it. These stories worked with many other stories—about Korea, the "loss" of China, corruption in the Truman administration, the character of Richard Nixon—to shape popular understanding of the 1952 race.

As the Cold War continued, certain stories recurred because they appeared to encapsulate and define the issues and tensions of an era. The accused spies Alger Hiss and Julius and Ethel Rosenberg became exemplars of Communist deviousness for one set of Americans, of persecuted innocence for another set. The American government found rebellion against a colonial oppressor laudable in some contexts (Hungary, Poland) and subversive in others (Vietnam, Nicaragua).

Issue narratives work best when they plug into powerful stories that people already know. Sometimes an entire set of stories can be triggered by a single line. Ronald Reagan used one such line with devastating effectiveness against Jimmy Carter in their 1980 debate. "Are you better off than you were four years ago?" he asked the American people, summoning up a whole set of ideas—secular dreams about rising living standards and individual improvement—and stacking them against the gnawing anxieties of rising oil prices, inflation, and taxes. The old story of America's unceasing upward path as an ever richer and more prosperous country seemed to Americans to be under threat in the late 1970s. In his disastrous "malaise" speech of 1979, Jimmy Carter had essentially tried to tell America: The party's over, there are limited resources, and we can't go on the way we've been going. A year later, Ronald Reagan offered a simpler and more reassuring message: If you're not better off today, it's not your fault or the fault of changing circumstances; it's Jimmy Carter's fault. The problem lay not with the people but with their leader.

Jimmy Carter offered a story in which the voters were the villains; Reagan offered one in which the voters were the blameless victims. Is it any wonder that Carter lost?

CHAPTER FIVE

WHEN STORIES COLLIDE: CAMPAIGNING FOR PRESIDENT

THE JOURNEY OF FINDING A VIABLE PRESIDENTIAL NARRATIVE AND emerging as a national figure can take decades. But in a campaign each candidate must quickly marshal a vast array of forces to publicize his stories while simultaneously combating the countervailing narratives circulated by opponents and produced by news organizations. A presidential campaign is a great festival of narration, with the press serving simultaneously as actor, chorus, and audience. The press interprets stories, has stories reinterpreted for it by political spin doctors, and responds (sometimes) to the public's appetite for new narratives. Campaigns are a high-velocity duel of story versus story that stretches out over months. New stories must constantly be developed, as old ones either are overturned or lose the public's interest. The successful candidate is the one whose stories connect with the largest number of voters.

The process has changed over time. John Adams acted his part to the small audience of prominent men of his day, and that was enough. Zachary Taylor was elected amid a patriotic din of parades and banners. Warren Harding was plucked from obscurity by the leaders of his party and then posed handsomely for the part, allowing others to decide what lines he should speak. Lyndon Johnson knew in 1968 that he could not overcome a negative story line and gave up trying, recognizing a force that even his will could not master.

The presidential campaign itself has become a stock story of American life, with familiar chapters—primaries, conventions, debates—and recurring themes. The candidate and his team must understand this story well and mold his story to take advantage of it.

Here the prize often goes to the candidate (and campaign) with the greatest ability to improvise. New issues regularly arise—brought on by world events, a gaffe, an opponent's stratagems, or a new revelation unearthed from the past. The ability to explain, revise, and recast an existing story often means the difference between victory and defeat. A gifted improviser like Bill Clinton can recover from stumbles and prevail, while a less fluid performer such as Michael Dukakis strides stiffly into defeat.

RULES OF THE GAME

The presidential game has become ever more expensive, time-consuming, and complicated. George Washington devised no electoral strategies, made no campaign trips, conducted no fund-raising, attended no nominating conventions, and kissed no babies, but he did establish some powerful traditions for future candidates. One was the tradition of the reluctant candidate, which survived for a century before finally falling into disuse. The other was the custom of stepping down after two terms, which survived until FDR's successful third-term race in 1940. So great was the alarm over Roosevelt's break with an unwritten rule that in 1951 it was made part of the fabric of the Constitution with the adoption of the Twenty-second Amendment.

The two-party system developed starting in the 1790s, and although it has occasionally faced challenges, it has remained central to the election process. The role and influence of the bosses of the two parties, however, has waxed and waned over time. Sometimes party leaders could dictate virtually every aspect of a campaign, as in McKinley's 1896 race, and other times party leaders were shoved aside, as in George McGovern's 1972 campaign. With the rise of broadcasting, and in particular television, the importance of raising funds to pay for campaign commercials has grown, and in recent years full-time fundraisers, direct-mail consultants, media buyers, ad makers, and Internet gurus have replaced party organizations as the principal conduits—and recipients—of campaign funds.

The rising importance of television has been the greatest change in campaigning in the past century, for television places a much greater emphasis on narrative. The world of strong party allegiances, disciplined and effective party organizations, and grassroots get-out-the-vote efforts is largely gone, replaced by well-financed fund-raising machines, constant polling, and cinematic campaign advertisements produced by film-school graduates and Madison Avenue pros. Old-fashioned party loyalties were based upon a few fundamental ideas—hostility to concentrated economic power (Jacksonian democracy, the Populists), allegiance to one side in the Civil War (the postbellum Republican party in the North, the southern Democrats well into the 1960s), hostility to taxation and related big-government notions (the modern Republican party). But as party loyalties have grown dimmer in recent decades, voters have increasingly needed to be presented with compelling reasons to vote for particular candidates, and campaigns gathered their resources and their wits to devise the best ways of getting an effective message across. As a result, modern campaigns focus on presenting the best possible series of life stories about one's own candidate while circulating the most effective negative notions about the opponent. Campaign ads, candidate appearances, press events, photo opportunities, and even leaks to the press are all orchestrated to make sure the campaign stays "on message," and that the message sent tells the best possible story to the largest number of likely voters.

The game has both its own rhythms and its own road map, and the most important early stop on the road is the New Hampshire primary.

THE PRIMARIES—NEW HAMPSHIRE AND AFTER

Certain steps along the campaign path are by now as well choreographed as a pas de deux in *Swan Lake*. Among them are the campaign kickoff, the early campaign trips and fund-raisers, the primaries, endorsements by party leaders and vanquished contenders, the national convention, the choice of a running mate, televised debates, and election day. Each step is its own collection of stories, eagerly watched and relentlessly compared with earlier versions of the same drama. Although the issues of the day are part of the meat of any campaign, much of the press coverage and of the public's attention centers on a campaign's success or failure at staging these episodes. The ability to run a well-choreographed campaign is considered vital evidence of skill at governance.

At least as far back as Eugene McCarthy's surprisingly strong showing against Lyndon Johnson in 1968, the New Hampshire primary has been the defining early moment of the election year. Once a candidate announces his candidacy—indeed, for many months prior to the official announcement—regular trips to New Hampshire are essential. There, at last, the presidential campaign moves beyond opinion polls and straw polls and Sunday-morning talk shows and the citizens actually get to vote—the most fascinating act of the drama, because campaigns cannot control it. For months the Granite State is overrun with candidates and reporters, as different issues and stories are tried out, their messages honed or discarded. The delivery systems vary—campaign rallies, interviews with local TV anchors, debates with the other candidates, and print, radio, and television advertisements. It is a harsh environment for a candidate. If you come from New England, you had better run well in New Hampshire—because if you do not, your campaign is likely finished. If you hail from elsewhere, you'd better spend a lot of time in the state, while still paying visits to states with subsequent primaries. In New Hampshire, what matters most is not the actual result of the voting but how the result differs from expectations. Do worse than anticipated, and you can expect to read articles predicting the date of your withdrawal from the race. Do better, and you might be the new front runner, with all the advantages and pitfalls that go with that position.

Yet winning in New Hampshire is no guarantee of success. In 1968 Lyndon Johnson won there as a write-in—he had not yet announced his decision on running for reelection—but Eugene McCarthy's strong showing (42 percent to Johnson's 49) turned the president's victory into a perceived defeat. Four years later Edmund Muskie took 46 percent of the vote in the Democratic primary, but the fact that he was from neighboring Maine caused news reports to downplay his showing and concentrate instead on the surprising strength there of South Dakota senator George McGovern, the eventual nominee. For the press, the interesting story was not the front runner's predictable victory but the emergence of the insurgent challenger. After two elections in a row, the surprise surge of an underdog became a stock story, and campaigns quickly realized that managing expectations was as important as the actual performance in a given primary. In 1976 Jimmy Carter and his team masterfully constructed the story of his campaign to fit the predilections of the press. Carter's strategist Hamilton Jordan wrote, "The press shows an exaggerated interest in the early primaries as they represent the first confrontation between candidates, their contrasting strategies and styles." Carter's people spent the year before the first caucuses and primaries preparing to take advantage of this "exaggerated interest." In addition to campaigning tirelessly in New Hampshire, they used the previously little-noted Iowa caucuses to give their man an early boost. Carter won a plurality at the caucuses, and *Time* suggested that he might be the front runner in a crowded post-Watergate Democratic field. When he also placed first in New Hampshire, both *Time* and *Newsweek* put him on their covers, and Carter was on his way.

The first battles of a presidential campaign often define the coming race. George H. W. Bush came into the 1980 New Hampshire primary after eking out an upset win in the newly important Iowa caucuses. Bush hoped to turn the campaign into a two-man race between him and the front runner, Ronald Reagan. But that plan backfired at a New Hampshire debate. Though the debate was scheduled to feature only Reagan and Bush, the Reagan camp, which was paying for the event, invited the other GOP contenders to participate. As Reagan argued for the inclusion of the other hopefuls, the moderator ordered his microphone turned off. Reagan snapped back, "I paid for this microphone, Mr. Green!" (Actually, the moderator's name was Breen, but the comeback was so well-delivered that the lapse was discounted.) George Bush, meanwhile, sat passive, mute, and inglorious. The next morning Reagan's quip, and Bush's wooden discomfort, became the story. Reagan won the primary handily, and Bush's campaign began to deflate.[1]

New Hampshire has four electoral votes. There is no constitutional, mathematical, or demographic reason that the opinions of its voters should matter much. But because it is such a powerful source of primary campaign stories, they do matter. New Hampshire is where scruffy college students came "clean for Gene" McCarthy, where Muskie wept, and where Bill Clinton was the "comeback kid." New Hampshire serves a vital purpose. Neither the press nor the public can possibly keep straight the multiplicity of stories generated by a field of eight or ten or twelve candidates. New Hampshire gives the press the chance to simplify the story by weeding out hopeless, hapless candidates. Its disproportionate power over the race for the presidency is a telling testimony to the power of stories in American politics.

Sometimes a clear front runner emerges from New Hampshire; sometimes the battle continues for weeks longer as delegates are chosen and campaign funds pour into one war chest, leak out of another. Those who withdraw are wooed by the remaining contenders, while the press assesses the value of each endorsement and seeks to unearth which quids were exchanged for what quos along the way. As spring approaches and flowers, the campaigns roll along like the Conestoga wagons of frontier days. And at the end of the trail lies the convention.

CONVENTIONS

Primaries have become increasingly important in recent years, as demands for greater participation in the nomination process have weakened the grip of party organizations. The power and spontaneity of conventions have declined accordingly. But for the choice of a running mate, conventions have become utterly without drama. It was not always so.

For better and worse, the Democrats have excelled at producing dramatic conventions. In 1844 the party had initially been expected to nominate Martin Van Buren for a third run at the presidency, but Van Buren's opposition to the annexation of Texas (which he viewed as just more territory for slavery) had undercut his early lead, and the convention was moving toward choosing Michigan's unscrupulous Lewis Cass. Then the historian and politician George Bancroft helped launch a surge of support for James K. Polk that won the Tennessean the nomination on the ninth ballot. News of the nation's first "dark horse" candidate was relayed to Washington from the Baltimore convention by Samuel F. B. Morse's new invention, the telegraph, and the swiftness of the news' arrival added to the surprise. The "dark horse" became one of the stock stories of conventions.

One of the ways for dark horses and other candidates to emerge as front runners at a convention was through the power of oratory. The event is set up for oratorical display. Before the leaders of his party, a man's name is placed in nomination: "Our country, crowned with the vast and marvelous achievements of its first century, asks for a man worthy of the past, and prophetic of her future; asks for a man who has the audacity of genius; asks for a man who is the grandest combination of heart, conscience and brain beneath her flag—such a man is James G. Blaine." So spoke Robert G. Ingersoll, a former attorney general of Illinois, when he placed Blaine's name in nomination at the 1876 Republican Convention. "Like an armed warrior, like a plumed knight, James G. Blaine marched down the halls of the American Congress and threw his shining lance full and fair against the brazen foreheads of the defamers of his country and the maligners of his honor." So tumultuous was the convention's response to Ingersoll's speechifying that the Republican bosses opposed to Blaine were saved from his nomination that year only by the late hour, which allowed an adjournment and then an overnight effort in favor of a dark horse, Rutherford B. Hayes, who prevailed. The success of his speech led Ingersoll to combine his successful law practice with a burgeoning career as a professional speaker. His great cause (after Blaine) was agnosticism, a sentiment that terminated his political career. When he died in 1899, the *New York Times* wrote, "death came swiftly to the famous infidel." But its editorial appreciation of Ingersoll spoke mostly of his nominating speech, which it found "tawdry and almost absurd in the reading, but it was as electrifying in the delivery as the 'effort' of Bryan twenty years later about the 'cross of gold.'"[2]

Impressive oratory would continue as a convention story throughout the twentieth century, but its preeminent example remains the *Times's* point of comparison in 1899—William Jennings Bryan's "Cross of Gold" speech of 1896. Bryan was just thirty-six when he rose to address the Democratic National Convention in Chicago. A lawyer and former congressman who had been defeated in a try for the Senate two years earlier, Bryan was editor in chief of the *Omaha World-Herald* and a champion of the inflationary pro-silver monetary policy that sought to free the United States from the gold standard because inflation would allow debt-ridden farmers to pay back loans more easily. Speaking to the convention in favor of a pro-silver platform plank, Nebraska's Bryan championed rural America: "Burn down your cities and leave our farms, and your cities will spring up again as if by magic; but destroy our farms and the grass will grow in the streets of every city in the country." His voice growing stronger, his delivery more dramatic, Bryan concluded with the famous words "You shall not press down upon the brow of labor this crown of thorns, you shall not crucify mankind upon a cross of gold." While he spoke the last phrases he held his hands out from his sides, then let them slowly drop. The arena exploded in cheers. In spite of his youth and his insignificant government experience, Bryan was nominated on the fifth ballot.[3]

Just as William Jennings Bryan's "Cross of Gold" speech propelled him to the nomination, other convention speeches have helped initiate national careers. At the 1948 Democratic Convention, Hubert Humphrey, the young mayor of Minneapolis, gave a bold speech in favor of civil rights that helped move the party away from its habitual deference to its segregationist southern wing. The speech thrust Humphrey into the national spotlight. Humphrey eventually became the party's vice presidential nominee in 1964 and its presidential choice in 1968. In 1984, New York governor Mario Cuomo delivered a keynote speech that attacked Ronald Reagan and enthralled the Democratic faithful. The urban Cuomo drew upon frontier imagery as he chided the former host of TV's *Death Valley Days:* "The Republicans believe the wagon train will not make it to the frontier unless some of our old, some of our young, and some of our weak are left behind by the side of the trail." In contrast, "We Democrats believe we can make it all the way with the whole family intact. We have. More than once. Ever since Franklin Roosevelt lifted himself from his wheelchair to lift this nation from its knees."[4]

Cuomo was deploying various stories in aid of his argument, and his speech itself became part of the lore of convention rhetoric, and of his own stillborn presidential career. Speeches have not always been the path to success, of course. At that same 1984 convention, Walter Mondale's acceptance speech included the following fateful lines: "Let's tell the truth. Mr. Reagan will raise taxes, and so will I. He won't tell you. I just did." This pledge may not have sealed Mondale's fate, but it certainly did not boost his chances of winning.[5]

In recent decades conventions have come to serve as coronations rather than places where serious political choices are made. The television networks accordingly have come to treat the process as less and less newsworthy, so candidates try to maximize their benefit from the shrinking amount of airtime available to them. At today's conventions, the central concerns have to do with who gets to speak in prime time (the nominee and his telegenic backers of all ages and hues), who is relegated to off-hours, and how to minimize the visibility of the party's fringe elements. Even the choice of a vice presidential nominee, once reliable grist for the convention news mill, is now staged before the gathering to pump up enthusiasm and garner maximum press coverage before the event. The news media will still have to cover the formal nomination and acceptance speech of the number two, so why not get another and fuller round of stories first?

Today's reporters, and many citizens, are aware of these calculations. Indeed, much of the press coverage of conventions today is less about the events themselves than about the strategies and staging behind the events. And it is not just the events that are manipulated—even the reasoning behind the spin is spun. It isn't politics anymore, or even metapolitics; it's meta-metapolitics.

FAITHFUL LANDMARKS
ALONG THE CAMPAIGN TRAIL

Presidential campaigning has its own traditions, some of them still honored, some of them vanished. One now abandoned nineteenth-century staple was the formal notification of the candidate of his nomination. The "reluctant candidate" would stay away from the convention, and then a delegation of party worthies would appear on the nominee's front porch, often many weeks after the nomination, and give official word to the candidate of the high responsibility his party was asking him to bear. The candidate would respond with a modest speech of acceptance, and the real campaign would commence. FDR delivered the deathblow to this ancient rite in 1932. Aware of doubts about how his physical condition might affect his ability to campaign and govern, Roosevelt flew to Chicago to accept the nomination in person. Commercial aviation was in its infancy, which made the move even more dramatic. The story of that flight put to rest countervailing stories about FDR's infirmities.

A more modern story is the "October surprise," an actual or feared late revelation or event that will scramble the scripted narrative. Ronald Reagan's team in the 1980 race lived in fear that Jimmy Carter would somehow manage to resolve the Iranian hostage crisis in time to lift him to reelection. Henry Kissinger's premature announcement that "peace is at hand" in Vietnam on October 26, 1972, undermined the last remaining hopes of the botched and sabotaged McGovern campaign. Four days before the 1992 vote, former Reagan defense secretary Caspar Weinberger was indicted in connection with the Iran-contra affair, and the foundering Bush campaign slipped beneath the waves.

Campaign dirty tricks are a staple of presidential lore, dating almost to the beginnings of the process. Not all have risen to the inspired heights of Nixon operative Donald Segretti, whose campaign-sabotage operation in 1972 cooked up such stunts as late-night calls to white New Hampshire voters before the primary claiming to be from the Harlem for Muskie Committee. Republican saboteurs in Florida papered a rally for a Democratic hopeful, George Wallace, with flyers reading "If you liked Hitler, you'll just love Wallace" and urging voters to support Muskie. Other races have also had their stolen briefing books, their trumped-up accusations, their phony mailings and bogus telephone calls.[6]

One of the most dramatic campaign deceptions was one inflicted by a still unknown hand against James Garfield in the 1880 race. Shortly before the election that fall an editor of a Tammany Hall paper in New York City found a mysterious letter on his desk. Addressed to "H. L. Morey," the letter contained, in what appeared to be Garfield's handwriting, an endorsement of unrestricted Chinese immigration, so as to provide "our great manufacturing and corporate interests" with a constant supply of cheap labor. The Democratic paper published the letter on October 20, provoking a controversy widely thought to have cost Garfield California and Nevada in the election. The letter soon proved to be a forgery, and no "H. L. Morey" was found to exist. Garfield won, but in a closer race the fake letter could have proved decisive.[7]

DEBATES

Convention stories have grown less compelling, and candidates no longer accept the nomination on their front porches. In the place of these venerable traditions the presidential debate has emerged as the new focus of fall campaigns. From the first Nixon-Kennedy debate to the Bush-Gore struggles of the 2000 race, the face-offs have proved rich in the narrative potential that can be crucial to the outcome of campaigns. Although voters clearly care what the candidates stand for, and often seem more eager than reporters to learn about the candidates' positions, few remember the debates for their discussions of policy. Our minds do not summon up images of Kennedy attacking Republican agricultural policies, or Ronald Reagan citing statistics about productivity growth in his first term. It is the signature moments, the gaffes and the zingers, that stick in our minds and that we use to construct the meaning of those encounters. They simply make the best stories.

What does the average person know about the first Nixon-Kennedy debate? That Kennedy looked handsome and relaxed, that Nixon looked shifty and was sweaty and unshaven, and that it is always a good idea to wear makeup on television. Being telegenic is not, one might think, the most important element one should look for in a leader. Nor is it true that voters who watched those debates paid attention only to appearances. But the story, and indeed the moral, of those debates is all about appearances. That story has shaped the master narrative of all subsequent presidential debates.

The debate tradition did not resume until 1976, a year that saw the enshrinement of the gaffe. In the second debate, Ford remarked, "There is no Soviet domination of Eastern Europe," a contention completely at odds with reality. Even so, viewers polled initially saw Ford as the winner by a margin of 44 to 35 percent. But after reporters and editorial writers made the mistake the lead story of the encounter, the numbers swung in Carter's favor by 61 to 19 percent. It took Ford a week to admit his error, which further solidified the story line. The press shaped the story into a narrative that fit with other unflattering parts of Ford's life story, including his image as a bumbler.[8]

The 1960 and 1976 debates prepared the press and ordinary viewers to concentrate on dramatic moments rather than the substance of the whole, and subsequent debates fit (or were shoehorned) into this frame. Ronald Reagan asked voters whether they were better off than they were four years earlier, and responded to an accusation from Jimmy Carter that Reagan wanted to cut Medicare with the line "There you go again." When Reagan tried to recycle the line in his first debate against Walter Mondale in 1984, Mondale was ready. "Remember the last time you said that?" Mondale asked. "Uh-huh," said Reagan. Mondale pointed out that Reagan had tried to do exactly what Carter had predicted he would: "You went out and tried to cut $20 billion out of Medicare, and so when you say, 'There you go again,' people remember this, you know."[9] What else do viewers remember? George H. W. Bush glanced at his watch in a 1992 debate and voters wondered what better things he had to do. Al Gore sighed theatrically in response to remarks by George W. Bush during their first debate in 2000, a silly tactic that made him look immature.

Reporters don't just cover the debates, they participate as moderators and questioners. In 1988 CNN's Bernard Shaw helped shape the coverage of the campaign when he asked Michael Dukakis what he would do if his wife, Kitty, were raped. "Would you favor an irrevocable death penalty for the killer?" Shaw took a complex set of issues and personalized them for Dukakis in a question so personal it bordered on the offensive. And Dukakis, to his detriment, responded with a wan explanation of his opposition to the death penalty rather than blasting Shaw for his question.[10]

Campaign staffs know that press coverage of debates is not primarily about issues discussed or programs presented. While Bill Clinton prepared for his debates in 1992, his aides worried that he was spending too much time mastering issues and sticking to specifics. After a particularly poor rehearsal for the first debate, one exasperated aide said, "He didn't tell a single story about his life." James Carville and George Stephanopoulos tried to get their candidate focused on fashioning a few electric "moments" in the debates, the sort of dramatic episodes that would attract news coverage and come to define the encounter. Debates, as Clinton's advisers understood, had come to be about gaffes and one-liners, humor and petulance, makeup and tie color—further testimony to the power of the story.[11]

SKELETONS

Probably no one in national life ever reaches a position of great prominence without having a few skeletons in the closet—youthful indiscretions, family unhappiness, impolitic statements, financial peccadilloes. In the past quarter century, much that used to be seen as rightfully beyond the public's need to know has been exposed, changing the character story in midcampaign. No reporter asked John Kennedy or Richard Nixon whether he had smoked marijuana or snorted cocaine in his college days, and a candidate's sexual escapades were the stuff of barroom and newsroom gossip, not headline coverage. Today, such intrusive queries—and the answers—are standard operating procedure.

The press feels entitled to ask such questions partly because candidates have lied to them in the past. John Kennedy suffered from Addison's disease, a glandular disorder with potentially serious consequences. During the week of the 1960 Democratic Convention, Lyndon Johnson's supporters, hoping that the convention would deadlock and go for Johnson, spread the story of Kennedy's disease. Kennedy's staff flatly denied the rumor. But as the historian Robert Dallek has revealed, Kennedy's health problems went far beyond Addison's disease. "The lifelong health problems of John F. Kennedy constitute one of the best-kept secrets of recent U.S. history—no surprise, because if the extent of those problems had been revealed while he was alive, his presidential ambitions would likely have been dashed," Dallek argued. Today, any kind of illness is seen as a matter that the public has a right to know, and today it is much more difficult for any candidate to conceal his medical history. Kennedy's illness was hidden from view by a culture of secrecy in which doctors were willing accomplices.[12]

Modern candidates face an ever changing problem: What does one admit to and what does one keep private? Which stories from a candidate's past ought to be leaked because they may unfold someday? What can be bottled up? The candidate must ask himself: Can I hope that my cheating on that college test, my drunk driving arrest, my old girlfriend's abortion, will never see the light of day? If so, I win. But if I bet wrong and the story comes out, I'm in trouble. When a skeleton gets dragged out of a closet, how one handles the charge is as important as the charge itself. What can successfully be portrayed as a mere youthful indiscretion, and what will be seen as a fundamental character flaw? During the 1992 campaign, Clinton managed to survive Gennifer Flowers's allegation that he had had a long-term affair with her. The candidate hastily arranged to be interviewed by Steve Kroft on CBS's *60 Minutes* and, with his wife, Hillary, beside him, he admitted "causing pain" in his marriage. Clinton's evasions were less than appealing, but however damaging the accusation by Flowers might have been, Clinton came up with a story that seemed to counteract it. He told Kroft and his viewers that they were using the wrong reference point. Clinton's was not the story of the philandering married man or the celebrity harvesting his crop of groupies. It was the story of a person with human failings, of an erring husband and father who was still committed to his marriage. Rather than choosing a story that set him apart from others, Clinton found common ground with his audience. Clinton was a sinner—along with everyone else. He admitted "wrongdoing," confessed that there had been "problems," but stressed, "This is not an arrangement or an understanding. This is a marriage." And with Hillary at his side, Clinton's version seemed to prevail, for the moment.[13]

The rules about coverage of a politician's private life began to shift in the aftermath of Watergate. That scandal, along with the long history of government deception during the Vietnam War, degraded the substantial trust between the press and government that had existed in the days of FDR and Ike. Once that trust was violated, everything was fair game. Current leaders were thoroughly investigated, and old heroes were brought down. Dwight Eisenhower was one of the first victims of the new spirit. In 1974 Ike's affair with his wartime driver, Kay Summersby, was revealed by Harry Truman in Merle Miller's "oral biography" of Truman. In a later book, Summersby herself corroborated the relationship. President Kennedy's affairs, rumored or actual, had become public property earlier, but the exposure of the grandfatherly Ike as a skirt chaser was a shock. And such revelations would continue.[14]

The story that really changed the ground rules was that of Colorado senator Gary Hart, who had emerged as a dynamic Democratic figure in the 1980s. Hart was poised to rejuvenate a party reeling from the defeats of Jimmy Carter and Walter Mondale, but he had certain problems in his own story. First, he had been the campaign manager for George McGovern, who had gone down to spectacular defeat as the 1972 Democratic nominee. More seriously, Hart was dogged by widespread rumors that he was a ladies' man. Hart made the mistake of challenging reporters who suspected him of philandering to prove it. Reporters from the *Miami Herald* took him up on his dare, and, having staked out his Washington town house, they found him, indeed, involved in an affair with a young woman named Donna Rice. Hart and Rice had also gone on an overnight cruise aboard a yacht called the *Monkey Business,* a spicy detail (with accompanying photo) that no self-respecting reporter could omit.

And so the rules changed again. The fact that Hart had invited the press to expose him was perceived by reporters as a license to pursue stories of affairs concerning politicians who had not extended similar invitations. Hart's downfall was not the fact that he'd had an affair so much as the fact that he'd invited people to prove that he'd done so. When they had, his political career was effectively terminated.

Hiding past medical problems worked for John Kennedy, but twelve years later the story was different. George McGovern's initial running mate, Senator Thomas Eagleton of Missouri, turned out to have a history of depression for which he had received electroshock therapy. When this story surfaced immediately after Eagleton's nomination, McGovern proclaimed himself a "thousand percent" behind his choice. But as article after article detailing Eagleton's medical history came out, McGovern gradually retreated. Within a week, he had dumped Eagleton for R. Sargent Shriver, the Kennedy brother-in-law who had helped start the Peace Corps. McGovern's mistake was not ousting Eagleton but doing so after having proclaimed his steadfast support for him.

McGovern would have been wiser to adopt as a model Dwight Eisenhower's cautious reaction to the accusations against Richard Nixon in the 1952 race. The *New York Post* broke a story that September 18 that Nixon supporters in California had raised money for a secret fund to aid Nixon in his political career. Dwight Eisenhower quickly made clear that he would not spend his own political capital to rescue his running mate. Nixon's response to those accusations was

WHEN STORIES COLLIDE: CAMPAIGNING FOR PRESIDENT

the most revolutionary single piece of crisis management ever carried off during a campaign. Nixon, demonstrating a firm grasp of the power of narrative, saved his career in a famous television address known as the Checkers speech. Accused of profiting personally from his high office, Nixon managed to transpose this accusation into an emotional key that a less imaginative politician would never have had the courage to attempt. He took the tale of a greedy politician and offered another story in its place. He talked about being a poor man, a humble man. He spoke of his wife, Pat, and the modest life they lived. He went into mawkish detail about their family finances ("I owe $3,500 to my parents") and spoke about how Pat didn't have a mink coat, just a "respectable Republican cloth coat. And I always tell her that she'd look good in anything." Nixon managed to play two cards at once, those of the humble workingman and the doting husband.[15]

But no part of the speech plucked the heartstrings more acutely than when Nixon spoke of the spotted cocker spaniel that a supporter in Texas had given his family. "And our little girl—Tricia, the six-year-old—named it Checkers. And you know the kids love that dog and I just want to say this right now, that regardless of what they say about it, we're going to keep it." Accused of financial impropriety, Nixon rallied to his side a puppy and two little girls. He did not so much evade the issue of misappropriation of funds as overwhelm it with emotion. It was one heck of a good story, and it worked. The public loved the speech, Eisenhower welcomed Nixon back into the fold, and in November they defeated Adlai Stevenson and Alabama senator John Sparkman by a decisive margin.[16]

ACTORS AND THEIR ROLES

Nixon managed to turn the story around that time, but eventually the press and much of the public assigned him to the role of trickster. The characters that stick tend to do so because, however crude, they do capture a truth about the candidate. And perhaps this aspect of American politics is actually not a bad thing. The voters are choosing between two men. Newspaper editorials may call on candidates to talk seriously about the issues and to use campaign ads to clarify stands on issues rather than to attack opponents, but voters don't spend a lot of time reading position papers. Life is short, and people are busy. Of course issues are important, and some voters will cast their votes based entirely on one issue—such as abortion or taxes—regardless of other considerations. But less ideological voters are often judging the candidates on the basis of character. Thanks to television, they can look at the contenders and say, "I like this person" or "I don't like that person" or "This person seems like a schemer; this person seems like an idiot; this person seems pretty good." Serious issues can be made to go away, not by evidence or reasoned argument but by playing the right card (and the right role) at the right time.

For example, after the first debate in 1984, President Reagan's mental fitness for office came into question. As he contended against Walter Mondale, he was so confused, so uncertain of his government's policies that he appeared lost onstage. The *Wall Street Journal* then ran an article questioning Reagan's ability to govern. Asked at the following debate to address the issue, Reagan responded, "I'm not going to exploit, for political purposes, my opponent's youth and inexperience." The quip got a big laugh; there was no follow-up question (it would have seemed discourteous and, worse, humorless), and the issue was defused. Reagan had finessed the problem by playing a role he was comfortable with and that America had bought into—that of a relaxed, paternal figure, at ease with who he was, even with his shortcomings. This response was hardly impromptu; the line was scripted and rehearsed. And Reagan performed well. He hit his mark and said his line. Americans thought that showed ability enough.[17]

On one level such superficial treatment of a serious issue is terribly depressing. When a real question is left unexplored because of a joke, the public is poorly served. On another level, though, Reagan's ability to deal with exactly that kind of problem showed an important aspect of leadership. The ability to manipulate a situation, to know what role to play at what time, is crucial to providing leadership for the country. Part of a president's role is to help decide what policies the government of the United States should pursue; but another, equally vital role is to execute the decisions the government has made. Managing public opinion is part of that process.

Prior to television, candidates' characters were conveyed and judged mostly through intermediaries. Today it's much more important for the candidate to be able to *play* the candidate. He must not only envision his role but must also perform it, onstage, to a vast and critical audience. But the role has to fit the actor: John Wayne didn't play bad guys, and Jerry Seinfeld does not play action heroes. Jimmy Carter, in his notorious 1976 *Playboy* interview, admitted that he'd felt "lust" in his heart many times for women other than his wife, giving Americans the chance to consider whether he was a playboy. The quote embarrassed the campaign, but that soon faded. Americans decided Carter was speaking honestly about common urges, not confessing to a life of promiscuity. Ultimately, Carter's remarks fit the role of preacher much better than that of rogue, and that's what people took away from his interview in *Playboy.*

Such roles cannot be chosen at random, of course. Family stories help establish the boundaries within which the presidential hopeful can function. And even the person who has moved a long way from his origins has to remain in tune with his past. In the 1992 election campaign, Bill Clinton made a great deal of his upbringing in Arkansas, of being "the Man from Hope." His intention may have been to shift attention away from his Georgetown/Oxford/Yale education, yet Bill Clinton really did grow up in a poor family in a broken home with an alcoholic stepfather in Hope, Arkansas. Clearly, his ability to empathize—to "feel your pain," as he once put it—flowed not just from a good political sense but also out of some real, fundamental experience, which is why it rang true for many people. Clinton was comfortable with the vocabulary of voguish psychological nostrums and twelve-step programs, and his easy empathy carried some of the flavor of a self-improvement infomercial. Yet Clinton's past did equip him to understand how it felt to be poor and unemployed far better than George H. W. Bush ever could. Clinton had the ability to project artificially what he felt genuinely. Because much of his audience believed that his empathy was real, Clinton was a remarkably effective politician.

Public figures and the world within which they operate are constantly changing, and the attributes that are essential to their makeup change, too. How Abraham Lincoln was seen by the people of Illinois in 1858 versus how he was seen by the nation in 1862 or 1864 or after his assassination is a complicated question. How then do we comprehend the "real" Lincoln? Which real Lincoln? Is he the humble rail-splitter, the bumbling war leader, "Father Abraham," or a fallen martyr, a redeemer who died that his people might live? Every president constantly moves between different characters, reflected in the press and weighed in the minds of voters.

MANAGING THE STORY

As new forms of mass communication developed, campaigns tried new methods of storytelling. In the early republic, well-founded accusations of sexual improprieties against Alexander Hamilton and Thomas Jefferson received scant circulation outside their original publication by the propagandist James Callender. Electoral politics was still largely confined to the elites, as were newspapers, and information often moved in small circles. In the time of William Henry Harrison and Abraham Lincoln, campaigns consisted of torchlight parades and mass meetings, pamphlets and broadsides. Later in the nineteenth century, in the days of McKinley and William Jennings Bryan, newspapers were tremendously important in conveying the ideas of the campaigns, not only through words but also through pictures and cartoons. When FDR and Herbert Hoover contended, radio was the emerging medium. At least from the days of Kennedy and Nixon, television has been the crucial realm of storytelling. As a result, politicians who master the art of television dominate the electoral process.

President Reagan's training as an actor was one of his most effective weapons. Bill Clinton, with a different background, proved equally effective. In the second presidential debate in 1992, George H. W. Bush was baffled by a question from an African American woman in the audience about how the current economic crisis was affecting him personally: "I'm not sure I get it—help me with the question and I'll try to answer it," Bush said. When his turn came, Bill Clinton walked toward the questioner and asked, "You know people who've lost their jobs and lost their homes?" She did. Clinton replied that he, too, knew the face of suffering. "In my state, when people lose their jobs there's a good chance I'll know them by their names. When a factory closes, I know the people who ran it. When the businesses go bankrupt, I know them." Clinton connected emotionally with both his questioner and the TV audience, which helped him win both the debate and the election.[18]

The science of campaign-trail story-spinning has changed with the development of the television campaign. The deferential press of the mid-twentieth century has been replaced by a very aggressive press whose members try to frustrate politicians' efforts to tell their stories. In return, politicians have become even shrewder in scripting their public appearances. Campaign staffs choose backdrops, themes, and stories with an eye to preventing the press from telling the story in any way other than how the candidate wants it told. A candidate journeys to a certain place, with certain characters, a carefully chosen background, and sets a scene. It may be a farm scene, a factory scene, or an inner-city scene. Whatever it is, it is scripted. And if a hardworking, inner-city high school student is part of the story, the candidate's staff will research that student's background very carefully to make sure there is nothing that could embarrass the candidate. If an incumbent president goes to a formerly run-down area that a federal program has helped, the TV cameras will be confined to a vantage point that demands that the scene be framed in a specific way, to show a story of improvement and optimism. Should an enterprising TV crew poke its lens behind the Potemkin façade, the candidate's press advisers will take note, and that crew may well find its future access restricted. Every picture tells a story; sometimes the stories are true, and sometimes they are not.

CAMPAIGN ADS

No candidate can win the presidency without seasoned advertising professionals to illustrate the core narratives of the campaign. Ad campaigns can be powerful storytelling. They appeal directly to voters, unmediated by any press coverage. They tell stories with considerable sophistication. Sometimes the advertisements tell a happy story about one candidate; sometimes, a damaging story about another. Often they will place one issue in the forefront, thus clouding or ignoring other issues. A war-hero president presiding over a faltering economy will emphasize the heroic past rather than address the troublesome present. His opponent will dwell relentlessly on the present.

In the earliest days of televised ads, the new medium was used simply to broadcast a campaign speech—Adlai Stevenson used TV this way, to poor effect, in 1952. The candidate was proud of his oratorical abilities, but his presentations sometimes took longer than the airtime his campaign had purchased, with the result that his thrilling summation would take place off the air. Campaigns quickly figured out more effective uses of the time they bought at ever greater cost. Lyndon Johnson's famous "daisy" ad of 1964 was, for better or worse, a watershed. In it a little girl counts the petals she is plucking from a daisy, and the count turns into an ominous countdown to a nuclear explosion. The ad suggested, none too subtly, that Barry Goldwater would recklessly involve the United States in nuclear war (though the ad did not mention Goldwater). The ad ran only once, but the news coverage it generated made its images and story familiar to any attentive American.

Recognizing the importance of ads, the press now covers them as news. Reporters routinely assess the accuracy of ads. Many of these stories also work to expose the thinking behind the ad campaign. The candidate puts out one story with his ads; his opponent counters, either with his own ads or by attacking the initial ad campaign; and the press tries to cover the story without becoming a tool of either campaign. Ultimately, there are so many players in this game that no one, however well funded, clever, or powerful, can control the story. But all candidates and their staffs must participate vigorously in the ensuing debate, lest they become victims of it.

Clever storytelling by a candidate can influence how a given narrative comes out. But the stories have a power of their own, and the heart of a campaign is the competition among them. Sometimes the determining factor is not the winning story's relevance or truth but its ability to qualify as the best story, the story people really want to hear. Whether or not it has anything to do with the problems the nation faces, if it's the story that seems revealing or somehow strikes a chord, pleasing or dissonant, it usually prevails.

In the 1988 campaign the Republican strategists Lee Atwater and Roger Ailes tried to associate the Democratic party with black urban America and crime. They linked Michael Dukakis with William Horton—dubbed "Willie" Horton by the Republicans—a convicted murderer who had raped a woman and beaten her husband while free on furlough from a Massachusetts prison. News organizations wrote examinations of the furlough program and retold Horton's story. Their reports pointed out the irrelevance of the furlough programs to the federal government and noted that Bush himself had supported such a program in Texas, as Ronald Reagan had in California. But there was a power to the story and to the mug shot photo of Horton, an exemplar of white America's fear of black criminals. Together these factors constructed a powerful narrative, against which reasoned argument didn't stand a chance. The Dukakis campaign finally responded with an attack ad of its own, which charged, "In 1968, George Bush helped an ex-convict fund a halfway house for early released felons in Houston, Texas. In 1982, one of those prisoners raped and murdered a minister's wife." It, too, was a cynical jab, but less effective than the punch the Republicans had already landed. The Willie Horton story rose to prominence not because it was pushed the hardest but because its imagery was so powerful.[19]

OF ALL THE SKILLS a contender has learned along the way, of all the qualifications he has amassed in his career, none is of greater importance to him in reaching the White House than the ability to cast his story in a favorable light. If he has a real gift for this, it will be an incalculable help in carrying out the duties of his office.

But the challenges of the White House will call for new kinds of storytelling. He must navigate a new set of tests, each by now codified into a set of narrative expectations—on relations with Congress, with the press, with the military, and with foreign heads of state. The new president must reach not only the American people but a global audience, with different expectations and different narrative traditions.

The victorious candidate is stepping onto a new, and larger, stage. But it is still a stage.

CHAPTER SIX

A BRAND-NEW STORY: ELECTION AND INAUGURATION

WINNING ELECTION AND ASSUMING OFFICE TRANSFORM THE CANdidate into the president, and that change is titanic. Vastly greater powers and responsibilities are now at hand, and the partisan candidate must now become the president of all the people and must start to weave his story into the ongoing history of the American presidency.

Today the process is chronicled in lavish detail. The candidates' trips to the voting booth, how and where and with whom they watch the returns, the details of the losing candidate's concession phone call to the victor, and countless other aspects of the drama are described and sifted for meaning. The rise of television and the dawn of the atomic age have created an aura of boundless consequence around the moment. But not so long ago, when both the nuclear age and the TV age were in their infancy, the process—and the story—was much simpler.

THE VERDICT

Late in the afternoon of Election Day, 1948, Harry Truman and his Secret Service detail left Truman's home in Independence, Missouri, slipped away from reporters and drove to the resort town of Excelsior Springs. Truman took a Turkish bath, then went to his room a bit after 6:00 P.M., had a ham sandwich and a glass of milk from room service, and listened to election returns from the East Coast. As he later recalled in his memoirs, when he went to bed, "I was reported some thousands ahead." He awoke at midnight and turned on the radio again, to hear the authoritative voice of the veteran NBC newsman H. V. Kaltenborn report that Truman was now ahead by 1.2 million votes but was nonetheless certain to lose. (The opinion polls were predicting a solid win for Thomas E. Dewey, Truman's Republican opponent, and Kaltenborn personally favored the Republican.) At 4:00 A.M. a Secret Service man woke Truman to listen again to the radio. Now he was leading by 2 million votes, but the commentator, in Truman's account, "continued to say he couldn't see how I could be elected." Truman could, and told his detail they had better head back to Kansas City, "because it looked very much as if we were in for another four years." At 10:30 that morning he received a congratulatory telegram from Dewey. Soon Truman was to have the pleasure of posing with the now famous *Chicago Tribune* with the headline "DEWEY DEFEATS TRUMAN." Kaltenborn was far from the only reporter counting Truman out in the race, and Truman is far from the only presidential contender to have to wait past election night for news of victory or defeat.[1]

Presidential campaigns are filled with moments of drama, although today many are carefully scripted. But the election itself remains a moment of genuine drama, when all the competing stories and forces converge and the voters decide the outcome—except in those years when the vote of the people is not enough. Four times—1800, 1824, 1876, and 2000—the vote of the people has been superseded by another authority, and in three of those instances the presidency was awarded to the candidate who came in second in the popular vote. (This triumph of the popular runner-up also happened in the 1888 race, when the Electoral College totals placed Benjamin Harrison ahead of Grover Cleveland, the incumbent, who had outpolled Harrison by more than 90,000 votes.) The 1800 and 1824 races were decided in the House of Representatives. A partisan electoral commission after the 1876 race delivered the election to the Republican Hayes, and a controversial 5–4 vote in the Supreme Court gave George W. Bush the prize in 2000, despite voting irregularities in Florida and the greater popular vote for Gore.

Drawn out as the 2000 vote was—the Court's ruling did not come until December 12—it was not the longest wait. The result of the November 1876 vote was not known until March 2, 1877, when the Electoral College at last certified Hayes as the victor with a one-vote majority. He had two days to prepare for his inauguration on March 4.

However long it takes, the vote concludes with two of the most familiar scenes in the political process, the defeated man's concession speech and the jubilant appearance of the winner. Both sides try to appear above partisanship, with the defeated man urging the nation to support its elected leader and the president-elect promising an inclusive administration. Behind the scenes, though, things can be less rosy. In 1956, after suffering a second thrashing at the hands of Dwight D. Eisenhower, Adlai Stevenson was slow to make his concession speech. Ike, growing impatient, complained, "What in the name of God is the monkey waiting for? Polishing his prose?" The concession speech must be difficult in ordinary circumstances, wrenching after a close race or when vital issues are at stake. None can have been more bitter to make than Al Gore's address on Wednesday, December 13, 2000, the evening following the Supreme Court's decision. Gore turned to the past for help, saying, "Almost a century and a half ago, Senator Stephen Douglas told Abraham Lincoln, who had just defeated him for the presidency, 'Partisan feeling must yield to patriotism. I'm with you, Mr. President, and God bless you.'" But

Gore's disappointment was palpable—not just his jaw but his entire body seemed clenched, and the effort he made to present a calm front was plain to see.[2]

The weeks between election and inauguration are filled with the assembly of an administration, picking and announcing members of the cabinet, choosing new ambassadors, signaling where the nation and the world can expect continuity and where to look for change. It is an odd period, during which the legal authority remains in the hands of the sitting president but the real power lies with his successor. It is a heady time for the president-elect. In the far simpler days of 1920, Warren Harding made a postelection trip to the Caribbean, and as he steamed toward the Panama Canal Zone he was accorded a submarine escort while American planes flew overhead. One observer thought Harding was powerfully moved by all the attention and noted, "He cherished an idea that when a man was elevated to the presidency, his wits, by some automatic mental chemistry, were increased to fit the stature of his office."[3]

ARRIVALS

The final drama of transition comes with the president-elect's arrival in the capital. When George Washington rode from Mount Vernon to New York to take office in 1789, his route was marked by numerous celebrations. Washington was concerned that the much debated new government be accepted by the people, and his procession to New York was both a measure and a reinforcement of that support. A bridge across the Schuylkill River at Philadelphia had been festooned with laurel and cedar by the artist Charles Willson Peale, and highlighted with laurel arches. When Washington stopped under one arch, Peale's daughter Angelica set in motion a contraption that lowered a laurel wreath onto the startled leader's head. Similar tributes lined the route from that capital-to-be to the nation's current capital. The last part of his journey was made aboard a lavish barge built especially for the purpose. The barge was powered by thirteen pairs of identically dressed oarsmen. As Washington crossed over from New Jersey to Manhattan, he was greeted with cannon salutes, banners, and waterborne serenaders, including a quartet singing,

Joy to our native land,
Let every heart expand,
For Washington's at hand,
With glory crowned.

So new was the nation, and so apparently short of musical talent, that the tune to which the words were set was that of "God Save the King."[4]

Eight years later Thomas Jefferson's journey to his new capital at Washington, D.C., was a much less grand progress, and he arrived with the outcome of the election still in doubt. Jefferson's route was chosen for its convenience, but as the nation's history developed so did the conscious appropriation of earlier symbols and sages for contemporary uses. One hundred and ninety-two years after Jefferson took office, a president-elect who had been given his name, William Jefferson Clinton, chose to highlight the link by re-creating Jefferson's journey, this time by bus, along a route lined with both supporters ("Bubbas for Bill," said one sign) and opponents ("You're Socialists, Stupid"). The choice of route was Clinton's way of laying claim to the democratic and idealistic legacy of his namesake. As we shall see, the mantle of Jefferson has been claimed by many, and for many purposes.[5]

On occasion the arrival of the president in Washington has not been so stately, or so happy. After being sworn in as president aboard

Air Force One, Lyndon Johnson flew back from Texas the day of Kennedy's assassination and was whisked through a grieving city to the security of the White House compound. The single most perilous arrival in the capital was that of Abraham Lincoln in 1861. Lincoln had been heading east from Illinois by train, delivering speeches along the way. A couple of days before he was scheduled to hit Baltimore, his aides learned of a plot to assassinate the president-elect when he passed through that city. Lincoln reluctantly agreed to travel through Baltimore in secret late at night. News of the threat and of Lincoln's response soon appeared in the papers, in embellished form. Cartoonists were merciless in their portrayal of a skulking Lincoln. The frontier rail-splitter was transformed into a timorous weakling, flitting through Baltimore disguised "in a Scotch cap and long military cloak." In New York the diarist George Templeton Strong lamented that "this surreptitious nocturnal dodging or sneaking of the President-elect into his capital city, under cloud of night, will be used to damage his moral position and throw ridicule on his Administration."[6]

INAUGURAL STORIES

Every president hopes to define himself with his inaugural address. Some use it as an opportunity to reaffirm their life stories, others to change them. And from George Washington forward, presidents have also used inaugural addresses to attempt to define the master narrative of their times. The first president was acutely conscious of the burden of defining so many aspects of his new office. He worried about how to make the presidency effective without allowing it to become tyrannical; about how to give the position dignity without adopting the trappings of monarchy; about how a man could both embody the state and represent the people.

In his inaugural address, delivered in New York on April 30, 1789, Washington gave voice to his ambivalence: "Among the vicissitudes incident to life no event could have filled me with greater anxieties than that [which informed him of his election]. On the one hand, I was summoned by my Country, whose voice I can never hear but with veneration and love, from a retreat which I had chosen with the fondest predilection, and, in my flattering hopes, with an immutable decision, as the asylum of my declining years—a retreat which was rendered every day more necessary as well as more dear to me by the addition of habit to inclination, and of frequent interruptions in my health to the gradual waste committed on it by time."[7]

Washington articulated the eighteenth-century notion that the role of the natural aristocrat was to serve his country out of duty rather than a desire for power or profit. Yet he knew that he had sometimes to temper his elitist instincts. And so he delivered his speech that day dressed in a suit of brown homespun to proclaim himself a man of the people—and in symbolic encouragement of domestic manufacturing, just as modern candidates are careful to wear American-made suits.

Aware that many citizens feared the power of the new government and its strong executive, Washington downplayed the powers of his new office. Rather than recommending measures to Congress, he said, "It will be more consistent with those circumstances, and far more congenial with the feelings which actuate me, to substitute, in place of a recommendation of particular measures, the tribute that is due to the talents, the rectitude, and the patriotism which adorn the characters selected to devise and adopt them." In the formal and circumlocutory language of public discourse in the late eighteenth century, Washington was saying that rather than trying to ram measures through Congress, he would defer to the judgment of those whom the people had elected.[8]

This proved to be a promise Washington could not keep. The

complex political world of the 1790s and the incipient struggles between Federalists and Republicans caused Washington to be a much more active and partisan president than he had contemplated at the time of his inauguration. The lack of partisanship that led to Washington's unanimous election didn't last long. Rifts emerged in Congress over domestic policy and in debates over how strong the central government should be and how great should be the powers reserved to the states. Even more divisive were the struggles over foreign policy, made urgent by the French Revolution and the revolutionary wars that swept across Europe, first under the French Republic and later under the empire of Napoleon Bonaparte. Thomas Jefferson was a leading advocate of the French republicans, while Washington's right hand, Alexander Hamilton, stressed the importance of American relations with Great Britain.

By 1800 political parties had begun to form in a way that was, if not truly modern, certainly recognizable to a modern student of politics. Jefferson had held high office under Washington and Adams, but had opposed many of their policies, and soon made himself the leader of the none-too-loyal opposition. In the election of 1800 he was a very strenuous partisan, although he claimed otherwise. In his inaugural address, Jefferson had a choice: he could stress his existing story and celebrate his victory, or he could try to change the story. Jefferson opted for change.

"Let us, then, fellow-citizens, unite with one heart and one mind. Let us restore to social intercourse that harmony and affection without which liberty and even life itself are but dreary things. And let us reflect that, having banished from our land that religious intolerance under which mankind so long bled and suffered, we have yet gained little if we countenance a political intolerance as despotic, as wicked, and capable of as bitter and bloody persecutions." True, the nation had seen partisan strife, "but every difference of opinion is not a difference of principle. We have called by different names brethren of the same principle. We are all Republicans, we are all Federalists." The truth was a bit harsher than the rhetoric. Jefferson envisioned a nation undivided by faction, but his idea of a harmonious world was one from which the Federalist party had disappeared.[9]

Jefferson's speech was a brilliant effort to revise the history of his own partisanship, and indeed to rewrite the political history of the previous ten years. In the American political world of the eighteenth century, the party politics that emerged in the 1790s was seen as profoundly undesirable. What political historians now see as the emergence of a healthy two-party system Jefferson was presenting (and sincerely viewed) as an unwanted flowering of the spirit of faction. For both Republicans and Federalists, a faction was not a legitimate opposition or an expression of one point of view on a matter about which reasonable men could differ. Rather, a faction was simply a group placing its own private interests ahead of the common good. To Jefferson, all Americans should be dedicated to the common good, as long as he was allowed to define it and to determine the measures that would secure it.

Jefferson was as gifted a politician as he was a writer. The Federalist party did disappear within fifteen years of his inauguration, the victim of measures implemented by Jefferson and of its own blundering. Yet despite the "era of good feelings" under President James Monroe (in office 1817–1825), Americans were not "all Republicans and all Federalists" but people with different visions of the nation and its policies. Jefferson and the so-called Virginia dynasty that succeeded him tried regularly to renew the appeal that he had made so persuasively in his 1800 inauguration: that all Americans should join together, that party spirit was faction, and that harmony could be found by rallying behind Jefferson and his successors, Madison and Monroe.

Yet disharmony emerged anyway. In the 1820s the Jeffersonian Republican party split into the fragments that eventually became the

Democratic and Whig parties. These groups would contest elections into the 1850s. Then that arrangement dissolved, unable to withstand the divisions caused by slavery. In 1860 the candidate of the new Republican party, Abraham Lincoln, won election only to face the gravest crisis in the nation's history.

In March 1861, with seven states already having voted to secede from the Union, war seemed inevitable. Lincoln saw in his inaugural address a chance to prevent bloodshed or, failing that, to rally support for the Union cause. Lincoln's speech recognized the seriousness of the accelerating crisis but professed hope that it could be resolved. "One section of our country believes slavery is right, and ought to be extended, while the other believes it is wrong, and ought not to be extended. This is the only substantial dispute." Surely this was an optimistic description of the problem that was to lead, within five weeks, to the outbreak of civil war. That there was only one "substantial dispute" was true, but saying so was hardly sufficient to do away with the problem. But Lincoln took care to stress that there were countless areas of agreement that existed between the states, like the shared tradition of the Revolution.[10]

Yet at the end of his speech Lincoln turned from explanation to entreaty and addressed the people of the seceding South. And here, in his summation, the language soared. "In your hands, my dissatisfied fellow-countrymen, and not in mine, is the momentous issue of civil war. The Government will not assail you. You can have no conflict without being yourselves the aggressors. You have no oath registered in heaven to destroy the Government, while I shall have the most solemn one to 'preserve, protect, and defend' it. I am loath to close. We are not enemies, but friends. We must not be enemies. Though passion may have strained it must not break our bonds of affection. The mystic chords of memory, stretching from every battlefield and patriot grave to every living heart and hearthstone all over this broad land, will yet swell the chorus of the Union, when again touched, as surely they will be, by the better angels of our nature."[11]

Thus Lincoln threw the onus of aggression onto the South. He would not start a war—indeed, God and his angels forbade it. In the days ahead, Lincoln went to great lengths not to fire the first shot. He carefully managed the crisis at Fort Sumter, the Union garrison in the harbor of Charleston, South Carolina, waiting until the Confederates shelled the fort, an act of aggression that led to the outbreak of war.

Bad times make for good inaugural addresses. Presidents who entered office at a time of general public satisfaction or national complacency speak without urgency, and their words are little remembered. Not so those leaders who took office amid national crisis. In 1933, facing an economic disaster of unprecedented gravity, Franklin Delano Roosevelt addressed the nation with these words: "This is preeminently the time to speak the truth, the whole truth, frankly and boldly. Nor need we shrink from honestly facing conditions in our country today. This great Nation will endure as it has endured, will revive and will prosper. So, first of all, let me assert my firm belief that the only thing we have to fear is fear itself—nameless, unreasoning, unjustified terror which paralyzes needed efforts to convert retreat into advance. In every dark hour of our national life a leadership of frankness and vigor has met with that understanding and support of the people themselves which is essential to victory. I am convinced that you will again give that support to leadership in these critical days."[12]

Roosevelt was suggesting a new story, that of the nation uniting behind the government in a time of peril. Never before had the entire nation looked to Washington, D.C., for salvation. If Roosevelt could convince Americans that this was a legitimate story line, he'd gain the support he needed to bend Congress to his will and mobilize the federal government behind an activist program. By working together the people and the president could revive the economy and restore prosperity. And if he fulfilled his side of the bargain—if he provided "leadership of frankness and vigor"—he expected support in return. FDR would not beg for help. He simply described America's past support for bold leadership. His language carefully echoed Lincoln (the nation would "endure as it has endured") and appropriated the solemn language of the courtroom oath ("the truth, the whole truth"). In his first 100 days he launched a vigorous program—public works agencies, banking and securities-industry reforms, agricultural relief programs— and won the backing that he had implicitly asked for in his inaugural address.

The addresses given by Washington, Jefferson, Lincoln, and Roosevelt had several things in common. They took place in times of political crisis. They were memorable. And they succeeded in creating new stories, new scripts, for their administrations to follow. But the worlds in which these four addresses were given were very different. Washington's inauguration was without precedent. By Jefferson's time, the inaugural address was understood as an emerging tradition. His words made their way slowly across the still small nation, surfacing in newspapers of varying political stripes, to be read quietly in the homes of the prosperous and aloud in the taverns and meeting places of the many.

By Abraham Lincoln's time, the inaugural address had been established as an oratorical tradition, the defining moment of a new administration. The development of the telegraph meant that Lincoln's words were transmitted across the nation for inclusion in the next day's newspaper, whether that paper was in New York, Chicago, or San Francisco. For Franklin Roosevelt, however, the transmission took place not overnight but instantly, through the medium of radio. Millions who listened took heart from the determination they heard in Roosevelt's resonant and patrician voice. He solicited "support to leadership" and then proceeded to govern as if he had that support. With the decisive actions of his first 100 days, he transformed his rhetoric into action and set a tone for his administration. FDR had established both a new political tradition and a legislative benchmark for a president's first three months in office.

At the time, though, perhaps Roosevelt's most important move was to break with the passive, lethargic style of his predecessor, Herbert Hoover. At his inauguration just seven months before the stock market tumbled into the Crash, Hoover told the nation, "I have no fears for the future of our country." FDR recognized the fear abroad in the land, but told his countrymen that their worries were excessive and harmful, and that with their support he would lead them out of the Depression.[13]

A generation after FDR, John Fitzgerald Kennedy took office during much better economic times. But they were still times of crisis, both in the Cold War and in the increasingly heated debate in America over civil rights. When Kennedy became president, he addressed the nation via both radio and television, which in the previous decade had displaced radio as the nation's electronic hearth. But with the emergence of the United States as a global superpower, Kennedy was also addressing an audience beyond America's borders.

The Cold War was Kennedy's great concern, and in fighting it he invoked the tradition of George Washington and of the Revolution, just as Lincoln had. "We dare not forget today," said Kennedy, "that we are the heirs of that first revolution. Let the word go forth from this time and place, to friend and foe alike, that the torch has been passed to a new generation of Americans—born in this century, tempered by war, disciplined by a hard and bitter peace, proud of our ancient heritage—and unwilling to witness or permit the slow undoing of those human rights to which this Nation has always been committed, and to which we are committed today at home and around the world.

"Let every nation know, whether it wishes us well or ill, that we shall pay any price, bear any burden, meet any hardship, support any friend, oppose any foe, in order to assure the survival and the success of liberty."[14]

When Kennedy spoke about a new generation of Americans, "born in this century, tempered by war, disciplined by a hard and bitter peace, proud of our ancient heritage," he was talking not only about his contemporaries but also about himself, the first president born in the twentieth century. "Tempered by war" referenced his heroic exploits in the Second World War. "Proud of our ancient heritage" summoned up the heritage of the prominent Kennedy family. The still young war hero was connecting his life story to those of his countrymen.

The most famous line in his address was his exhortation to his fellow citizens, "Ask not what your country can do for you—ask what you can do for your country." Less well remembered is the next line: "My fellow citizens of the world: ask not what America will do for you, but what together we can do for the freedom of man." Here Kennedy set himself apart both from the passive government of the Eisenhower years and the activism of FDR. The statement appealed to Democrat and Republican alike, an important consideration for a president elected by a very thin margin. As Jefferson and Lincoln tried to do, Kennedy used his inaugural address to get the nation on his side, and to try to heal the divisions of party and section. As Roosevelt did, Kennedy sought to encourage a troubled people. And as all presidents do, Kennedy used the speech to connect his story with that of the nation.[15]

The rest of the inaugural day's festivities allow the new president to set a tone and mark a new beginning. The parade is a cavalcade of inclusion, the evening's parties a chance to emphasize home-state virtues and affirm longtime political bonds. They too can advance the story of a new president.

Jimmy Carter won election as an outsider, someone untainted by

Vietnam or Watergate. He had loudly criticized the Washington infrastructure of lobbyists and influence peddlers. In his speech to the Democratic Convention, Carter charged that under Nixon and Ford, "we've seen a wall go up that separates us from our own government." He stressed the same themes, in gentler tones, at his inauguration, and pledged to try to run an administration that would allow "our people to be proud of their own government once again." To highlight his distance from the imperial pomp of the Nixon era, after his inaugural speech Carter eschewed his bulletproof limousine and walked the parade route, to the consternation of his Secret Service detail but the delight of many citizens and commentators.[16]

Carter would continue this studied casualness. He carried his own garment bag on presidential journeys and addressed the nation from the White House wearing a cardigan, Fred Rogers with his finger on the button. Reporters soon came to treat these down-home touches as simply another form of artifice. Carter learned that though voters may like an informal candidate, they want their president to look, well, presidential.

And as his administration progressed, Carter also discovered that power brokers and influence peddlers were far easier to criticize than to do without. The very distance from Washington that helped to ensure his election compromised his ability to govern, and the fact that he actually did see the Washington power structure as corrupt prevented him from changing tack in time to rescue his presidency. His old story worked for the campaign, but Carter needed a new story to run the nation. He never found one.

TAKING CHARGE

Having strived for years, sometimes decades, to reach the Oval Office, the new president must be eager to exercise his new powers. In order to succeed, he must carry public opinion with him in ways that will persuade Congress to advance his program. But how does a president get his message out? And what forces are arrayed against him? He gives speeches, holds press conferences, visits sites around the country that are relevant to his programs—a factory assembling new jets, a long-planned dam, a cleaned-up river. The president commands a vast government and, like Rumor in ancient myth, has a thousand tongues to spread his message. But a thousand is not always enough.

That vast government apparatus is filled with competing interests, conflicting ambitions, and personal agendas, all of which make it difficult to project a clear message. Washington politics fits Thomas Hobbes's description of the basic condition of man, "a condition of war of everyone against everyone." The president's staff would seem to be a safe haven, but the White House is a Hobbesian whirlpool of self-promotion, flattery, and feuding. The president, vice president, and First Lady all have their own staffs, who may not work well with one another, or with the rest of the executive branch. Like monarchs of old, presidents have their courtiers—loyal advisers, steadfast allies, flatterers, knaves, and fools. Presidents must maintain control over their staffs, particularly to prevent unwanted contact with the press.[17]

In the government agencies, presidential appointees struggle to gain control over entrenched bureaucracies without sacrificing access to the institutional memory and expertise they need to make their departments run. Members of the cabinet have their own agendas, too—their own careers and reputations, winning a larger share of the budget, and getting the president's attention for the issues they care about. Their subordinates, too, have pet programs they wish to advance, protégés they would like to promote, and favors they would like to do, or have done for them.

Then there is Congress, 535 robust egos striving for press attention, campaign dollars, and the love and votes of their constituents. A good number of them have considered what it would take to put them in the Oval Office, and even remote hopes are difficult to extinguish. Every member of Congress has a press staff eager to draw attention to their boss, and hoping to advance along with him or her.

Part of the government, but distinct from it and powerful in its own right, is the vast military establishment. Here, too, are countless individual agendas, interservice rivalries, and deeply held beliefs. The military is a powerful interest group, especially when its financial desires are at stake. Although the armed forces answer to the president, when differences of opinion arise between the military and the White House they seldom are secret for long. Dissent about strategy and tactics easily leaks out of the corridors of the Pentagon and the deliberations of the Joint Chiefs of Staff. Outright defiance of the president, such as Douglas MacArthur demonstrated during the Korean War, is rare; but subtle opposition and relentless undermining are not.

Outside the bounds of the government itself are corporations, labor unions, advocacy groups, trade associations, religious organizations, foreign governments, and freelance gadflies all seeking to influence the debate in Washington. And all these groups try to get their messages out to the people. They use direct-mail campaigns, newsletters, and magazines, advertorials, sponsored broadcasts, Web sites, and telemarketing. When they can, they use the mainstream press to spread their points of view.

This scrum of messages is a formidable challenge for any new president, but the fact that he has won election indicates that he and his aides can handle the press in a campaign. Now they must adapt that ability to governing.

HONEYMOONS

No matter how challenging the road to the White House, once in office a president can leave the campaign behind and build a new record. Americans want their president to succeed, since presumably they will be better off if he does. There may be problems with this presumption; it is, however, the reason that the press and the public generally grant the new president a "honeymoon" at the start of his administration.

The presidential honeymoon is treacherous. The fantasy that all will go smoothly adds to the disappointment when reality intrudes. A fractious Congress, a hypercritical press, and events beyond the president's control can cause the honeymoon to end in a hurry. The honeymoon tradition is a trap. The greater the presumption of success at the start, the higher the optimism, the more vivid the disappointment when things go awry.

For some presidents, the honeymoon never even happens. John Quincy Adams entered office in March 1825 to face its opposite. The disputed 1824 election left Jacksonians crying "bargain and corruption," and Adams's administration never shed this air of illegitimacy. What had briefly been the greatest victory of Adams's career proved to be his most salient defeat. Adams was never one to be cowed by the odds against him, a trait he shared with his father. In December 1825, he presented Congress with an ambitious agenda for America, one that involved the most active federal government since the time of Washington and Hamilton. Yet the cloud over his administration ensured that none of his promises could be fulfilled, and his administration experienced a long, gray defeat.

The economy has blighted several presidencies early on—the financial crises of 1837, 1893, and 1929 came fatally early in the terms of Martin Van Buren, Grover Cleveland (his second time around), and Herbert Hoover. Nothing undermines a presidency as effectively as a bad economy, and none of these men enjoyed political success after the economic ax fell.

The honeymoon is a vital but perilously short time for establishing the new story for the president. A quick victory can set a positive tone for the new administration, and an early defeat can seriously tarnish the new leader's image. In January 1961, John F. Kennedy came to office having advocated a stronger defense and more vigorous prosecution of the Cold War. In his first weeks in office JFK unwisely embraced one legacy of the Eisenhower administration, a planned invasion of Fidel Castro's Cuba. On April 17 a force of 1,700 ill-trained opponents of Castro landed at the Bay of Pigs. In a vain effort to preserve his ability to deny involvement, Kennedy canceled plans to offer covert air support for the invasion. The invasion was a military disaster and an international embarrassment for the new president. The invading troops were swiftly captured, and subsequent American efforts to deny involvement proved laughable. The Bay of Pigs stigmatized the Kennedy administration and its conduct of foreign policy for more than a year. Members of the administration made efforts to throw the blame back upon the Eisenhower White House and CIA director Allen Dulles, an Eisenhower holdover. These efforts failed, and the Bay of Pigs went down as a clear defeat for the new president.

Thirty-two years later, Bill Clinton, a Democrat inspired by JFK, was inaugurated. The Clinton administration came to power in January 1993 and suggested that an early priority would be establishing the right of homosexuals to serve openly in the military. But the initiative encountered greater opposition than the Clintonites expected, particularly from the career military. As opposition mounted, Clinton backed down, and the administration found itself supporting a weak compromise that said the military shouldn't ask for, and its members shouldn't volunteer, information about their sexual orientation. Though the White House claimed it was a step forward, many found this "Don't ask, don't tell" policy morally vacuous. It helped solidify Clinton's incipient reputation as a trimmer, a man whose soul was in the compromise.

Just as early defeats can be debilitating, early victories can set a tone for an entire term. Franklin Roosevelt took office decisively. He declared a bank holiday to deal with a panicked run on bank deposits, and followed that with an unprecedented 100 days of legislative activity. FDR's activism and willingness to experiment set a tone of achievement for his administration strong enough to survive subsequent setbacks.

The most successful president since Roosevelt in establishing his agenda and remaking American politics was Ronald Reagan. His most important early victory was a personal one—surviving an assassination attempt by a lunatic named John Hinckley Jr. on March 30, 1981. The single bullet that struck Reagan nearly killed him—it lodged just an inch from his heart, and he lost half his blood. Yet Reagan was spectacular—walking from his car into the hospital before collapsing, and joking with the doctors before his operation, "Please tell me you're Republicans." Reagan's courage and humor in surviving the attack established a twin legacy of bravery and of luck. An outpouring of public support followed the assassination attempt and helped him achieve substantive policy victories in tax cuts and increased defense spending that reshaped American politics. There was a new sheriff in town, with a new set of values. The story that showed this most clearly was his handling of the strike later that year by the Professional Air Traffic Controllers Association, or PATCO. That August, PATCO went on strike for higher wages and a shorter work week. Rather than taking the more conciliatory approach to labor troubles favored by earlier presidents, Reagan ordered the strikers—who as federal employees could not legally strike—back to work. If they did not comply, he said, they would be fired. Then he followed through. Within forty-eight hours, Reagan had fired the vast majority of PATCO workers and proclaimed a lifetime ban on rehiring them. Reagan's action may have jeopardized the safety of air travel for years afterward, but it did show that he was decisive. Here again was an early victory that set the tone for the entire Reagan era.[18]

EARLY INNINGS

Presidents can change their standing upon reaching office. The honeymoon period and the first year present opportunities for them to recast themselves, marrying their existing narratives to the stature and tradition of the office they now hold. Warren Harding believed that some sort of wondrous transformation elevated the abilities of a man upon reaching the presidency, and Americans look hopefully for such a metamorphosis in new presidents, particularly those who unexpectedly arrive in office. Gerald Ford had a reputation in Congress for rather plodding partisanship. But upon suddenly becoming president after Richard Nixon's resignation in August 1974, he was briefly seen by a newly supportive press and public as a statesman with hitherto undiscovered depth. Worn out by the intense months of investigation into the Watergate affair, both press and public gave the new president the benefit of the doubt. Weary of Nixon's imperial style, reporters dotingly noted that Ford toasted his own English muffins in the morning. But Ford inflicted a major defeat upon himself at the end of his first month in office. On September 8, 1974, he granted Nixon what he called a "full, free and absolute pardon." That decision abruptly ended his honeymoon and squandered the goodwill he had been granted.[19]

Ford had the advantage of succeeding the most disgraced president in American history, but a very different situation faced Harry S. Truman, coming to office after FDR's eventful twelve years in power. For many of the 12 million men and women then serving in the armed forces, Roosevelt was the only president they could clearly remember. Truman himself was stunned by his ascension, saying to reporters the day after Roosevelt's death that when he heard the news, "I felt like the moon, the stars, and all the planets had fallen on me." Yet many observers found him to possess qualities that were significant and presidential, although vastly different from the habits of his predecessor. Even in the eyes of people who had been close to Roosevelt, some aspects of the change were even quite positive. In his diary, Henry Stimson, the secretary of war, marveled following a meeting with the new president that "there were no long-drawn-out 'soliloquies' from the President and the whole conference was thoroughly businesslike so that we actually covered two or three more matters than we had expected to discuss."[20]

Within four months of taking office, Truman had presided over the successful conclusion of the Second World War with the defeat of Germany in May and the surrender of Japan three months later. He had met in conference with Churchill and Stalin at Potsdam, his frank midwestern countenance in the place the world was accustomed to seeing Roosevelt occupy. And he had approved, and defended, the use of the atomic bomb, the device that transformed the powers of his office beyond the imagination of his predecessors. A combination of circumstances and his talents stamped Truman indelibly as the new leader of his nation. Yet some could never forget Truman's roots as a Democratic machine politician, and critics harped on the perceived stature gap between Truman and Roosevelt.

CONTINUITY AND CHANGE

Truman ultimately succeeded in making the transition because the way he handled his presidency was consistent with the man he was. He did not try to become patrician, nor did he renounce his Missouri roots, even though some thought those roots still encrusted with dirt. Shortly after Truman was inaugurated as vice president, his longtime political ally and patron, Boss Tom Pendergast of Kansas City, died. The loyal Truman attended the funeral, in spite of Pendergast's 1939 imprisonment on a federal income-tax charge. Some tried to portray

Truman's attendance as evidence of a permissive attitude toward political corruption, but the idea that he was just doing the decent thing for an old friend rang truer.

Truman was not so helpful to his successor, Dwight Eisenhower. In 1952 Ike had pledged, "I shall go to Korea," and with the election won, he did. Douglas MacArthur, chafing on the sidelines after Truman had removed him from command, volunteered that he had a plan to deal with the stalemate there. An incensed Truman denounced Ike's trip as demagoguery and said that if MacArthur had any plans he should discuss them with Truman, who was still president. Eisenhower was privately furious at Truman's criticism but took the high road in public, expressing puzzlement over the president's attack and declaring that he would not interject himself into the argument between Truman and MacArthur.[21]

From the pledge to the trip to the reaction to Truman's blast, Ike's actions were all consistent with the qualities that had gotten him elected: military leadership, a reputation for diplomatic tact, and the ability to hold his tongue when angry. The *New York Times* editorialized upon Ike's return, "The obligation that General Eisenhower willingly assumed in that pledge has been honorably discharged." "Mission accomplished" was the newspaper's verdict on the trip, adopting the sort of military idiom that would reinforce Eisenhower's army credentials in the reader's mind.[22]

First impressions matter. A national hope that a new president can grow in office buys a short honeymoon, but reality soon intrudes, and woe to the leader who cannot adapt to his new circumstances. First impressions may be swiftly formed, and often wrong, but they are not easy to overcome.

CHAPTER SEVEN

THE WHITE HOUSE AS MOVIE SET

THE ELEVATION TO THE PRESIDENCY MAKES THE SUCCESSFUL CANDI-
date into a new character, and the White House becomes the stage
upon which he, his family, and his aides act out their various parts.

He also has new audiences for his performance as well. As president he plays to an international crowd, and stories and characters
that may have worked in domestic politics can prove inappropriate in
the larger context. Much of his energies must go to taming and entertaining a veteran audience of Washington reporters, familiar with the
town's ways and linked by custom and interest to the permanent
power brokers of the city. The new president must figure out how to
address these and other new audiences without alienating the followers who elected him.

Presidents are not monarchs, but they are heads of state, and they
and their First Ladies are measured both against previous inhabitants
of the White House and the stories of regal couples drawn from history and legend, so that John Kennedy's assassination recalls both the
death of Lincoln and the elegiac strains of the musical *Camelot.* The
White House set today requires a certain stature of the actors who

stand on it, and the stories that are now acted out must be found worthy of these mighty surroundings.

HUMBLER BEGINNINGS

Yet it was not always so. The presidency used to be a much less august office, and its occupants were less inclined—or even adamantly opposed—to any regal pretensions.

When Woodrow Wilson was a young graduate student at Johns Hopkins University in the 1880s, he chose as his thesis subject the operations of the United States government. The resulting work was called "Congressional Government," a title that proclaimed Wilson's conclusion about where power lay in Washington. Wilson's judgment would have heartened the men who wrote the Constitution in Philadelphia in 1787, concerned as they were about excessive executive power.

Washington and other Federalists worried about the dignity of the office and whether the democratic instincts unleashed by the Revolution might result in mob rule. They felt the office needed some majesty in order to command respect, and during the early weeks of the new government Congress devoted considerable energy to debating the proper forms of address for the new leader. Vice President John Adams complained that the title "president" brought to his mind the leader of a fire company or a cricket club, and a Senate committee proposed that the chief executive be referred to as "His Highness the President of the United States of America, and Protector of their Liberties." This suggestion was wisely rejected. Adams was mocked for his pomposity and his critics dubbed him "His Rotundity."[1]

Thomas Jefferson was certainly a sophisticate, one whose experience at European courts had honed his taste for the finer things, including the best French wines. But he ignored both diplomatic convention and common courtesy in his entertaining at the White House. From the start of his presidency, Jefferson declared, in the words of Henry Adams, that "he would admit not the smallest distinction that might separate him from the mass of his fellow-citizens." For his inauguration, he had simply walked from the boardinghouse where he was staying to the Capitol. Washington was then a city under construction, and a small and dirty one at that. However such informality played with the voters of that time, it was entirely new, and offensive, to the European diplomats selected to endure the pestilential weather and scant comforts of the new American capital.[2]

The most consequential diplomat was the British minister, who in 1803 was Anthony Merry, a young man whose appointment had been connived at by the American minister in London, Rufus King, because he felt Merry would be good for relations between the two countries. Upon his arrival in Washington, Merry came to present his credentials to Jefferson, stopping first to pick up James Madison, the secretary of state. Merry was dressed, as the occasion required, in full diplomatic uniform, a rather splendid sight in those days. But Jefferson greeted the new ambassador in his customary garb, which was described by an American senator of the time as follows: "He was dressed, or rather undressed, in an old brown coat, red waistcoat, old corduroy small-clothes much soiled, woollen hose, and slippers without heels." The senator thought Jefferson was a servant, and Anthony Merry took Jefferson's manner of dress as an intentional affront, both to Merry and to the government he served.[3]

Matters got worse when Jefferson gave a dinner party for Merry and his wife. First of all, the president invited—indeed, urged the attendance of—the French minister, even though France and Britain were then at war, and such a joint invitation was most inappropriate for a small dinner. Then, when it came time to be seated, Jefferson did not take Mrs. Merry in to dinner, as custom and courtesy dictated, but Dolley Madison, and sat her to his right. Merry grew even more infuriated when he went in himself and, as he later recounted in his report back to London, "I was proceeding to place myself, though without invitation, next to the wife of the Spanish minister, when a member of the House of Representatives passed quickly by me and took the seat, without Mr. Jefferson's using any means to prevent it, or taking any care that I might be otherwise placed."[4]

Members of Jefferson's cabinet later tried to repair the damage and show the Merrys more traditional courtesies, and Jefferson himself explained that this was simply his standing social practice of using the "rule of pell-mell" (or, as he put it, *pêle mêle*) in such situations. But Merry was not convinced, and relations between Britain and the Francophilic Jefferson deteriorated.

Jefferson would never admit that his action was inappropriate, but neither did he manage to establish the "rule of pell-mell" as the standard for the White House. However fundamental the notion that "all men are created equal" may be to the country's history and self-image, the American people today seem to want their president to be a bit more equal than others. Yet for most of the nineteenth century Congress remained first among equals, and the executive branch stayed small and relatively powerless. There were exceptions: the imperious Andrew Jackson bent Congress to his will, and the exigencies of the Civil War led to a swift, if largely temporary, expansion of executive power in the 1860s—but by and large the action was in Congress. Leaders of the House and Senate like Henry Clay, John C. Calhoun, and Daniel Webster had presidential ambitions but wielded power for decades as legislators and probably shaped the nation at least as much from the Capitol as they would have from the White House. Later power brokers, such as the Gilded Age Republican senator Roscoe Conkling and the despot of the House in the early twentieth century, Speaker "Uncle Joe" Cannon, enjoyed exercising their vast powers from more secluded vantage points than the Oval Office.

This all began to change when Theodore Roosevelt's outsized personality and imperial ambitions gained the White House a more prominent place on the national and world stages. And that chronicler of "congressional government," Woodrow Wilson, himself oversaw a vast expansion of government powers during the First World War. But it was Teddy's cousin Franklin who turned the White House into the most important beat in Washington, and Washington into a place for a young reporter to win a reputation.

THE FOURTH ESTATE

Before the Depression and the New Deal, news organizations, headquartered mostly in New York, saw little need to spend much money covering the doings of government. As late as 1932 the *New York Times* found it hard to recruit a new Washington bureau chief because the assignment was seen as a career dead end. All that began to change, according to Senate historian Donald Ritchie, when in June 1932 the Depression brought the Bonus Expeditionary Force to the capital. The so-called bonus army was made up of veterans from the First World War. Their cause was to demand the early payment of the "adjusted compensation certificates" that Congress had voted as a bonus for their military service. The certificates were supposed to come due in 1945. The veterans, broke and with hungry families, were marching to ask for the payment to be made immediately. They were a patriotic crew whose rules included "no panhandling, no drinking, no radicalism," and they marched from as far away as the West Coast to make their case to the federal government.[5]

The bonus marchers had some support in Congress, but President Hoover refused to meet with them and largely ignored their existence. His secretary of war fretted that the men were so well behaved that he had been given no excuse to declare martial law and move them out. A small Communist force among the marchers tried to whip up more violent protest, largely without success. But when a panicky police-man fired into a crowd, the government had its excuse to move against the campsite where the bonus marchers had settled.

The force that attacked the veterans included cavalry troops with sabers drawn, tanks, tear gas, and infantry with fixed bayonets. Among the officers leading the attack were Douglas MacArthur, Dwight Eisenhower, and George S. Patton (who helped drive from the camp-ground a veteran named Joe Angelo, who fourteen years earlier had saved Patton's life in France, winning the Distinguished Service Cross). Reporters used to writing their stories based on government docu-ments or briefings suddenly had to cover a story happening on the streets, and they discovered to their disgust that the government whose handouts they had printed so faithfully was capable of lying to them. The secretary of war denied that the soldiers had set the marchers' shanties on fire—but the reporters had seen them do it. Paul Y. An-derson of the *St. Louis Post-Dispatch* told of troops hauling drums of kerosene to start the fires. Fearful of civil unrest, many newspapers backed the president's action in ordering the assault, but newsreel footage showing the attack on the veterans did not win Hoover much support.[6]

It was a big story, but the new medium of radio wasn't prepared for it. Although radio broadcasting had begun in 1920, in the summer of 1932 there were still no radio reporters assigned to the nation's capi-tal, and the stations scrambled to get some sort of coverage.

The election that fall of Franklin Roosevelt marked the beginning of a new era in press coverage of the capital. By 1933 the Great De-pression had fanned fears about the stability of America's economic and political systems, and Roosevelt's New Deal programs involved a vast enlargement of government's role in American society. In a year when Stalin and Mussolini were consolidating their regimes in the So-viet Union and Italy, and Hitler was coming to power in Germany, the United States seemed more threatened than it had since the Civil War—and that made events in Washington big news.

Radio reporters were soon ensconced in the capital, and newspapers devoted greater resources to what was becoming a glamorous beat. The reporters found colorful personalities to cover—the president above all, as well as his wife, Eleanor, who turned the job of First Lady into a public platform as well as a ceremonial responsibility. There was Hugh Johnson, the former general who headed the National Recovery Administration, along with the famous "brains trust" of university experts who helped devise economic policy and social programs. There was Frances Perkins, the new secretary of labor and the first woman to serve in the cabinet, and Harry Hopkins, who headed two "alphabet agencies" of the New Deal before becoming commerce secretary in 1938 and then Roosevelt's all-purpose diplomatic envoy during the war years. Such characters made great copy. The constant array of new programs, the legislative and court battles they triggered, and their effects on the nation provided ample subject matter for ambitious journalists.

The coming of the Second World War only heightened the need for more reporting, and the propaganda machine that developed in wartime taught new and lasting lessons on how the government and the press could work with—or against—each other. The sense of common purpose engendered by the war and its successful conclusion helped to create a climate of trust and shared values between reporters and government officials that persisted for two decades afterward. Those decades saw a further expansion of Washington coverage as the Cold War and the maintenance of a large defense establishment, combined with social programs passed under Roosevelt and Truman, greatly enlarged Washington's role in the life of the average citizen. Military bases, public housing projects, federally funded highways, and weapons-procurement decisions all had concrete effects on jobs, prices, and other aspects of daily life around the nation. The public wanted to know about how government decisions would affect them, and elected officials wanted to make sure that voters knew that they were working to bring home the pork.

In the 1950s television joined radio, wire services, and newspapers in offering daily coverage of events in the capital, and by the 1960s the nightly television newscasts had emerged as a crucial molder of public opinion. In the 1990s the growing number of twenty-four-hour cable news channels and the rise of the Internet turned the already hectic pace of Washington reporting into a ceaseless maelstrom.

Not all the reporting was taking place at the White House, of course. Congress remained an important beat, and representatives and senators and their staffs labored hard to generate stories that would attract attention to themselves and their issues. Some news organizations devoted the resources to covering the important but often obscure activities of executive departments and regulatory agencies, where lobbyists were concentrating increasing amounts of their own time and resources.

But the powers of the modern presidency had moved the spotlight inexorably away from Congress, the Supreme Court, and the agencies and toward the White House. It was the glamour beat, and the choreography of press and president has evolved over the decades into a quadrille of ever greater elaborateness. For a new president, everything he, his family, and his administration did was news, so he and his aides had to plot each step with care. But in such plotting, they also had to bear in mind the history of the office, and of the White House, and work within (or consciously against) the conventions of the office.

As a new president takes control of the government, a new cast of characters moves onstage. Distinguished members of the cabinet, home-state contributors, political strategists, and campaign veterans stake their claim on offices and responsibilities, turf and perks. Washington gossips, in the press and out, sift for clues to where the power lies with assiduousness and sophistication. At the center of it all is the White House itself, and at the center of the White House is the president's family.

FIRST LADIES

So much is written about the candidate's family during a campaign that the possibility of further news from that front would seem exhausted. Yet the reality is that the scrutiny of the president's family actually intensifies once they move into 1600 Pennsylvania Avenue. Now they are expected to perform their lives before a worldwide audience, rather than merely live them. A new friend, a new hobby, even a new haircut become newsworthy, and all are interpreted for what they might mean for the administration. Every dinner guest is a potential controversy, every entertainer at a White House banquet a potential political liability. (Did he ever sing at an IRA rally? Did she ever pose topless? Did the band ever take drugs?) And the figure presiding over all this is the First Lady.

Before the White House became the center of media attention in Washington, the president's wife was relied upon to help host dinners, run the household, and generally perform the domestic duties assigned to wives in wealthy families of the nineteenth century. If she performed these adequately, little attention was paid to her. When things went wrong—as when the cares of the Civil War crushed the fragile mental balance of Mary Todd Lincoln—the attention increased but was still slight in comparison to what would happen today.

By far the most powerful First Lady ever was Edith Bolling Wilson, Woodrow Wilson's second wife, who married him in December 1915. The following year, the *Washington Star* reported that "Mrs. Wilson has accompanied the President everywhere on his campaign trips," and, noting her apparent influence over the president, the *Louisville Courier-Journal* suggested, "Omnipotence might be her middle name." When President Wilson suffered a paralytic stroke during his 1919 whistle-stop campaign to drum up support for the Versailles Treaty, Edith became, in essence, the acting president for the balance of his term, although she took care to conceal the extent of her powers.[7]

It was the 1920 election that first saw women vote nationwide, as a consequence of the enactment of the Nineteenth Amendment. Edith Wilson did not vote that year, but millions of women did, and one of the things that influenced their votes was the character of the First Lady. The rise of female political power made the First Lady an increasingly important part of her husband's life story.

Broadcasting accelerated the rising importance of presidential wives. Eleanor Roosevelt was the key figure here, in significant part because her arrival in the White House coincided with the coming-of-age of radio. Her experience defined the new realities of being First Lady and illustrated the limits of the role—and the price a woman would pay for transgressing those limits. In 1933, FDR's first year in the White House, Eleanor traveled 40,000 miles around the country, visiting schools, factories, and hospitals and spreading hope and drumming up support for her husband's New Deal programs. At first, the presence of such an active First Lady was seen as a refreshing change. *The New Yorker* ran a cartoon in its June 3 issue depicting a coal miner, deep in a shaft, saying, "For gosh sakes, here comes Mrs. Roosevelt!"[8]

But FDR's reforms and Eleanor's own crusades for, among other things, the rights of women and blacks earned both the Roosevelts the enmity of many Americans, particularly the wealthy. Just three years later another *New Yorker* cartoon showed a group of well-dressed socialites—the women in furs, the men in dinner jackets—hailing another group through the open window of a stately home: "Come along. We're going to the Trans-Lux to hiss Roosevelt." And Mrs.

Roosevelt was a particular target for this antagonism. Critics mocked her buck teeth and physical awkwardness, and her interest in the rights of blacks and women was subject to lewd and snickering interpretation. A group of southern opponents of the Roosevelts distributed a photo of Eleanor with some ROTC cadets at Howard University with the caption, "A picture of Mrs. Roosevelt going to some nigger meeting, with two escorts, niggers, on each arm." She and her husband were attacked in verse as well:

You kiss the negroes,
I'll kiss the Jews,
We'll stay in the White House
As long as we choose.[9]

Eleanor's activism was seen as entirely inconsistent with the wifely role of First Lady, and she drew criticism not only from snide Republicans but also from her husband's loyal adherents. Harold Ickes, while head of the Public Works Administration, wrote that he wished she would "stick to her knitting." Ickes worried that Eleanor was "not doing the President any good. She is becoming altogether too active in public affairs and I think she is harmful rather than helpful. After all, the people did not elect her President, and I don't think the country likes the thought of the wife of the President engaging in public affairs to the extent that she does." FDR's press secretary, Stephen Early, worked hard to distance the president from his wife's campaign for racial justice.[10]

There were, however, many Americans, liberals in particular, who were inspired by her activism and heartened by her embrace of unpopular causes. Mrs. Roosevelt showed particular courage in her efforts to champion an antilynching bill being pushed by the NAACP in the 1930s. In many states, and the South particularly, most lynchings were never prosecuted—indeed, local authorities often condoned them. The NAACP bill would have made lynching a federal crime, taking such cases away from the states and moving them into federal courts. Mrs. Roosevelt acted as an important intermediary between Walter White, head of the NAACP, and the president. At one White House meeting, whenever FDR objected to some portion of the bill, White had a ready response. "Somebody's been priming you," Roosevelt said testily. "Was it my wife?" In his account of the matter, White wrote, "I smiled, and suggested that we stick to our discussion of the bill."[11]

In 1939 Mrs. Roosevelt again found herself in the middle of a civil rights debate. That year the great contralto Marian Anderson was refused the use of the auditorium in Washington owned by the Daughters of the American Revolution (DAR). Anderson was then invited to sing at the Lincoln Memorial, and Eleanor Roosevelt resigned her membership in the DAR. In her regular newspaper column, "My Day," she explained that to remain in the DAR "implies approval" of its action, "and therefore I am resigning." Marian Anderson praised the First Lady as "one who really comprehends the true meaning of democracy." A Gallup poll showed that about two-thirds of the nation supported the resignation.[12]

Harry Truman was a more vigorous champion of black rights than his predecessor, taking the landmark step of desegregating the armed forces. But his wife, Bess, was strongly averse to crusading in the tradition of Eleanor Roosevelt. In the fall of 1945, the DAR invited her to a tea in her honor at Constitution Hall. But it soon came out that another black singer, Hazel Scott, the wife of Harlem congressman Adam Clayton Powell Jr., had recently been turned down in her effort to sing at the hall. Powell raised the matter with the president and his wife, but Bess refused to boycott the event, saying that "acceptance of the hospitality is not related to the merits of the issue which has since arisen." Powell derided Bess as the "last lady," for which he was declared persona non grata in the Truman White House.[13]

Mrs. Truman was different from Mrs. Roosevelt in other ways as well. Although she was politically aware, and some thought acute, she was never seen as a meddler. In fact she was seen as having no influence over her husband's policies. Yet even the most placid and matronly First Lady can draw fire. In 1952, Dwight Eisenhower had to face down accusations (floated by the camp of Robert Taft, his Republican opponent for the nomination) that his wife, Mamie, was a problem drinker. A Republican convention delegate from Nebraska asked Ike about Mamie, saying flat out, "We hear she's a drunk." Eisenhower kept his composure and replied that she had not had a drink for more than a year.[14] In the 1950s such an accusation was heard more often in whispers than in public, and seldom did such matters make it into the press. The situation was far different in the 1970s, when drugs, alcohol, and mental illness had all become more acceptable subjects of public discussion. Gerald Ford's wife, Betty, became a hero for speaking and writing frankly about her own problems with chemical dependency. As a prominent advocate of treatment, she helped found a major center for the treatment of drug and alcohol abuse, which bears her name.

First Ladies are expected to avoid political controversy, but they are permitted to champion a few wholesome and inoffensive causes. Lady Bird Johnson made highway beautification her crusade, Nancy Reagan focused on drugs, and Laura Bush, a former librarian, has emphasized literacy. But although a president's wife may be allowed her pet causes, and can prove a useful campaigner (Lady Bird Johnson, for example, conducted her own whistle-stop campaign on her husband's behalf in 1964), the story changes when she is seen as influencing government policy. The president's wife then becomes Lady Macbeth. The two First Ladies to have recently been cast in the role are Nancy Reagan and Hillary Rodham Clinton.

The women appear opposites in most ways. Hillary was the striving lawyer, the feminist, the child of the sixties; Nancy, the devoted wife, the actress who abandoned her career to support her husband's, the smiling ornament to her husband's success. But what appear to be very different stories bear closer similarities below the surface, as each woman was a crucial influence on her husband's career. It is, of course, extremely hard to gauge the influence of one spouse on another from outside the marriage.

One way Nancy Reagan made her presence felt was by altering the president's schedule on the advice of her astrologer, Joan Quigley, to whom she had been referred by her friend Merv Griffin, the former talk-show host. Presidential aide Michael Deaver was often charged with implementing inconvenient last-minute schedule changes that the First Lady dictated after consultation with Quigley. Nancy Reagan took pains not to flaunt her behind-the-scenes influence. But there were moments, such as her very public power struggle with Chief of Staff Donald Regan, where it became impossible to hide her power. In return, Regan revealed Nancy Reagan's astrological obsessions in his memoirs.[15]

No such reticence about influence marked Hillary Rodham Clinton during her time as First Lady. Hillary's assertiveness proved troublesome for her husband's candidacy and his presidency. During the primaries in 1992, she responded to concerns about her career and her influence on her husband by remarking that she supposed she could have just "stayed home and baked cookies," an unfortunately vivid line that seemed to denigrate all of America's homemakers and became an enduring political liability. In May 1992, the reporter Maureen Dowd wrote in the *New York Times* that Mrs. Clinton had to assure "doubters that she is not Lady Macbeth in a black preppy headband." Once in the White House, President Clinton appointed his wife to head the biggest reform agenda of his presidency, the push for a comprehensive national health-insurance system. The First Lady's active involvement in this effort contributed to its defeat. Both the fact and the style of her advocacy on this issue gave ammunition to the opponents of the move, who were numerous and well financed.[16]

For many Americans, women and men, Hillary Rodham Clinton is an impressive, dynamic woman who has managed to make a career for herself despite working diligently to promote her husband's ambitions. Others are put off by what they see as an aggressive, know-it-all air, and simply find her political views too liberal for their tastes. Still others find in her a perfect symbol of the moral decay of the country, an unfeminine threat to patriarchy and social order. And some just don't like her. The Republican speechwriter Peggy Noonan says that for her Hillary is the "kneesocked girl in the madras headband" in high school who "mention[s] to a teacher that they're smoking in the girl's room again."[17]

If Hillary Clinton paid the price of violating the accepted story line for First Ladies, and her husband later got into trouble for his infidelities, they did at least stay married. It is only in the past generation that divorce ceased to be an automatic disqualification of a candidate, perhaps because a society in which divorce was so common could hardly continue to anathematize those who had gone through it. And yet of the forty-three presidents to date, only Ronald Reagan has been divorced. As we have seen, a generation back, Nelson Rockefeller's progress toward the 1964 Republican nomination was derailed by his divorce and then his 1963 remarriage to a much younger woman who was herself a divorcée. More recently divorce has been less of an issue, although it remains a potential liability, a "negative" blip on the candidate's résumé (as it was, in the 2000 primaries, for the Republican contender John McCain).

Sometimes a happy marriage itself is not enough. The signature moment of the 2000 Democratic National Convention was when Al Gore embraced his wife, Tipper, on the convention stage and kissed her. It was Gore's way of defusing the accusations that he was a wooden, bloodless candidate. No moment of Gore's convention got a more positive response, and the kiss became one of the campaign's defining images. A couple of years later, Gore himself parodied the moment in an appearance on *Saturday Night Live.* He and Tipper were seen in a long clinch—endless, almost—which finally concluded with the Gores reciting the trademark opener, "Live from New York it's *Saturday Night!*" The next day, Gore announced he would not run for president in 2004. When you know you are going to opt out of the presidential story, you acquire the freedom to parody it.

First Ladies come and First Ladies go, but the definitive story belongs to Jackie. Jacqueline Kennedy parlayed youth and beauty, proficiency in French and an intimate knowledge of Parisian couture into mythic status. Perhaps coming after Eleanor Roosevelt, Bess Truman, and Mamie Eisenhower, the youthful socialite seemed even more beautiful than she was. Certainly the sight of a pregnant wife on the campaign trail with her candidate husband was a rare and heartwarming picture. Her televised tour of the White House brought average Americans into the presidential mansion in a new way. Today her career as First Lady is defined by the black trappings of her husband's funeral, all of her outfits distilled into the pink suit she was wearing in Dallas that day, and the remainder of her life—marriage to the Greek tycoon Aristotle Onassis, raising her children, a career in New York—is simply the long coda to the heady days of Camelot. It is the story line of story lines for First Ladies, as unapproachable as it is undesirable to approach.

OTHER PLAYERS

The rest of the president's family also garners attention from the press and public. Sometimes the glamorous lives First Families lead provide vicarious satisfaction for those consigned to less glorious activities and locations. At other times, we find comfort in the ordinariness of presidential relatives, and in the everyday sorts of troubles and embarrassments they encounter. Against the magisterial progress of a presidential life story, these moments of comic relief can prove remarkably refreshing.

Parents, siblings, and children of presidents all get their own kind of attention. Parents are consigned to the background, even when one parent is a former president (at times George H. W. Bush has seemed the only member of his own administration not playing an active role in his son's government). The elder John Adams was much deteriorated by the time his son ran for president in 1824. That summer, the Marquis de Lafayette was touring the United States and visited his old comrade in Massachusetts. "That was not the John Adams I knew," Lafayette commented after the meeting—although Adams said the same thing about him.[18] The Peace Corps experiences of Lillian Carter and the hard-knocks life of Bill Clinton's mother, Virginia Kelley, cast a leavening influence over their sons' White House lives.

Siblings are generally permitted to live their own lives in peace, except when they seek the spotlight. The Kennedys set the standards for presidential brothers and sisters. The hearty elegance of touch football on the lawn at Hyannis and the appointment of Robert F. Kennedy as his brother's attorney general guaranteed that this dynastic family would remain a big part of the president's story.

In addition to the gaudily successful Kennedy brothers, there are the more recent Bush brothers, one president, the other governor of Florida. There are also the family embarrassments, such as Jimmy Carter's beer-swilling brother, Billy, and Bill Clinton's drug-troubled half-brother, Roger. (As governor of Arkansas, Bill Clinton once had to approve the arrest of Roger on a cocaine charge.) Such family embarrassments are sometimes referred to in aid of partisan cheap shots or late-night TV yucks, but in general the achievements and foibles of brothers and sisters are a peripheral part of the presidential life story.

Perhaps citizens and the press acknowledge that presidents are, after all, human, and cannot choose their relations.

Children are another matter. Here the constant tug between national curiosity and personal freedom is felt acutely. Grover Cleveland was one of three presidents to marry while in the White House (Wilson and John Tyler are the others), and in 1891, as Cleveland was preparing to retake the presidency he had lost in November 1888, his wife, Frances, gave birth to their first child, a daughter named Ruth. In the small article the *New York Times* ran about her christening, the paper commented that her "birth and subsequent conduct and condition have excited widespread and general interest among the people of the whole country." When the Clevelands returned to the White House in 1893, "Baby Ruth" was a celebrated figure—it was front-page news when she got the measles in 1896—and the nation later mourned her death, from diphtheria, in 1904. So fondly was she recalled that in 1921 a candy bar was named for her, which remains a staple of candy stores today. Her story connected people to Cleveland intensely, bringing the distant and exalted office of president tragically into human scale.[19]

A baby in the White House humanizes the presidential occupant like nothing else. The photos of John-John Kennedy gamboling in the Oval Office remain vivid images of the imagined Camelot of that administration. President Kennedy was aware of this effect and had the pictures taken and publicized in spite of the objections of his wife. Another life story was being generated, without the young boy's having any say in it.

Adolescents are a tougher group to handle, with their growing pains and the enormous tension between the desire to rebel and the political need to conform. Adolescence is difficult under the best of circumstances, but imagine it played out in the news, as has been the case for the likes of Chelsea Clinton and Amy Carter. The decision about whether Chelsea Clinton would attend public or private school was subjected to intense public scrutiny and a crucial part of a young girl's life was made a litmus test of her parents' principles. George and Laura Bush's daughters, Barbara and Jenna, were hardly unique in having pursued underage drinking, and if every person under twenty-one found with a fake ID (as Jenna was) were written up in the newspapers, Canada would be short of trees. Yet in large part the press respects the wishes of presidential parents and leaves the private lives of children unexamined. When those lives do come under scrutiny, however, it is usually in connection with some variation from the straight and narrow.

THE WHITE HOUSE AS SET

The White House is the home in which the president's family lives, but it is also the workplace of the president's closest staff and the location of various routine and ritual functions, from cabinet meetings and press events to formal dinners. Parts of the complex—the Oval Office, the Rose Garden, the press briefing room—are familiar sites, and sights, with multiple associations drawn from fact and fiction. The building has witnessed real courtship (between Edith and Woodrow Wilson) and fictitious romance (Kevin Kline and Sigourney Weaver in *Dave,* Michael Douglas and Annette Bening in *The American President*). It has hosted celebrations of peace (such as the Camp David Accords of 1978) and acts of war (the British attack on the building in 1814). It has been dressed up (each Christmas and Easter) and blown apart (in the film *Independence Day*). And it is has served as the raison d'être for one of the most sophisticated programs ever shown on network television, *The West Wing.* Every time an actual event takes place at the White House, our view of it is colored by all the previous images of it we carry—real or fictitious, noble or venal, present or past.

With its elegant proportions and imposing size, the building establishes a grandeur that quickly affects the way we see its inhabitants. Some respond by fighting against it—Bess Truman never felt truly at home there—others take to it quite naturally. Jackie Kennedy thought the place run-down and gathered antiques (mostly donated) with which to furnish the public rooms properly. Richard Nixon, eager to make the place even grander, commissioned new uniforms for the White House guard that looked like something out of *The Prisoner of Zenda;* he was soon shamed into abandoning the Austro-Hungarian chic he had hoped to introduce.

The television networks are happy to embrace and promote the conventions of White House iconography. After all, a correspondent has to work hard to get assigned to that beat and wants the glory of standing on the lawn, with the colonnaded portico behind, and intoning the news of the day. The fact that that news may have been carefully processed and prepared by the White House press office is just part of the price of standing there.

This big stage transforms all who play upon it. The president's story is no longer that of an individual, but of a ruler. The welfare of the nation depends upon both how good his choices are and how well he explains them. A president who can impose his story on the nation stands on a brightly lit stage and plays a starring role in the history of his time.

CHAPTER EIGHT

WINNERS AND LOSERS

THE PROBLEMS A PRESIDENT FACES IN OFFICE ARE COMPLEX. BUT THE press and the public have little patience for complexity. Just as a great novel loses its subtlety when adapted by Hollywood, so the difficult issues of public policy are reduced to simple, easily remembered stories when processed by the news media and absorbed by voters. And one of the simplest ways of looking at political life is to sort its participants into winners and losers.

This sorting is a familiar part of the coverage of presidential campaigns, and it carries over into the coverage of the conduct of a new administration. As the press has moved from its long-ago partisan roots to embrace "objectivity" as a goal, it has found it difficult, indeed wrong, to reach its own conclusions on any issue, except on the editorial page. (So firm is this principle that many papers now expect their reporters and editors to avoid participation in public life—no serving on the school board, or on the board of the local environmental group. The *Washington Post*'s editor personally refrains from voting.) Reporters are unwilling to assess in a news story whether a particular stand on an issue is right or wrong, or even to indicate whether the evidence supporting one side or the other is true or false. So journalists often become mere scorekeepers, ruling on who won a legislative wrangle in Congress or lost a treaty negotiation overseas.

Such tallyings promote a culture of competition rather than cooperation, and presidents and their staffs become fixated on how to "win" a particular issue, often seeking ways to recast the matter at hand so as to appear victorious even if the original goal gets lost in the process. Faced with complex issues, political strategists generally care less about how to solve the problem than how to declare victory. The original point of the conflict is shoved aside, and the story is boiled down to a simple win/loss column. Almost forgotten is the question of what effects these decisions have on the lives of those affected by government action. It becomes the job of historians to sort the matter out decades later, revising the provisional verdict announced in the press.

VICTORY IN WAR, AND THE RHETORIC OF WAR

If election to the presidency is the clearest sort of triumph an American politician can achieve, a president once in office must look for other victories and hope that they provide a useful climax to important narratives. The most obvious kind is defeating an enemy in war. Three of the least martial American presidents—Abraham Lincoln, Woodrow Wilson, and Franklin Roosevelt—led the nation to its three most important wartime triumphs. Neither Lincoln nor Roosevelt lived to savor victory, and Wilson's concern was less to celebrate the victory than to become master of the peace process. The deaths of Lincoln and Roosevelt, the war leaders who had become symbols of the nation, clouded the victories of 1865 and 1945.

No victory is final, of course. Wilson presided over America's triumphant role in the victory over Germany in 1918, but his intense interest in the shape of the postwar settlement caused him to invest all his hard-won political capital in the treaty process, first at Versailles and then in the United States Senate. Having won the war, Wilson managed to lose the peace by refusing to compromise with members of the Senate less committed than he was to internationalism.

Avoiding war can also be a form of victory, as can being a peacemaker. The high point of Jimmy Carter's presidency was the September 1978 signing of the Camp David Accords, an important step toward peace in the Middle East. For a time this agreement between Egypt, Israel, and the United States significantly lowered tensions in the region. Jimmy Carter eventually was awarded the Nobel Peace Prize, in large part for that achievement. Theodore Roosevelt, perhaps the most bellicose of American presidents, won the Nobel Peace Prize for helping negotiate the settlement of the Russo-Japanese War of 1904–1905. Such diplomatic achievements can help establish a record of success for a presidency or redeem in part an unsuccessful legacy.

Because victory in war can have a clarity often lacking in less bloody pursuits, the language of war is often adopted for other confrontations. Andrew Jackson fought the so-called Bank War with Nicholas Biddle, head of the Second Bank of the United States. In the 1830s, Jackson moved to destroy the bank—and succeeded. For him, the fight was nothing less than the struggle for control of the nation, and he took it personally: "The Bank, Mr. Van Buren, is trying to kill me, but I will kill it," he told his future vice president in the summer of 1832. He would do so in part with the powers of rhetoric. Fanning the flames of class warfare, he vetoed the bill Congress had passed extending the bank's charter and wrote in his veto message that government was in the wrong when "the laws undertake . . . to make the rich richer and the potent more powerful." In such circumstances, "the humble members of society—the farmers, mechanics, and laborers . . . have a right to complain of the injustice of their Government."[1]

Daniel Webster, speaking for the opposition, denounced Jackson's address: "It manifestly seeks to influence the poor against the rich. It wantonly attacks whole classes of the people, for the purpose of turning against them the prejudices and resentments of other classes." But Jackson wanted war; he got it, and he won. And his use of dramatic language—he called the bank a "corrupting monster"—worked for him in important ways. It made what might have seemed an abstract contest into a momentous confrontation. And the idea of conflict, of a bank "war," reminded Americans of Jackson's existing identity as a war hero. The radiance of his 1815 victory could thus cast its glow over his presidential actions in the 1830s.[2]

POLITICAL VICTORY

The rhetoric of war fit Jackson's past, but some presidents earn reputations as winners without having tasted victory on the field of battle. One of the most gifted politicians ever to sit in the White House was Lyndon Johnson, and in his pre–White House career as a U.S. senator he fashioned for himself a reputation as a brilliant and successful tactician. But all of his engagements were fought in the halls of the Capitol, not the halls of Montezuma. Perhaps the greatest and most difficult victory was the passage of the Civil Rights Act of 1964. Johnson's predecessor, John F. Kennedy, had taken tentative steps toward supporting civil rights, in almost every case his hand forced either by the aggressive tactics of the civil rights movement or by the active resistance led by southern governors. In spite of Kennedy's lukewarm support for civil rights, his assassination crowned him with a halo of martyrdom, and his cautious advocacy of civil rights was soon being recalled as much more forceful than it had been at the time. Thus the cause of civil rights was transformed into a major aspect of his legacy, a central part of his story. Soon after Kennedy's death, the civil rights leader A. Philip Randolph said JFK's place in history "will be next to Abraham Lincoln." But however emotional the tributes to Kennedy, the real progress on civil rights came under his successor.[3]

For Johnson, succeeding where Kennedy had failed became both a personal challenge and a political imperative. The Civil Rights Act—designed to end discrimination based on race, color, religion, or national origin—was a personal triumph for Johnson. He was himself a man of the South; Texas had been in the Confederacy. And it would be, in his eyes, a measure of his achievement that he not only overcame the prejudices of his home state but also effected reforms that had been blocked for a century. Johnson wanted to be measured against the greatest hero of the modern Democratic party's pantheon, Franklin D. Roosevelt. It was an ambition he had harbored for years. Decades earlier, when he was in the House of Representatives, Johnson had asked his aide Horace Busby to refer to him in press releases by his initials: "FDR–LBJ, FDR–LBJ—do you get it? What I want is for them to start thinking of me in terms of initials."[4]

But the Civil Rights Act of 1964 was much more than a personal triumph. It began an important new chapter in the history of the United States, and signified the end of an old and ugly one. The movement from which it sprang had also inspired a profound rewriting of the story of the Civil War and Reconstruction. The war's centenary generated a flood of books in the early 1960s, which changed the way Americans thought about the Civil War. The old narrative had treated the war as the dreadful cataclysm it was but had considered the aftermath as of less moment and generally either ignored or condoned the swift curtailment of the rights of the freed slaves through violence, Jim Crow laws, and other mechanisms of segregation and oppression. The "moonlight and magnolias" view of the antebellum South (as in *Gone with the Wind*) and the racist portrayals of black Reconstruction governments (as in *Birth of a Nation*) were being put out to pasture. So when Lyndon Johnson aligned the national Democratic party firmly behind the 1964 Civil Rights Act he changed something fundamental to the party. He broke definitively with the party's racist path, but at a price. After he signed the legislation, he said to an aide that he thought they had just handed the South to the Republican party. They had.

Johnson's victory with the Civil Rights Act and the many other pieces of legislation he passed as part of his Great Society programs transformed and deepened the story of Lyndon Johnson. Once he was merely the politician stock character, the wheeler-dealer, the Texas horse trader. Now he was something more—a leader. Lyndon Johnson's life story—that of a backslapping congressional power broker from Texas—had carried him to the vice presidency. But by itself it might never have taken LBJ all the way to the Oval Office; the death of John Kennedy was required for that. Once in office, though, Johnson changed—perhaps it was the office itself that changed him. In 1964 he used his new power to transform America—and himself. Employing his negotiating skills in pursuit of a remarkably ambitious agenda of reform, LBJ had chosen to fight a difficult fight. He made it his top priority upon taking office after Kennedy's death. And a little more than halfway through that first year in office, Johnson had his historic victory.

KEEPING SCORE

A victory isn't a victory if the press doesn't label it so. In the last fifty years, perhaps the most spectacular short-term triumph in international relations was John Kennedy's performance in the Cuban Missile Crisis. In October 1962, American reconnaissance photos revealed the presence on the island of Soviet medium-range missiles that were capable of carrying nuclear warheads, and a showdown with the Russian leader Nikita Khrushchev quickly followed. After a heated White House debate over the best response, Kennedy ordered a naval blockade of Cuba. Although he resisted the entreaties of his generals to invade Cuba, he still came close to provoking nuclear war. But when Khrushchev agreed to withdraw the missiles, Kennedy achieved a tremendous victory in the eyes of the American public and, indeed, the world. In the global nuclear competition between the United States and the Soviet Union, Khrushchev had blinked first. This victory saved Kennedy's presidency while illustrating the new and deadly serious politics of nuclear war. Kennedy showed that a nuclear threat could succeed, but only by taking the world to the brink of war. When it was over, the Cuban Missile Crisis established two stories: one about Kennedy's steely resolve and one about the exercise of power in the nuclear age.

The missile crisis shows how familiar stories and stock characters shape not only the public's understanding of events but also the actions of those making the decisions. For Kennedy and his advisers, two familiar stories framed their understanding of the crisis: Munich and Pearl Harbor. The attempt of British prime minister Neville Chamberlain to blunt Adolf Hitler's aggression by negotiating an agreement with the German dictator at Munich in 1938 had become the cardinal lesson in the dangers of appeasement. President Kennedy had mastered the subject at an early age: "Appeasement at Munich" was the original title of his undergraduate essay that formed the core of his book *Why England Slept.* The Japanese surprise attack at Pearl Harbor in 1941 was the most reviled act of war in the memory of postwar America, and when it was suggested in 1962 that a surprise attack on the Soviet missiles in Cuba would solve the problem, Bobby Kennedy and other advisers fretted over the possibility that it would be labeled another Pearl Harbor. Concerns about how the world would interpret White House decisions lingered long after the events.

After the missile crisis, President Kennedy himself helped to leak information about the deliberations of his security advisers, and an article appeared alleging that his United Nations ambassador, Adlai Stevenson, had favored large-scale withdrawals of American missiles from overseas bases as a concession to win Soviet withdrawal of the missiles in Cuba. The article, written by two journalists friendly with the president and published in the *Saturday Evening Post,* quoted an anonymous administration official saying "Adlai wanted a Munich." The source of that quote was John F. Kennedy himself. The Kennedy folks had chosen both a story that worked and a likely scapegoat whose actions only made the Kennedys look wiser and more resolute. As far back as 1952, Richard Nixon had attacked Stevenson as "Adlai the Appeaser," and the Kennedys didn't hesitate to pile more dirt on top of Nixon's spadework.[5]

The Cuban Missile Crisis victory revitalized Kennedy's presidency because until that point his record had been one of modest achievement and one spectacular failure, the Bay of Pigs invasion. But this victory in Cuba removed the taint of the Bay of Pigs and branded Kennedy as a winner. To win, of course, someone else has to lose. Khrushchev, Castro, and Stevenson were the fall guys.

Choosing the right antagonist is a vital part of presidential success. For the first President Bush, Saddam Hussein seemed a perfect adversary—a brutal dictator who with his invasion of Kuwait in August 1990 had alienated many Arab leaders who had supported, or at least tolerated, Iraq's long war against its non-Arab Islamic neighbor, Iran. Saddam Hussein was also far less potent militarily than was thought; his vaunted Republican Guard troops proved no match for U.S. and allied forces in the 1991 Gulf War. The stunning victory of the American-led forces in Operation Desert Storm seemed to provide a perfect story line for the first-term president, a powerful contrast to the seeming impotence of the Carter administration during the Iranian hostage crisis a decade earlier.

SEEDS OF DEFEAT

Yet something about such absolute and easy victories tends to produce problems down the road. The one-sided victory in the Gulf War of 1991 provided a stark contrast with the domestic economic miseries the nation was experiencing at the same time its military was making mincemeat of the Iraqi forces. This contrast made it easy for Bill Clinton and other Democrats to make political headway with the charge that President Bush's attention was too much engaged with military and diplomatic matters, and insufficiently concerned with the everyday lives of average Americans. The very ease of the victory abroad highlighted the tenacity of the difficulties faced at home.

The classical explanation for the way victory prepared the way for defeat was the idea of hubris, the blinding pride that came with inordinate success. Whether the image is of Icarus flying too near the sun or Napoleon marching on Moscow, life and literature offer ready examples of the perils of pride. So does presidential history.

In the 1936 election Franklin D. Roosevelt did not merely win, he crushed his opposition, collecting 523 electoral votes to Republican Alf Landon's 8. Roosevelt carried all but two states, and the returning Congress would be top-heavy with Democrats—the party outnumbered Republicans by more than three to one in both the Senate and the House. Flush with victory, Roosevelt decided to finish some unfinished business from his first term. His historic 100 days legislative program of 1933 had been designed to fight the Depression through decisive federal action. But some of the most important pieces of that legislation were overturned by the Supreme Court in a series of decisions handed down later in Roosevelt's first term. So in 1937, Roosevelt proposed more vigorous and radical reforms that were soon dubbed the Second New Deal. Crucial to its success, Roosevelt thought, was a realignment of the Supreme Court. Since the justices are appointed for life, Roosevelt concocted a plan to appoint one additional justice for each sitting justice over the age of seventy.

Roosevelt's "court-packing" plan, as it became known, allowed political opponents and journalistic commentators to emphasize a different aspect of his life story. He was no longer Franklin Roosevelt, champion of organized labor, friend of the farmer, enemy of concentrated capital, but rather Franklin Roosevelt, dangerously strong president and threat to the balance of powers of the American Constitution. The court-packing scheme was a political disaster that defined and undermined his second term. It made Americans wonder whether Franklin Roosevelt was a danger to the Constitution—a danger all the more plausible, Republicans said, because of the magnitude of FDR's electoral victory.

And aspects of Roosevelt's life story that had formerly proved useful now seemed to fit this new narrative. Roosevelt had gotten tremendous mileage from his confident, aristocratic bearing, his eloquence, the authoritativeness of his voice during his "fireside chats." These traits calmed Americans when Roosevelt took office in 1933. Roosevelt's activism in those early days inspired great admiration. In spite of Roosevelt's disability, from those first days of his presidency editorial cartoonists routinely portrayed him striding forcefully forward, borne by two healthy legs. But after four years of concerted federal action, the rise of the alphabet agencies of the New Deal, the landslide election of 1936, and above all the botched court-packing plan, Americans saw a Franklin Roosevelt who had become too forceful, too powerful. During a decade of dictators, with Hitler and Stalin and Mussolini strutting the world stage, apprehension about dictatorship was understandable. Congress rejected the court-packing plan, a humiliating defeat for Roosevelt and a perfect example of how a story line can turn bad.

Yet turns can turn again, and Roosevelt overcame this defeat, going on to win reelection twice more. The political defeat of the court-packing plan has obscured the fact that soon after FDR announced the plan, the courts became much less hostile to New Deal initiatives. They began to allow the more expansive interpretations of the commerce and general-welfare clauses in the Constitution that were vital to the success of his programs, affirming the permanent expansion of federal power that would be the New Deal's most lasting legacy. Roosevelt and his aides adapted following the defeat of the Court plan, and won new victories.

HANDLING DEFEAT

The ability to handle defeat and hardship is central to the character of the successful president. No matter how privileged a person's background, how effortless his early success in his career, how unblemished his electoral record, every president has faced difficulties. That is inevitable. What matters—and what becomes a part of the life story—is how the president overcomes those difficulties. If he overcomes them. Consider Washington's defeat at Fort Necessity, Lincoln's loss to Douglas in the 1858 Illinois U.S. Senate race, or Franklin Roosevelt's polio; each challenge could have served as an explanation of—or excuse for—merely moderate success in life and career. But those who face such defeats and obstacles and move beyond them produce a narrative of a very different kind.

In stories with happy endings, the power of the denouement comes not from the final happiness alone but from the contrast between that happiness and what might have happened—and the more imminent the disaster, the farther into the jaws of defeat the hero is plunged before extricating himself, the more effective the story. The innocent prisoner saved from unjust execution at the last moment is a more compelling character than the one acquitted at trial.

Some defeats are easier to turn into winning stories than others. Franklin Roosevelt's return to public life after being stricken with polio was undeniably heroic. So dramatic and inspirational was the story that it provided the basis for the play (and film) *Sunrise at Campobello,* which related the story of his rehabilitation. His successor in the White House, Harry Truman, also faced his own early defeats, including his failed haberdashery, which made for a memorable but inglorious story.

Perhaps the most remarkable series of recoveries from defeat in American presidential history is contained in the career of Richard Nixon. The 1952 scandal over his secret campaign fund threatened an early end to his career until the Checkers speech saved him. His defeat by John F. Kennedy in 1960 was a severe blow, but his next defeat, by Edmund G. "Pat" Brown in the 1962 California governor's race, seemed to slam the door on his political future. Nixon himself thought so: "You won't have Nixon to kick around anymore, because, gentlemen, this is my last press conference," he told the press after that campaign. Nixon had attained a seemingly indelible status as a political loser. His name was synonymous with defeat, a punch line for easy jokes.[6]

Nixon moved to New York, practiced law at a Manhattan firm, and nursed his wounds. Over the next half-dozen years he worked tirelessly to support local Republican candidates across the nation in their election struggles, and created a reserve of goodwill and IOUs within the Republican party. In the late 1960s, with the Democratic party fracturing in the face of the twin challenges of the Vietnam War and the civil rights movement, Nixon reemerged and completed his political rehabilitation by winning a narrow victory in 1968. So complete was his revival that in 1972 he won an electoral victory nearly as crushing as Roosevelt's defeat of Landon a generation earlier. But Nixon went on to pay the price of his own hubris, and less than two years after his smashing 1972 win he was forced to resign his office owing to the Watergate scandal.

His successor, Gerald Ford, was swiftly branded a dolt. Facing intractable economic problems, Ford tried to fight inflation and unemployment with slogans and cheerleading. Exhorting Americans to "Whip Inflation Now," Ford had WIN buttons produced and hoped to solve the nation's economic troubles by persuading workers to make concessions in labor talks and businesses to hold off on raising prices. This moral suasion proved futile, and Ford's popularity plummeted. A Roper poll taken the month after Ford took office gave the new president a 40 percent positive rating on his handling of the economy, with 20 percent negative and the rest undecided. But two years after Ford's ascent to the White House, a Harris poll found that 79 percent of Americans had a negative opinion of Ford's handling of the economy. Ford had the misfortune to experience several public pratfalls (stumbling down steps, etc.), and the comedian Chevy Chase had ignited his acting career by imitating the accident-prone president. The pratfalls and the WIN button helped construct an identity for Ford as a bumbler, an identity he never shed.

Jimmy Carter faced similar economic problems and experienced some similar embarrassments that won him, too, a reputation for ineptness. Two 1979 incidents cemented his loser's image. That April, Carter told staffers that a rabbit had swum toward his boat while he was fishing, and that the rabbit had bared its teeth and hissed. The press churned out deadpan accounts of the president battling an "attack rabbit," and Carter came off second best in the contest. Then in September, Carter collapsed while trying to complete a ten-kilometer road race in Maryland, and the photo of the collapsing president sent a message of weakness. By the time the American embassy staff in Teheran was taken hostage that November, Carter's role as loser was already indelible.

PRIVATE HEALTH, PUBLIC HEALTH

Ford's clumsiness and Carter's 10K collapse would seem irrelevant to their fitness for office. Neither was the result of any serious medical problem, and each was the sort of incident that happens to every-one. But because the essence of the bond between leader and voter is identification, each blemish on the nation's leader can be (and of-ten is) construed as a blemish on the nation and its citizens. Just as the pope personifies the Roman Catholic Church, political leaders repre-sent their nations. Many successful leaders of the twentieth century were thought to personify the traits of their nation—Churchill's stead-fastness, de Gaulle's arrogance, Gandhi's humility, FDR's optimism. Weaker leaders also create bonds of identification, which makes their frailties, when revealed, troubling. Just as Shakespeare made Lear's madness a symbol of the disorder of his realm, voters interpret the stumble of a president as a concern of state. This explains why Bob Dole's fall off a platform in California during the 1996 presidential race proved the one enduring image of that pallid contest.

Presidents know how harmful the appearance of weakness can be, and they have a long tradition of concealing health problems. After the shooting of James Garfield on July 2, 1881, the press and the pub-lic anxiously followed the condition of the wounded president. Garfield's doctors issued frequent medical bulletins, but they gave al-most no indication of Garfield's fitness to govern. He died that Sep-tember, and the nation mourned. A decade later, when President Cleveland was found to have a cancerous lesion in his mouth, the sur-gery was carried out in secrecy, aboard a ship, and the story did not become public until 1917. The tradition of secrecy continued with Woodrow Wilson's illness at the end of his second term, and then with the elaborate protocols surrounding FDR's disability, and the press's willing complicity in playing down his handicap—avoiding photos that showed him using crutches, for example. Dwight Eisen-hower's 1955 heart attack launched a new openness on the subject of presidential health, but the concealment of Kennedy's Addison's dis-ease, the Eagleton mess in 1972, and the long avoidance of the issue of Reagan's mental acuity during his second term attest to the continuing power of this tradition. Presidents (even fictional ones, like Martin Sheen's President Josiah Bartlet on *The West Wing*) know that any illness can be interpreted as a systemic weakness, and so they conceal their vulnerabilities and aspire to project images of youth and vigor.[7]

SHADOWS AND SUBSTANCE: DEFEAT IN VIETNAM

Symbolic weakness can hurt a president, but actual weakness, as demonstrated by actual defeat, is even more harmful. A military defeat can be even more devastating than a high-profile political loss. The United States has won many wars, but along the way it has lost its share of battles. The War of 1812 was a series of defeats for American forces, although Americans tend to remember only the occasional naval victory or Andrew Jackson's victory at New Orleans in 1815. The rare disaster is recalled—Japan's attack on Pearl Harbor, Britain's 1814 capture of Washington and burning of the White House and the Capitol, Jimmy Carter's botched mission to rescue the American hostages in Iran. But such transitory setbacks do not inevitably tarnish the reputation of the president on whose watch they occurred. The consequences depend in part upon the expectations the public has of the president in question, in part upon the circumstances of the setback. Nobody thought of James Madison as a military leader, so the burning of the White House has not harmed his historical reputation, which rests upon his role as architect of the Constitution. And although efforts have been made to find FDR culpable for Pearl Harbor—it has even been suggested that he knew the attack was coming and allowed it to happen in order to bring the United States into the war—the Pearl Harbor story has remained one of Japanese perfidy rather than one of presidential neglect or malfeasance, and the eventual triumph of the United States in the Second World War has prevented the taint from becoming an indelible stain.

A much more complicated dynamic surrounds the greatest defeat in American military history, the Vietnam War. The American defeat there was drawn out over more than a decade and was the consequence of many complex factors in domestic and international relations. As a result, neither Kennedy, who initiated significant American military involvement, nor Johnson, who escalated it, nor Nixon, who "Vietnamized" it, nor Ford, who presided over the endgame, is seen as the principal architect of that defeat. But association with Vietnam harmed the political careers of each. It tarnished Kennedy's legacy. Lyndon Johnson's handling of Vietnam ended his political career. Richard Nixon tried his best to engineer an American withdrawal that could be presented as a victory, but in the process of attempting to dictate American foreign policy, stifle dissent, and preserve American credibility he overreached and planted the seeds of his own destruction. Gerald Ford was a weak president facing a resurgent Congress that had chafed too long under the imperial presidencies of Lyndon Johnson and Richard Nixon. Congress refused Ford's request for more money for South Vietnam's army, and the North Vietnamese achieved victory in April 1975.

Understanding the defeat in Vietnam in relation to each of these four characters reminds us of the importance of each individual's narrative. At the root of Kennedy's involvement in the Vietnam War was his infatuation with the Special Forces, with commandos and cloak-and-dagger operations, with the idea that the great levers of history could be moved with small forces deployed very deftly. Kennedy thought that elite groups of American advisers could help the South Vietnamese defeat the Viet Cong and the North. That model was on the way out even before Kennedy's assassination as the Communists proved more determined, and the South Vietnamese less so, than Kennedy had thought. Lyndon Johnson's answer to Vietnam, like his answer to America's social ills, was to throw vast amounts of government resources at it. He increased the size of the American military and spent billions transporting that vast military presence to Vietnam and engaging in a kind of pork-barrel nation building that he knew from patronage politics in Texas and in the United States Senate. Build them a school, or a road, and they'll vote for you forever. The notion that the Vietnamese might want to decide for themselves what should be built, and where, seems not to have occurred to LBJ. He stuck to the story he knew, but it didn't work in Vietnam the way it had in Texas.

For Richard Nixon, who always imagined himself a world-historical figure, the Vietnam conflict was merely a shadow on the cave wall. His larger game was the Cold War and the rivalry with the Soviet Union and China. His playing field was the realm of appearances. For Nixon, reality was irrelevant; credibility was all. What mattered to Nixon was for America to extract itself from Vietnam and persuade the world that it had done so triumphantly. The story itself, not the real outcome, was what mattered. The future of Vietnam (or Cambodia) was insignificant. When Watergate laid bare Nixon's vast apparatus of deceit, the twisted thinking behind his policies was exposed for all to see, like the Wizard of Oz after Toto pulls back the curtain.[8]

For Gerald Ford, Vietnam was just another pratfall in the progress of the "accidental president." Vietnam was simply another obstacle for him to trip over, adding a note of tragedy to his farce. Ford had been appointed to office, discredited by his pardon of Nixon, and marginalized by a resurgent Congress. The final defeat in Vietnam was merely another chapter in the book of Ford's own shortcomings.

Richard Nixon was not wrong about the politics of perception. Defeat, although inevitable, is what a president, his handlers, his opponents, and the press make of it. Each defeat can be presented in a number of ways. No one person, no cabal of people, is powerful enough to establish a hegemonic story. In each situation, many different stories will spring forth. A president's supporters might argue that a given action shows his decisiveness, even as his foes portray it as proof of his overbearing nature. One story line might be that the president is weak; another might be that he is seeking a partnership with Congress in order to build consensus. The key for a president is to know how to recover from defeat—which means defining a defeat in a way that renders it as harmless as possible.

Stories of victory and defeat have power because they are simple and memorable. Yet the circumstances out of which they arise are murky and complex. For all of the American presidents involved in the Vietnam War, Vietnam itself was just a bit player in a larger tale, one about empires and ideas, communism and democracy, freedom and tyranny. The notion that for the people of Vietnam the war might fit into a different master narrative, one about self-determination and independence from colonial oppressors, never got much traction, in spite of the parallels to the American experience in the Revolutionary War. Each presiding narrative reduced the swirl of motives and interests to a black-and-white portrait, excluding shadings of gray. A similar urge to simplify lies behind the reduction of historical moments and presidential life stories to a struggle between good and evil.

CHAPTER NINE

GOOD AND EVIL

THERE ARE, OF COURSE, ISSUES AND EVENTS WHERE THE CATEGORY of winners and losers proves insufficient, and some moral judgments can and must be made. Domestic scandals are one such area, and foreign affairs is another. Here, instead of picking winners and losers, the press and the public select good guys and bad guys. Indeed, the entire issue of presidential reputation can be boiled down into a simple chart with an X axis running left to right and a Y axis running top to bottom. Place Loser at the left end of the X axis, and Winner at the right. Place Good at the top of the Y axis, and Evil at the bottom. This sets up four quadrants, with the best presidents assigned to the upper right corner of the chart, and the worst in the lower left. This creates four categories—Good Winners, Evil Winners, Good Losers, and Evil Losers. Much of what passes for journalistic and historical judgment on presidents and their reputations is dedicated to sorting the presidents along these two axes. Of course, such a chart is not static, and any given president's coordinates can move as time passes and historians reexamine his record, or as his life story comes to fit the mood of a new time. Truman, one notable example, has now moved far into the positive zone, despite having very low ratings soon after leaving office.

SCANDAL

The journalistic canon of "objectivity" restrains reporters from delving much into the realm of good and evil when assessing contemporary presidential careers, but this restraint lessens when journalists uncover a good juicy scandal. Just as a parched man will gulp water too quickly and a starved one bolt his food, a reporter set loose on the field of scandal may pursue his or her trade with abandon at first, reveling in the energy of a big story. But the reporter will soon adjust to the new terrain, and here again events from the past and characters from literature provide bearings both for the journalist and for the public imagination. And so each new scandal is viewed in light of preceding ones: the Teapot Dome affair under Harding is compared to the scandals of the Grant administration, Nixon's crimes are likened to Teapot Dome, and post-Watergate misdeeds, big and small, are subjected to the leveling device of the "-gate" suffix.

Scandal makes for good stories. Sex makes for a gripping plot, whether the man possessed by desire is Othello or Bill Clinton. Greed for money, too, evokes literary and historical precursors, as does lust for power.

Reporters are often charged with being overly fond of bad news and profoundly indifferent to good news. Nowhere is this accusation borne out more dramatically than in the press's insatiable hunger for scandal. Scandal comes in many forms—sexual, financial, constitutional—and the literary and historical precedents each type draws on help to broaden and deepen each scandal's meaning. In this way already vivid events are given even greater resonance. Because the presidency is such a highly personal office, and presidents are chosen as much for their perceived "character" as for any ideological identity or public record of accomplishment, a scandal can damage the career of a president far more than a mere defeat. A defeat, after all, can stem from bad luck. Honorable men can be defeated. But a scandal arises out of bad character and bad judgment.

SEX

Sexual scandals are the most entertaining, of course. And a sexual scandal can be fatal to a presidential career. The sexual scandal is one of the longest-standing traditions of American politics, with some of its most lurid examples dating from the time of the Founding Fathers, and involving two of the most important of them, Alexander Hamilton and Thomas Jefferson.

Hamilton was the first to have his transgressions publicly exposed. The treasury secretary had been approached in the summer of 1791 in Philadelphia by a handsome woman named Maria Reynolds, who claimed that her husband had abandoned her and asked Hamilton to help her return to New York. The two went to bed together the day they met. Fairly soon the supposedly vanished husband reappeared and applied for a job at the Treasury Department. Wary of the man's character, Hamilton declined to hire him and soon sought to break off his relationship with Mrs. Reynolds. Mr. Reynolds promptly began blackmailing Hamilton, at the same time placidly encouraging the secretary to renew his attentions to his wife. At the end of 1792, Reynolds and his associate, Jacob Clingman, were arrested and charged with fraud in an unrelated case. They asked Hamilton to use his influence to quash the charges, and when he refused they made sure that word of Hamilton's affair reached his political opponents, including James Monroe, then a senator from Virginia. Clingman also claimed that Hamilton was guilty of speculating in government financial instruments. An investigation ensued; Hamilton managed to persuade Monroe and the others of his innocence on the speculation charge but revealed the reason that Reynolds felt it possible to blackmail him. He gave Monroe and his colleagues detailed evidence of his affair with Mrs. Reynolds until the embarrassed investigators begged him to stop.[1]

There the matter might have ended, had not Monroe had Hamilton's papers copied by an untiring Jeffersonian partisan named James Beckley, and had Hamilton not appeared, in 1796, to have a chance of becoming president. Beckley gave his copies to the notorious journalist James Callender, whose arrival in the United States from England had been prompted by his desire to escape a charge of seditious libel. Callender printed an account of Hamilton's affair and pointedly implied that Clingman's accusations of financial improprieties were as well founded as those of the affair had proved to be. When Hamilton defended himself, Callender responded with another attack, referring to the extensive exchange of letters and documents that ensued back when the charges were originally raised in 1792: "So much correspondence could not refer exclusively to wenching. No man of common sense will believe that it did. Hence, it must have implicated some connection still more dishonourable, in Mr. Hamilton's eyes, than that of incontinency. Reynolds and his wife will affirm that it respected certificate speculations."[2]

It is not clear what role Monroe or Jefferson had in Beckley's actions, but Beckley was a faithful Jeffersonian partisan. Jefferson would soon have reason to regret that he ever heard the name of James Callender. In September 1802, Callender published a story in the *Richmond Recorder* that Jefferson had "kept, as his concubine, one of his own slaves" and had had children by her. The slave was named

Sally, Callender added. Callender was promoting a story that had been quietly circulating for some time in the vicinity of Jefferson's home at Monticello and among political figures in Washington. "There is not an individual in the neighborhood of Charlottesville who does not believe the story," Callender wrote. But Callender's effort to wound Jefferson failed. The charge appears not to have been used against Jefferson in the 1804 presidential campaign, and certainly did not dilute his support—he won 162 electoral votes that year, to his opponent's 14, and even managed to carry the staunchly Federalist state of Massachusetts. The young John Quincy Adams wrote a poem satirizing the affair, a fact that was later used against Adams in his 1828 presidential campaign. By then, Jefferson had become a revered figure, dead and so above politics, and Adams's attack was portrayed as a serious transgression against a great leader of the founding generation.[3]

For their part, the forces supporting Adams in that 1828 campaign were not above exploiting allegations of sexual misbehavior involving his opponent, Andrew Jackson. Like the Thomas Jefferson–Sally Hemings story, one of these allegations involved the violation in the most serious way possible of the racist code then dominant in the United States—through interracial sex. A Cincinnati newspaper claimed, "General Jackson's mother was a Common Prostitute, brought to this country by the British soldiers. She afterwards married a Mulatto Man with whom she had several children, of whom General Jackson is one." Harsh (given the times) as this was, it was not the most stinging of the accusations, at least for Andrew Jackson. He was also accused of being a bigamist, and this accusation carried just enough truth to torment Old Hickory and his beloved wife, Rachel.[4]

The facts were that Jackson had met Rachel while a boarder in a house also inhabited by Rachel and her husband, Lewis Robards. Eventually, Robards asked Jackson to leave, accusing him of having improper relations with his wife. Jackson did leave, and Rachel later followed. When they eventually married, Rachel believed that the divorce she had long sought against her husband had been granted. It had not. Rachel was technically a bigamist until the divorce finally did come through, at which point Jackson and Rachel renewed their vows. But the Jacksons had to endure the bigamy accusation throughout the 1828 campaign. It was extremely painful to Jackson, and his pain deepened when Rachel died soon after the election. Jackson blamed her death on the scandal and never forgave Henry Clay, John Quincy Adams, and others whom he felt could have silenced the allegations had they troubled themselves to do so.[5]

Perhaps the most famous presidential campaign sex scandal was that involving Grover Cleveland in 1884. Cleveland was accused of having had an affair with, and a child by, a woman named Maria Halpin. Cleveland did not deny having sex with her and took responsibility for the child's welfare, although Maria had been promiscuous and the issue of paternity was far from clear (and Cleveland never admitted to it). In July of that year, the *Buffalo Evening Telegraph* ran an article headlined "A TERRIBLE TALE," which recounted the story of Cleveland's dalliance and his supposed illegitimate son. When Cleveland's flustered campaign managers went to him to ask how to handle the story, Cleveland reportedly said, "Tell the truth." And that is what his campaign managers largely proceeded to do. Republicans gleefully recited the famous campaign couplet "Ma, Ma, where's my Pa?" "Going to the White House. Ha! Ha! Ha!" But the laugh was on the Republicans, because Cleveland had defused the charge by admitting to it. The story of Cleveland the truth-teller trumped that of Cleveland the libertine.[6]

Cleveland also escaped harm because of then current attitudes concerning class and gender. The ratification of the Nineteenth Amendment, granting women the right to vote, was still twenty years in the future. Had the woman with whom Cleveland was alleged to have had a child come from a higher station in life, the entire affair would have been taken more seriously. For Cleveland, as for Jefferson, there was a code that discounted a sexual liaison with a woman of lower social standing. Such behavior was judged to be unbecoming but unimportant.

It also helped Cleveland that his opponent in the 1884 race, James G. Blaine, was dogged by accusations of financial improprieties. One political observer noted that Cleveland was generally recognized to have led a blameless public life—he was a reform-minded mayor of Buffalo before becoming governor of New York. Blaine, on the other hand, was thought to have a scrupulous private life but tainted public doings—he was accused of profiting improperly from his ties with railroad companies. So, this political thinker concluded, "We should elect Mr. Cleveland to the public office which he is so admirably qualified to fill and remand Mr. Blaine to the private life which he is so eminently qualified to adorn."[7]

For most of the twentieth century, much greater press reticence with regard to presidential romances was the rule. The movement of major newspapers away from the early-nineteenth-century tradition of being party organs toward much higher standards of truthfulness made investigating the personal lives of presidential candidates—an activity with such a partisan past—seem somehow unsavory. There developed a consensus that a man's public life merited the utmost scrutiny, but that his personal life, unless it impinged upon his public duties, deserved to remain private.

Many twentieth-century leaders benefited from this trend. Elected president in 1920, Warren G. Harding pursued extramarital affairs, including one long liaison with Carrie Phillips, the wife of a friend from Marion, Ohio. When that relationship ended, he had an affair with another Marionite, Nan Britten, with whom he once, in a careless moment, had sex in New York City's Central Park. The extramarital affairs that Franklin Roosevelt, Dwight Eisenhower, and John

Kennedy, among others, are now known to have had were not reported in the contemporary mainstream press. Such scrutiny of their private lives was not part of the political equation with which they had to deal as presidents.[8]

As we have seen, the rules for candidates were rewritten in the Gary Hart/Donna Rice scandal, but the rules changed again, even more dramatically, with the advent of Bill Clinton and the Gennifer Flowers affair. Early in 1992, Flowers, a lounge singer, sold her story of a long-term affair with the Arkansas governor to *The Star*, a supermarket tabloid then owned by Rupert Murdoch's News Corporation. When Clinton managed to recover from this revelation and finish a surprisingly strong second (to Paul Tsongas, a Massachusetts senator) in the New Hampshire primary, he proclaimed himself "the comeback kid." Clinton's aides Mandy Grunwald and Paul Begala crafted the line that transformed an allegation of sexual scandal into a test of character that Clinton the candidate passed with flying colors. It was a masterly stroke, particularly as this was an area in which he would have the opportunity to make a number of comebacks. Later, an Arkansas state employee named Paula Jones charged Clinton with having sexually harassed her in a Little Rock hotel room. Most famously and most damagingly, a young White House intern named Monica Lewinsky told her friend Linda Tripp, in a series of telephone conversations taped by Tripp, that she had had some sort of sexual relationship with Bill Clinton.[9]

Bill Clinton practiced rather less than Grover Cleveland's forthrightness when dealing with such matters. Yet despite the toxicity of charges of sexual scandal and what was, in the case of Monica Lewinsky in particular, a tawdry abuse of his office, Clinton managed to remain in the White House. His ability to survive owes much to the powers of narrative and narrative expectations. Bill Clinton already had a reputation as a ladies' man in Arkansas. On the campaign trail he did not harp on the importance of "traditional family values." And he carried himself with a kind of insouciance that helped shield him from damage when the charges came out.

When, during the *60 Minutes* interview with Steve Kroft early in 1992, Bill Clinton confessed to "causing pain" in his marriage, he expected that viewers would know that he meant that he had been unfaithful, but he refused to come out and say so. If the phrasing was not exactly direct and honest, it was at least some kind of admission of guilt—a signal, but not a full confession. The fact that Clinton was not a proselytizer for family values, that he was not out on the stump opposing birth control and arguing in the schools for sexual abstinence, as were some of his Republican opponents, at least made it difficult to accuse him of hypocrisy. And that lack of hypocrisy helped Clinton escape conviction on the impeachment charges on which he was ultimately tried in the United States Senate. If Clinton was not quite an open playboy, it is also true that few alert voters could have failed to perceive that part of his personality; and if that was the man America elected, the logic of Clinton's acquittal seemed to be, then more of the same was not sufficient cause for turfing him out of office.

His cause was also helped by the major countervailing story of the Clinton years—the flush financial times that were enriching many Americans beyond their fondest expectations. Against the story of Clinton the libertine was arrayed the story of Clinton the competent manager of the American economy, a tireless worker who brought the Democratic party back into the political mainstream, erased the budget deficits of the Reagan-Bush years, and presided over a time of giddy prosperity.

MONEY

Sex scandals may be the most fascinating to editors and reporters and to the general public. But financial scandals are the most common journalistic fare, giving reporters license to sort presidents and their aides into the just and the unjust, the honest and the corrupt, the good and the bad. Financial corruption has been seen, since the beginning of the republic, as a clear measure of a person's unfitness for public office. Alexander Hamilton was being investigated for financial impropriety when, to prove the falseness of those charges, he revealed his affair with Maria Reynolds. Although James Callender tried to revive those charges when he went after Hamilton in 1797, no reasonable evidence of such a scandal has tainted Hamilton's reputation.

Financial scandal could topple even the most revered national figure, or at least permanently darken his reputation. In both of his administrations, Ulysses Grant was plagued by greedy subordinates who clouded the reputation Grant had won as a Civil War hero. Vice President Schuyler Colfax, Secretary of War William Belknap, Grant's brother-in-law Abel Rathbone Corbin, and Grant's private secretary were all implicated in financial scandals between 1869 and 1876. This cavalcade of miscreants helped set a tone for the late nineteenth century in American government, making financial scandal seem not the exception in public life but the rule. Political machines in the immigrant-filled cities bought police, judges, and voters, while large corporations purchased influence in the House and Senate, to say nothing of entire state legislatures. The callous and brazen way in which public officials displayed the fruits of their graft made the Gilded Age the enduring standard for corruption in American public life.

So extreme were the misdeeds, and so eager were the perpetrators to flaunt their profits, that journalists began to delve into their secrets as a matter of course. By the turn of the century a new kind of journalist, the muckraker, was at work (the label was applied, not admiringly, by Teddy Roosevelt). Ida Tarbell, Lincoln Steffens, the gifted caricaturist Thomas Nast, and many others helped create a new set of stock characters, from the buzzardy Boss Tweed of New York City's

Tammany machine to the top-hatted personifications of the emerging great corporate trusts. Tweed was greatly upset by Nast's depictions of him, and is said to have ordered his subordinates: "Stop them damn pictures. I don't care what the papers write about me. My constituents can't read. But, damn it, they can see the pictures." And Tweed understood how powerfully pictures could tell stories.[10]

Financial tomfoolery, wheeling and dealing in office, gifts of dubious intent, all are part of American political life. There was the gift of a vicuna overcoat to Sherman Adams, one of Dwight Eisenhower's closest advisers, who was forced to resign in 1958. There were the boasts of Lyndon Johnson's aide, Billy Sol Estes, who once bragged to a contact that he could have any FBI investigation squelched by simply calling his friend the vice president.[11] There were the improprieties of Jimmy Carter's Office of Management and Budget director, Bert Lance, and a string of allegations about gifts received by the Clinton family during and after their time in the White House.

But financial scandals have been less influential in contemporary politics than their prevalence would indicate. The most carefully examined scandal of recent years, the Arkansas real-estate deal involving Bill and Hillary Clinton that was called Whitewater, proved ultimately to have little substance behind it. So relentless was the investigation, and so expensive were the inquiries, that the entire notion of a special prosecutor was tossed aside, and the Watergate-era provision for such a position was allowed by Congress to lapse (particularly after the Whitewater investigation became sidetracked by the Lewinsky affair). The real problem with most financial scandals today is that they are too complicated to provide a story line that is easy to follow. And it is difficult to get the sort of dramatic evidence that seals a person's guilt in the public mind. Direct evidence of financial corruption, like the videotapes of congressmen taking bribes in the Abscam scandal of 1980, produces immediate and harsh consequences. But the matrix of campaign contributions, favors to contributors, and nepotistic hirings are too murky and complex to win much of a place in the media limelight. Their complexity resists treatment in an 800-word news story in a newspaper, or a 90-second TV report. And so they fade from sight.

POWER

The most important scandals in the United States involve violations of the Constitution. These are, fortunately, rarer than the sex and money scandals. But their seriousness for the nation far outstrips the other kinds of scandals that punctuate American history. These are the scandals that get to the heart of things—they are about power. Sexual scandals raise the specter of debauchery, and financial ones sound a warning of corruption, but the danger that lurks behind constitutional scandals is that of tyranny.

Watergate remains the definitive American constitutional scandal. It single-handedly redefined both the dimensions of scandal and the role of press coverage. Before Watergate few Americans thought a president might systematically subvert the Constitution, or that the press had the ability to bring down a president.

What we today refer to as Watergate includes a variety of misdeeds: campaign dirty tricks, misuse of campaign funds, and efforts to use those funds to buy the silence of criminals. But ultimately, the most significant aspect of Watergate was the Nixon administration's use of the powers of the presidency to pervert the constitutional process. Congressional and other investigators and members of the press had uncovered numerous abuses of presidential power as the Watergate crisis unfolded in 1973 and 1974. But the final and fatal revelation— the so-called smoking gun—was the White House tape of the June 23,

1972, conversation in which Nixon ordered an aide to have the Central Intelligence Agency quash an FBI investigation into the Watergate affair. The tape was released on August 5, 1974, and Nixon announced his resignation three days later.

No president was ever more concerned with managing his and the nation's narrative than Richard Nixon. It was to him a central duty of a president in the atomic age. In the world of nuclear strategy, the "doctrine of credibility" holds that America's nuclear shield is only useful if foreign rivals believe that the president might actually use it. Nixon thought that strategic success depended on persuading your opponents that you were thinking the unthinkable. Nixon even thought it might be in the country's best interests if the Soviets thought he was a little crazy—the "madman" theory of nuclear deterrence. In October 1969, Nixon even put a global nuclear alert into effect in an effort to scare the Russians into pressuring North Vietnam to make concessions in peace negotiations. (It didn't work.)

In spite of the lessons of Watergate, in spite of the obvious problems of a president's ignoring the separation of powers in the Constitution, only a decade later, another president, Ronald Reagan, was deeply involved in another constitutional crisis. Contrary to official policy, the United States was selling missiles to Iran in return for the actual or hoped-for release of American hostages in the Middle East. To make things worse, the proceeds from those arms sales were being funneled (in violation of American law) to Nicaraguan contras, right-wing rebels who were trying to unseat the popularly elected radical Sandinista government in that Central American country. How much President Reagan was involved in the plot may never be fully determined, in part because Reagan did not use a White House taping system. The military chain of command kept its silence and Ronald Reagan kept his job. Reagan's reputation for lack of attention to detail served him well in this instance. All those stories about his naps and his detachment from the duties of his office helped to keep him in that office. Reagan never was able to accept that he actually had traded arms for hostages—he persuaded himself somehow that he had not, perhaps allowing his own admirable feelings of concern about the hostages' plight to excuse his administration's actions.[12]

GOOD AND EVIL ABROAD: AMERICAN FOREIGN POLICY

One of the striking things about the Iran-contra scandal was the complete lack of remorse the principals showed when their actions were exposed. Oliver North, the White House aide most vividly associated with the scheme, became a hero to many Americans because of (not in spite of) his unrepentant testimony before Congress. Others implicated also demonstrated little or no shame, and indeed made it clear that they thought they were serving the country faithfully even as they violated its laws and deceived its legislative leaders. Although the contempt for Congress that the Reagan administration officials showed was unusual, moral certainty of this sort has been a trademark of American foreign policy. The roots of this narrative lie far in the past. Its theme has been the exceptional nature of the United States, an idea implanted as far back as John Winthrop's "City upon a Hill" address of 1630, and played out in such notions as the Monroe Doctrine, Manifest Destiny, the imperialism of the Spanish-American War, Wilson's moral complacency at Versailles, and the Cold War.

One eloquent champion of America's moral mission in the world was Thomas Jefferson. In his case, it was part of a larger campaign against not merely the political and religious repression of the Old World but also the pervasive European condescension toward America. Jefferson, as a naturalist, was particularly offended by the dismissive remarks made by the French scientist the Comte de Buffon about all things American. In his *Notes on the State of Virginia*, Jefferson discussed Buffon's accusations: that animals found in both Europe and America are smaller in the New World; that animals indigenous to the Americas are smaller than comparable beasts in Europe; that European animals domesticated in America are degenerate versions of the originals; and that there are fewer species in America. Jefferson's response to Buffon was both passionate and meticulous. He drew up a table to demonstrate the virtues of the animals of the Americas and made learned observations about the sizes of bears, elk, and other creatures of the forest. He stood up for domesticated animals as well as wild ones. Jefferson insisted that a horse described by a Frenchman as "a middle sized horse" would in America be "deemed a small horse."[13]

Jefferson's nationalism extended beyond the fatuities of French naturalists to include fatuities of his own. As war raged between England and France in the early 1800s, with serious consequences for American ships and sailors caught in the middle, Jefferson dismissed European notions of how to fight a naval war. England and France had built dozens of huge ships of the line, carrying 74 guns or more, and scores more frigates—smaller, more maneuverable warships that might boast 32 or 40 large cannon. Such boats were expensive and required large crews but reflected the supreme naval technology of the day. (They could also threaten havoc to any city located within cannonball range of the sea.) Jefferson, however, favored small, inexpensive gunboats, which had proved useful as defensive vessels in the Revolution but had little applicability to serious naval challenges to the United States. But Jefferson thought the gunboats would be sufficient, because he had a larger strategy of how to deal with European bellicosity.

ISOLATION

Jefferson's idea was economic warfare, and in the Embargo Act of 1807 he declared a nearly total cessation of American shipping. Americans had used economic warfare against Britain in the run-up to the Revolution, embracing various "nonimportation" schemes to deny markets to British goods and thereby bring pressure on Westminster. Jefferson's notion, a more extreme one, was to deny Britain and France American exports. Perhaps he was recalling a line used by Thomas Paine in *Common Sense* three decades earlier: Paine had told Americans that they need not worry about finding a market for their exports, "while eating is the habit of Europe." Thinking to bring Britain and France to their senses, if not their knees, by cutting off American exports, Jefferson imposed the embargo. To back it up, he had his gunboats.[14]

European leaders thought such a naval strategy lunacy. With vast empires to manage, they needed to support transoceanic trade and defend that trade against hostile nations and pirates. A gunboat-based force could only defend shipping that did not venture out of its own ports. In open waters, their small size and lack of speed would doom them. The embargo did have a crippling effect, but unfortunately it was upon American port cities, not European politics. (Indeed, British landholders were pleased by the action, since it drove up food prices there, further enriching them.) Meanwhile, American merchants were devastated.

Federalist pamphlets denounced Jefferson as a despot, and smuggling became the favored pastime of New England. Attacks on Jefferson flowed from the pens of Washington Irving and William Cullen Bryant, who though just thirteen years old won a wide readership for his poem "The Embargo." Bryant later dismissed this juvenile effort as a "foolish thing," but Irving's attack was deft, as he made an earlier

Dutch governor of New Amsterdam his stand-in for Jefferson, and wrote of how this governor told his subjects that "he had been obliged to have recourse to a dreadful engine of warfare, lately invented, awful in its effects, but authorized by dire necessity. In a word, he was resolved to conquer the Yankees—by proclamation!"[15]

For all his love of free speech, Jefferson was none too welcoming of criticism—indeed, he encouraged state prosecutions of Federalist editors for "seditious libel." This part of Jefferson's life is an awkward and dissonant part of his own story, and thus is often skipped over as requiring too much time and trouble to reconcile with his beatified image. But Jefferson was never one to let inconsistency trouble him. Against the might of Europe, however, neither gunboats nor proclamations proved sufficient; the British navy seized American ships and impressed seamen it considered to be deserters, and the result was the War of 1812. Jefferson's reputation as a military thinker, never high, sank lower. But his view of the United States as good, and the Old World as evil, proved attractive, and the notion that the United States could remain detached from Europe would survive for another century.[16]

One of the principal ideas underlying the isolationist impulse was John Winthrop's notion of America's place as a beacon of righteousness for the corrupt Old World. Winthrop hoped that the Massachusetts Bay Colony and the religious life there would prove an inspiration and example to the corrupt religious practices he and the other Puritans saw in England. For Jefferson, and others of the revolutionary era, the nation was to be a shining example of a political, not a religious, idea. The Founders hoped that the example of an egalitarian republic, without an established religion or titles of nobility, would prove a shining beacon of liberty in a despotic world. That hope was one of the reasons Jefferson and his political followers were so delighted with the French Revolution, in spite of its excesses—surely it demonstrated that others were following the American example.

American isolation took many forms, but nearly all of them included a sense of America's moral superiority and righteousness. In 1823, James Monroe promulgated the famous doctrine that bears his name, a statement of the United States' interest in keeping the Western Hemisphere free of further European interference. (The United States had recognized the independence of Latin American countries that had rebelled against Spain, and the matter was causing consternation in Europe.) Monroe's statement proclaimed that the United States would view any European attempt "to extend their system to any portions of this Hemisphere, as dangerous to our peace and safety." In return, it was America's intention to steer clear of interference in European affairs. Republican government would become the norm in the Americas, and Europe could look to its own knitting. Or so hoped Monroe and his secretary of state, John Quincy Adams, who was the principal architect of the new doctrine.[17]

But Adams's notion had been that this approach would be laid out in private diplomatic exchanges with European governments, rather than as a proclamation. It was Monroe who decided to include the notion in his 1823 State of the Union message. Monroe originally wanted to include comments on European affairs, including an ongoing French invasion of Spain and the struggle for Greek independence. Adams persuaded the president to drop that language, arguing, "The ground I wish to take is that of earnest remonstrance against the interference of European powers by force in South America, but to disclaim all interference on our part in Europe; to make an American cause, and adhere inflexibly to that."[18]

Monroe's statement was popular at home and won him plaudits from abroad as well—Lafayette wrote John Quincy Adams to praise "the protecting genius of America, to shield both Columbian Continents, against the covetousness of colonization, the intrigues of counter-revolutionary corruption." With Monroe's statement, one of the master narratives of American history was publicly declared.[19]

The Monroe Doctrine clothed American self-interest in the appealing robes of self-determination and anticolonialism. But harsher sentiments were often more prominent in public discourse. As western expansion pushed white Americans into increasing conflict with native peoples, the denigration and dehumanization of the Indian inhabitants of North America became a public imperative. Each armed response by Native Americans to the invasion of their lands became an excuse to brand them as bloodthirsty savages and seize their territory. Britain, of course, was long the principal villain of American foreign relations, and the image of the grasping, bullying John Bull became a staple of popular imagery. When Mexico stood in the way of American territorial ambitions, the seething animosities of nativism, already deployed against the arriving immigrants from Ireland, were focused upon their fellow Catholics in Mexico and Spain. Anti-Catholic politics mixed with pornography as Americans of the middle nineteenth century made the *Awful Disclosures* of Maria Monk, a prurient supposed tell-all about depravities within a Quebec nunnery, into a best seller. Depicting enemies as evil predictably inflamed passions, while the use of ethnic, racial, and religious stereotypes justified war and genocide.

For most of the nineteenth century, the foreign enemy was more imaginary than real. Foreign policy routinely played a tiny role in the careers of nineteenth-century presidents. American expansionism did involve both diplomatic and military efforts—the Louisiana Purchase, the war with Mexico, treaties with Britain and Spain and Russia concerning such matters as the border with Canada, ownership of Florida, and the territory of Alaska—but the Monroe Doctrine provided a justification for American supremacy in the Western Hemisphere and indifference to European affairs, and that was pretty much how things stayed. The weakness of the American military largely prevented the nation from seeking conquest to the south other than through the Mexican War. Attempts to diverge from this plan seldom got very far; James G. Blaine, Garfield's secretary of state, called in 1881 for a meeting in Washington of all the nations of the Americas, but before it could go forward Garfield was assassinated. Under the new president, Chester A. Arthur, the invitations were rescinded and Blaine resigned his office. Even within the hemisphere, apparently, isolationism was the nation's policy. It was the established story line, and an appealing one. But within two decades of Blaine's ouster the entire equation was overturned and the United States had emerged as an imperial and colonizing power, turning away from principles that the country had been founded upon.

IMPERIALISM

In 1898 the United States enthusiastically embarked upon war with Spain. The short conflict resulted in an easy American victory that left the nation with imperial holdings stretching from Cuba to the Philippines. Isolationism was, at least for a time, dead. How did such a reversal take place? How did William McKinley and Theodore Roosevelt manage to transform the foreign policy of the United States? How did the story of American foreign policy get rewritten so swiftly?

First of all, there was much continuity in the new policy. The sense of moral superiority that Jefferson had expressed in his views about the Old World was still in evidence, but was now combined with other ideas, including some drawn from the work of Charles Darwin. To the already strong notions of the United States as a "city upon a hill" and as the champion of republican government was added the idea of survival of the fittest, which in the cruder nostrums of social Darwinism meant pretty much that might made right, and that light-skinned Americans were meant to rule over darker peoples in Cuba and the Philippines.

Second, a series of intellectual currents converged in the early 1890s to provoke a reassessment of America's traditional isolationism. The determination following the 1890 census that the American frontier, that mythic symbol of American possibility and redemption, had closed (as determined by a census official) inspired the historian Frederick Jackson Turner to present his "frontier thesis" of American history at a meeting in Chicago in 1893. Turner saw much of the democratic flavor and entrepreneurial energy of the United States as having arisen from the challenges and opportunities of the frontier. Here was a new master narrative for the nation that both flattered Americans and seemed to explain much about the nation's history and character. But it also generated a worry: What would happen now that the frontier was closed? Would America's virtues wither, particularly when each year vast numbers of immigrants were arriving from the Old World, many of them Catholics and Jews from southern and eastern Europe? That Turner's paper was delivered as the nation was entering a severe depression only made the questions more pressing. Into this intellectual ferment was drawn an 1890 book, *The Influence of Sea Power upon History,* by navy captain Alfred Thayer Mahan, which declared that a nation could not flourish in the world without a navy to project its power overseas.

Republican intellectuals like Theodore Roosevelt and Henry Cabot Lodge were very much part of this ferment, and when Cubans favoring independence took arms against Spain, they considered it a perfect excuse to move boldly abroad. William Randolph Hearst's *New York Journal* and Joseph Pulitzer's *New York World* competed to see which newspaper could portray Spain's rule over Cuba in the most damaging light. When the American battleship *Maine* exploded in Havana harbor on February 15, 1898, these elements coalesced; war was soon declared. Within months, Cuba, Puerto Rico, and the Philippines were part of the new American empire.

A century's tradition of anti-imperialism could not be abandoned so quickly without some people noticing. In 1900, William Jennings Bryan ran against McKinley on a platform opposing imperialism. The Democrats cited the principles of the American Revolution in opposing the new policies, and in his speech to the Democratic Convention Bryan cited Jefferson's dictum: "If there be one principle more deeply rooted than any other in the mind of every American, it is that we should have nothing to do with conquest." Webster and Clay, Franklin and the Golden Rule were all deployed by Bryan to make the case against imperialism. But racism, the lure of conquest, the fear of national stagnation in the absence of new frontiers, and the hope of potential profit were together far stronger than the legacy of the Revolution, and McKinley prevailed handily.[20]

Isolationism was not entirely routed, of course. There was real opposition to American entry into the First World War, and the backlash against that involvement in the affairs of corrupt old Europe helped doom Wilson's hopes for American leadership of the postwar League of Nations. And the America First movement and other isolationists helped slow Franklin Roosevelt's response to the rise of fascism in Europe and the outbreak of war there. The Japanese attack on Pearl Harbor shredded the isolationist case. And though isolationism retained a following in American politics, it would never again be dominant. Its story was over.

THE COMFORT OF VILLAINS

The power of stories to simplify and vilify is perhaps most easily seen in the way that through the years Americans—public officials, journalists, and ordinary citizens—have so easily drawn upon national stereotypes in manufacturing villains for American righteousness to confront. Britain, France, Spain, Germany, Japan, and China have all been pilloried, and not merely their governments but their citizenry and, indeed, their very identities have been classified as dangerous and vile.

France, the first ally, the necessary help to victory in the American Revolution, was long revered for her historic assistance, and for the shared sacrifices of two world wars. But as her fading imperial hopes brought forth rancor and then assertiveness against the new American hegemon, the land of liberty, equality, and fraternity has been recast as the land of "cheese-eating surrender monkeys." Twinned with France in American mockery in recent years has been Germany, her traditional enemy. In the United States, the image of Germany has remained that of the Hun of the First World War and the Nazis of the Second, in spite of the increasing irrelevance of those stereotypes. But the simple and bad old story is too easily recalled, so that German criticism of American policies can be derided as sour grapes, the whining of the superpower that failed.

Japan and China remain locked within American stereotypes rooted in habitual ignorance and modern prejudice. Whether as pliant (but devious) lackeys or as scheming, cruel adversaries, both nations endure as examples of the Other, strange and therefore fearsome opponents. The old Soviet Union, too, was subject to such easy categorization.

In the present day, heroes are largely confined to fiction. Does any leader today command the sort of respect that Churchill and Roosevelt once enjoyed? Villains, unfortunately, are much easier to mint. In American political discourse, issues are rendered both apparently comprehensible and emotionally engaging by peopling them with villains.

The nation's history is a parade of villains—George III and his ministers gave way to Catholics at home (Irish immigrants) and abroad (Mexico), to the Slave Power (or the evil abolitionists, depending on one's home state and hue), Labor or Capital, the Spanish dons in

Cuba or the Huns in Belgium. Then it was the Communists at home and abroad, and Fascists. For some, today's domestic villains are spineless Liberals; for others the fault can be found with the lies and liars of the American Right.

So powerful is this tendency that President Reagan could brand the Soviet Union an "evil empire," and George W. Bush could identify an "axis of evil" at work today. Simple antimonies like good and evil, winner and loser, get their message across quickly and powerfully. What does it matter that the message is so often inadequate to the complexities of the world?

CHAPTER TEN

EXITS

"*S*IC SEMPER TYRANNIS!*" CRIED JOHN WILKES BOOTH AFTER HE SHOT President Lincoln at Ford's Theater on the night of April 14, 1865—Good Friday. As the president lay bleeding to death, Booth jumped to the stage, delivered his Latin exhortation—thus always to tyrants—and made his getaway. The story of the murder of Julius Caesar had clearly inspired Booth. Not only was he a Shakespearean actor but his father, Junius Brutus Booth, was named for Caesar's assassin. In the play, immediately after Caesar has been stabbed and has called out *"Et tu, Brute?,"* another conspirator cries, "Liberty! Freedom! Tyranny is dead!" In the same spirit, Booth had found his biggest role.[1]

We are taught in *King Lear* that "ripeness is all," and that it is hard to take leave of power even when the time is ripe. Presidents have exited their office in a variety of ways: deaths violent and natural, electoral defeats, refusal to run for reelection, successful completion of two full terms, and one resignation in disgrace. Each of these exits is both a story in itself and an occasion for recasting the president's entire narrative. With power ebbing from their hands, departing presidents often seize the chance to make one last effort, when still armed with the might of office, to tell their story their way.[2]

Of course, those who die in office are deprived of the opportunity, but the facts of their deaths often prove the greatest boost to their reputations. And each presidential death builds on and is compared with those that have come before, so the dead president takes on an added dimension.

A reelection defeat is a kind of death-in-life for a president, but unlike an actual death it does not result in an elevated reputation. For a nation and a press so hooked on keeping track of wins and losses, this is the most painful kind of loss, involving not merely defeat but a public repudiation of the previous four years' work. Such defeats cement a version of the politician's life story that is hard to rewrite.

But defeated presidents try nevertheless, using their waning powers to make yet another attempt to tell the story their way. George Washington wanted his farewell address to deliver a cautionary tale to the nation and to recast the story of the partisanship that plagued his second term. Later presidents appropriated the device—sometimes, like Washington, a departing president would use the opportunity to issue warnings, other times just for the opportunity to offer his own summation of his time in office.

Even for the president who leaves office voluntarily, with a record of accomplishment and public approval behind him, relinquishing the power he has held makes a sad story of a particular kind, one that permeates life after the White House.

And around each of these departures there has developed a whole set of stories and narrative expectations. All presidential exits, whether triumphant, tragic, or pathetic, are framed by precedents both specific to the office and embedded in much broader historical and literary traditions. The dramas and rituals of leave-taking have become part of the script for American public life, to be enacted as appropriate, and understood without effort.

FATAL EXITS

Lincoln's assassination was part of a larger conspiracy against the Union government in the closing days of the Civil War. One conspirator attacked William Henry Seward, Lincoln's secretary of state, that same night in his home and grievously wounded him. A nation that had suffered more than 600,000 deaths, North and South, somehow found new meaning in all of the previous losses through the death of Abraham Lincoln. To Lincoln's stricken followers, his death seemed the greatest single loss of the Civil War. Some turned to the Bible in an effort to comprehend this tragedy. The fact that he had been shot on Good Friday did not go unremarked, and new closing lines were added to the Union anthem "The Battle Hymn of the Republic": "As Christ died to make men holy, he died to make men free while God is marching on." And in Springfield, Illinois, the *Illinois State Register,* a newspaper that had not always been friendly to Lincoln, wrote, "Just in the hour when the crowning triumph of his life awaited him; when the result for which he had labored and prayed for four years with incessant toil, stood almost accomplished; when he could begin clearly to see the promised land of his longings—the restored Union—even as Moses, from the top of Pisgah looked forth upon the Canaan he had, for forty years, been striving to attain, the assassin's hand at once puts a rude period to his life and to his hopes." A nation struggling with loss turned to the Bible, to familiar tales of Christ and Moses, to try to comprehend the dimensions of its loss.[3]

A century later, John F. Kennedy was assassinated. To many, it seemed that the story of Lincoln had repeated itself; a president who had taken up the cause of African Americans was slain. Lincoln's death had been part of a conspiracy, so Kennedy's, too, must be part of a conspiracy. A cottage industry soon emerged of conspiracy theorists who found uncanny links between the two events. It was a field day for numerologists, who exclaimed over the following coincidences: each president's last name had seven letters; John Wilkes Booth and Lee Harvey Oswald (Kennedy's assassin) both went by three names, and each assassin's name had fifteen letters; both presidents were succeeded by men named Johnson, each of whom was born in a year ending in '08. Labored as these exercises were, they reflected a strong link in the public imagination between the two slain presidents. The connection between the two murders was summed up most vividly in the widely published drawing by the great Second World War cartoonist Bill Mauldin, which showed the statue of Lincoln at the Lincoln Memorial, the marble martyr cradling his head in his hands as he wept.

For others, the narrative of the Kennedy assassination lay not in the parallels to Lincoln but in the slain president's youth and promise. This part of the story was given particular emphasis by his widow. A couple of weeks after Jack Kennedy's death, Jackie invited the journalist Theodore White to the Kennedy family compound at Hyannisport, Massachusetts. She mentioned that the president had, as a boy, loved to read about King Arthur, and that he also loved the musical based on those stories called *Camelot,* which had opened on Broadway just weeks after Kennedy's 1960 victory over Richard Nixon. She told White that Kennedy had liked to play the record in his bedroom at night, and was fond of the lines:

Don't let it be forgot
that once there was a spot,
for one brief shining moment
that was known as Camelot.

To the tale of Lincoln was added the legend of King Arthur.[4]

Presidential deaths, of course, have not always been of such tragic proportions; some have been merely pathetic. William Henry Harrison's pneumonia was perhaps triggered by excessive time in the cold during his inaugural events and while pursuing his custom of doing the White House shopping himself. Zachary Taylor's death has been attributed to typhoid-bearing refreshments he consumed at a July Fourth celebration in Washington. Although both were mourned nationally and posthumously celebrated for their achievements as army generals, no recollections of King Arthur were entertained in connection with their deaths.

Not all natural deaths in the White House were so easily borne. Franklin Roosevelt's death, on April 12, 1945, was for millions of Americans a harsh and sudden blow, for which all the evidence of his declining health had left them unprepared. The parallel with Lincoln—the war leader dead with victory in sight—was widely noted. A New Yorker named Victor H. Lawn wrote a lengthy letter to the *New York Times* on April 19 that pointed out numerous parallels between the careers of Lincoln and FDR, from the timing of their deaths in mid-April to their wartime experiences and their values: "There was a close parallel in their unreserved devotion to democracy. Each was free of any taint of bigotry or prejudice." And Eleanor Roosevelt, riding in the train carrying FDR's body back to Washington—it arrived there on the eightieth anniversary of the shooting of Lincoln—recalled a poem called "The Lonesome Train." It told of "A slow train, a quiet train, / Carrying Lincoln home again . . ." Later, the train that took Roosevelt home to New York for burial traveled the same route Lincoln's funeral train had taken on the start of its long journey home to Illinois.[5]

Roosevelt's increasing feebleness in his last months had worried some of his advisers, who fretfully considered the steps they might have to take if the president was no longer fit to govern. It was a situation the nation had faced just a quarter century earlier, when Woodrow Wilson's stroke left him an invalid in the White House and placed his wife, Edith, in a position of unprecedented power. Wilson's vice president, Thomas R. Marshall, learned of Wilson's illness not through any official source but from a Washington reporter. Mrs. Wilson did her best to keep Marshall, and the threat he represented to her husband's (and her) power, as far from the White House as she could. With the posthumous publication in 1934 of the memoirs of Irving "Ike" Hoover, the chief usher at the White House, the story of Wilson's invalid presidency was widely circulated. The notion that the power of the presidency had been wielded by an unelected person— worse, a woman—sent an alarm through the country.[6]

The image of such a regency returned, very quietly, near the end of the second Reagan administration. In March 1987 the president was so depressed by his administration's Iran-contra troubles that, according to his biographer Edmund Morris, he was "failing to read even summaries of important work papers, constantly watching TV and movies." Some Reagan aides gave serious consideration to invoking the Twenty-fifth Amendment, which has provisions for succession in case of presidential incapacity (and was itself inspired in part by the example of the last months of the Wilson presidency). The diagnosis some years later that Reagan was suffering from Alzheimer's disease has only made this incident more troubling.[7]

When a president is incapable of doing his job, the practical consequences can be dire. But the way the president serves as the embodiment of his nation makes his incapacity that much more deeply felt. And the closer the identification between the people and the president, the greater the worry about his illness and the deeper the mourning at his passing.

DEFEATED AND DISCARDED

The first two presidents to be driven from office by the will of the voters were the Adamses, and they set an early and dyspeptic example of how not to hand the reins of office over to a successor. The first

Adams lost a close and rabidly partisan election to Thomas Jefferson, who some Federalists thought would ruin the country by following his pro-French, godless predilections. Defeated, Adams used his remaining days in office trying to protect the Federalist agenda by filling vacant judicial slots, including naming John Marshall as Chief Justice of the United States. On the morning of Jefferson's inauguration, John Adams slipped out of the capital at 4:00 A.M. to begin his journey home to Massachusetts. Adams's biographer David McCullough puts things in the most positive possible light by observing that, in the absence of a tradition for how a defeated president should behave, Adams may simply have felt unwelcome. However, the criticism of Adams that followed at the time makes it clear that the pre-dawn departure was taken as the bitter act of a bitter man. A correspondent for the *Massachusetts Spy* observed, "Sensible, moderate men of both parties would have been pleased had he tarried."[8]

John Quincy Adams was equally discourteous to his successor, Andrew Jackson, following the 1828 campaign, one far more bitter and filled with scurrility than the 1800 race. On March 3, 1829, the day before Jackson's inauguration, Adams began his diary entry, "Close of the Twentieth Congress, and of my public life." That afternoon he moved his family to a friend's house outside Washington. The following day he avoided any connection with Jackson's inauguration, although he did later read over a copy of Jackson's inaugural address, which he thought was "written with some eloquence, and remarkable chiefly for a significant threat of reform."[9]

The worst aspect of the threatened reforms appeared to be prefigured in the celebrations at the White House that accompanied Jackson's inauguration. As Jackson's adherents poured into the capital to pursue appointments to federal office, members of the old guard lamented the sight. Daniel Webster said, "I never saw any thing like it before. . . . They really seem to think the Country is rescued from some dreadful danger." After the inaugural ceremony at the Capitol, crowds followed the new president back to the White House—never mind such formalities as invitations—and turned the planned reception into a "regular saturnalia," according to one of Martin Van Buren's informants. The crowd was eventually dislodged from the president's house by moving the punch out onto the lawn. Certainly John Quincy Adams was glad to miss that scene.[10]

Later presidents vanquished from office learned to leave town with greater grace than the Adamses. But for any man who has achieved the pinnacle of the presidency, to be cast down from that office by the voters is agony. The sight of the strained, defeated president's face as he witnesses his rival's inauguration is one of the classic images of American politics. In recent years we have watched George H. W. Bush endure the ascension of Bill Clinton, and Jimmy Carter sit through Ronald Reagan's installation, that event made more bitter for Carter by the simultaneous, long-delayed release of the American hostages in Iran. But perhaps no president has looked less happy riding to the inauguration of his victorious rival than Herbert Hoover, seated next to a jubilant Franklin Roosevelt in March 1933. A *New Yorker* cartoon by Peter Arno deftly captured FDR's toothy smile and Hoover's tight-lipped endurance. Hoover spent the balance of his long life working on his story, striving to prove how unfairly he had been treated by fate and the voters, trying to wipe that smile from Roosevelt's face.

PARTING WORDS

But it is not just vanquished presidents such as Hoover who strive to define their legacies; successful presidents also want to have their say. George Washington's example is again paramount. There has been no more gracious departure from the presidency than the first. When Washington finally stepped down after two terms, as he had hoped to do after one, he delivered a farewell address that itself became both a tremendously important document of American political history and a key element in the narrative of presidential departures.

Washington gave serious thought to how best to leave office. He considered it presumptuous to say that he was not a candidate for re-election; such a statement, in his view, would reflect a conceited assumption that the public was eager to have him. He did, however, find a rhetorical solution, saying, "It appears to me proper, especially as it may conduce to a more distinct expression of the public voice, that I should now apprise you of the resolution I have formed, to decline being considered among the number of those out of whom a choice is to be made."[11]

Washington's message, which he released to the press in September 1796, stressed his long-standing desire to set aside the cares of office. "I constantly hoped that it would have been much earlier in my power . . . to return to that retirement from which I had been reluctantly drawn. The strength of my inclination to do this, previous to the last election, had even led to the preparation of an address to declare it to you; but mature reflection on the then perplexed and critical posture of our affairs with foreign nations, and the unanimous advice of persons entitled to my confidence, impelled me to abandon the idea." This strenuous modesty, combined with a powerful notion of individual duty, was consistent with Washington's life story as citizen-soldier, ever reluctant to assume political power.[12]

With this personal matter disposed of, Washington went on to discuss the nation's diplomatic affairs and to warn of what he called "entangling alliances." Much of Washington's two administrations had been roiled by the politicking surrounding the French Revolution and ensuing struggles between England and France. Because he was George Washington, and because he spoke out on a crucial aspect of American foreign policy, his speech became not only a model for the farewell address but also for a jeremiad about America's involvement in world affairs. (That is not what Washington intended, as Stanley Elkins and Eric McKitrick pointed out in their book *The Age of Federalism,* but it was the simplest version of the story, and so one that could be used by isolationists for their purposes.) During the interwar period of the 1920s and '30s, Washington's farewell address was frequently cited as a nearly scriptural authority on the wisdom of disengagement from the rest of the world, and from Europe in particular.[13]

Of the many presidential good-byes, only two farewell addresses made real contributions to American public life. One is Washington's; the other is Eisenhower's. Eisenhower spent eight years in the White House. Before that he had been a career military officer, and as president he had presided over a vast military establishment. And yet, at the end of his term, he used his departure as an opportunity to warn against what he called "the military-industrial complex." Concerned that the logic of the Cold War would inevitably increase the power of the military and of the corporations that supplied equipment to the military, Ike cautioned, "In the councils of government, we must guard against the acquisition of unwarranted influence, whether sought or unsought, by the military-industrial complex. The potential for the disastrous rise of misplaced power exists and will persist." Eisenhower surprised many with the passion with which he warned against these dangers. Like Washington, he gave a farewell address that has taken on a life of its own in American politics. Eisenhower's stature as a military hero made his warning all the more credible and powerful. It has been cited ever since by those opposed to the power of the Pentagon and defense contractors.[14]

The parting words of other two-term presidents do not linger in memory; no others made statements as important as Washington's or Ike's. For most of the nation's history, in January of a year when a new president is assuming office the departing president did not report to Congress on the State of the Union. That norm has been violated five times, by Truman, Eisenhower, Lyndon Johnson, Ford, and Carter.

With the exception of Ike, each left office disappointed, and each chose to deliver a farewell State of the Union message.[15]

Lyndon Johnson had withdrawn from the presidential race at the end of March 1968, telling the nation that he wanted to put politics aside and concentrate on solving the problems in Vietnam. When his efforts to negotiate an end to the war had not borne fruit by the following January, he felt the need to get in a last word. Concerned about his historical legacy, Johnson used the address to make a persuasive case for his achievements in health care, education, and other aspects of his Great Society program. The rather long speech contained only a few lines about Vietnam. Even as he left office, Johnson was busily trying to control his story, seeking to celebrate the victories of his administration rather than dwell on his defeats. He knew that others would be happy to do that for him.[16]

Gerald Ford, departing after only two years in office, made a bittersweet reference early in his last State of the Union address to the way "our vigilant press goes right on probing and publishing our faults and our follies, confirming the wisdom of the framers of the First Amendment." One wonders how enthusiastic about press freedom Gerald Ford truly felt at the time, but it was a gracious and wise thing to say. The speech, however, went downhill very quickly, so that soon Ford was enumerating such achievements as having "avoided protectionism during recession." Finally, Ford invoked George Washington, borrowing the narrative of a more successful man to gild his own life story. "Like President Washington," Ford said, "like the more fortunate of his successors, I look forward to the status of private citizen with gladness and gratitude."[17]

One of the oddest of these final State of the Union addresses was Jimmy Carter's. Early in the speech Carter said, "I firmly believe that, as a result of the progress made in so many domestic and international areas over the past four years, our nation is stronger, wealthier, more compassionate and freer than it was four years ago." Carter was responding to the devastatingly effective question Ronald Reagan had posed in the debate the previous fall, "Are you better off than you were four years ago?" The voters had answered that question in the negative. But Jimmy Carter, leaving office, felt compelled to give a positive answer. Carter's speech was very long and filled with detailed recommendations on such matters as federal regulations and tax legislation. There was something delusional about the care with which Carter advised deferring a planned cut in income taxes for a couple of years because of budget problems. Days before Ronald Reagan, who had proclaimed his passionate interest in lowering taxes, was scheduled to take office, Jimmy Carter was still pretending to be able to set the agenda.[18]

The most pathetic farewell was the talk Richard Nixon gave to his staff just before he left the White House the morning after he announced his resignation. Nixon spoke of the servants in the White House and how kindly they had treated him. He then went on, in a way reminiscent of the Checkers speech, to talk about his mother. Eyes moist, he spoke of what a wonderful woman she was. Nixon told how she had nursed some of her children as they were dying of tuberculosis, and how she encouraged her surviving children to do well in life. He reflected that probably no one would ever write a book about his mother; he averred at one point that she was a saint. Surely Richard Nixon felt all these things deeply. But it almost seemed as though he was trying to make those who had driven him from office feel that they had somehow hurt his mother. But for Nixon, pathos had become a cliché, and what was once effective drama had turned into self-parody. And so, beaten and dogged by scandal, Nixon left the presidency for private life in as painful and embarrassing a way as possible.[19]

The image of this devious and powerful man at the moment of his disgrace, revealing himself in such an emotional and vulnerable way, left a lasting impression. Nixon's departure is the only example of a president forced from office in midterm and in disgrace. And it is sure

to be the standard of comparison the next time a president must resign. Nixon's resignation is the foundation story of disgraced presidents, just as Abraham Lincoln's assassination became the model on
which all subsequent presidential assassinations would be understood.

Some farewells are premature. Theodore Roosevelt could easily have
won reelection in 1908, but on the night of his election in 1904 he
had pledged that he would not run again. Since he had served all but
six months of the second term that William McKinley had been elected
to in 1900, he felt it was in keeping with Washington's tradition to step
down in 1909. But soon he was regretting his pledge, and in 1912 he
threw his hat in the ring and returned as candidate of the Progressive,
or Bull Moose, party. Defeated then, he continued to play an active
public role as a writer and adventurer, and during the First World War
tried mightily to obtain government permission to raise a volunteer
regiment that he could command in Europe.

Roosevelt set a new model for the postpresidential career. Rather
than retiring to his farm and plow, he turned to the pen and the cruise
ship. He wrote various accounts of his travels and big-game hunts
(with titles like *African Game Trails* and *Through the Brazilian Wilder-
ness*) and an autobiography and shared his thoughts on current affairs
(*America and the World War* and *The Foes of Our Own Household*). He
did this partly for financial reasons, but perhaps even more out of a
deep-seated hunger to be heard and taken note of in the world of public debate. Roosevelt wanted to keep his narrative before the nation
and the world, hoping to retain his hold on the public imagination
even though he could no longer inhabit the Oval Office.

AFTERLIVES

Teddy Roosevelt was ill suited to the role of ex-president. He was just
fifty years old when he left the White House, filled with energy and

continuing ambition. But if leaving office was hard on TR, it hasn't been easy for anyone. The moment a president leaves office, his life changes in ways that are difficult for outsiders to understand. On his last day in office, Dwight Eisenhower met with incoming president John Kennedy. Eisenhower thought he ought to demonstrate to Kennedy exactly what the powers of the presidency meant. Seated at his desk, he pushed a button on the phone and said to an assistant, "Send a chopper." Several minutes later, a helicopter settled on the White House lawn. "Mr. Kennedy seemed pleased," Eisenhower notes in his memoirs. One senses, too, that Ike would miss such perquisites.[20]

If departing presidents must surrender the perks of office, they also get to relinquish heavy cares. Harry Truman, the first president of the nuclear age, was acutely aware of this weight being lifted from his shoulders, since he had approved the nuclear destruction of Hiroshima and Nagasaki. In his memoirs, he stated that as president "the one purpose that dominated me in everything I thought and did was to prevent a third world war."[21]

Other ex-presidents have expressed the same concern. Early in his administration, President Nixon held a state dinner in California to honor the president of Mexico. Former president Johnson attended the dinner, as did the then governor of California, Ronald Reagan, and his wife. Nancy Reagan turned to Johnson and asked how it had felt to leave the presidency. Johnson told her, "When Richard Nixon took the oath, I had the greatest burden lifted from me that I ever carried in my life. There was never a day that went by that I wasn't scared that I might be the man who started World War III."[22]

It seems hard to fathom that in an instant, at noon on January 20 following a presidential election, a man suddenly relinquishes that power. Each of these rituals becomes part of the mythology surrounding the presidency, each farewell remark of a president builds on those before, each last walk to the helicopter on the White House lawn becomes a reenactment of earlier dramas. As the now ex-president flies off to his retirement, the plane in which he is riding is no longer Air Force One (that designation is reserved for whatever aircraft is carrying the president).

The ability of a president to leave town quietly, as the Adamses did two centuries ago, has vanished. Now when a president leaves his office for the last time, it becomes, not an event in itself, but a staged happening, a pseudoevent, in Daniel Boorstin's phrase. In *Dutch,* his imaginative biography of Ronald Reagan, Edmund Morris recounted making a point of waiting outside the Oval Office to see Ronald Reagan leave it at the end of his last full day as president. The next day, Morris ran into Colin Powell. That morning, Powell told him, he and other advisers, having forgotten to have Reagan's actual last moments in office photographed, had taken Reagan back to his office to reenact leaving it. Back Reagan went, one more time, for no other purpose than to pose for the camera and play the role of the president leaving office. The man who has the power to start World War III does not have the power to escape the photo opportunity.[23]

For Ronald Reagan, the old western hero, the closing images were as if he had orchestrated them. As he went up the steps of the plane taking him to California, the sun came out from behind a cloud to gild his departure from the scene. Riding off into the west, he managed one last time to turn his presidency into a production. It may have been a cliché, but it had real power. More than any other president, Reagan understood the world in terms of stories. So it is fitting that his exit from center stage had a perfect Hollywood ending.[24]

CHAPTER ELEVEN

MEMOIRS AND SECOND ACTS

THE QUESTION FOR AN EX-PRESIDENT IS ALWAYS, WHAT NOW? MORE
and more, the answer is the presidential memoir. These volumes
have become a staple of the postpresidential career. Most recently, Bill
Clinton's departure from the White House resulted in a frantic competition for his memoirs, which were eventually bought for an advance reported to exceed ten million dollars.

Even without such enormous book deals, presidents have been
recording their post–White House thoughts for two centuries. Some
(Washington and John Adams, for example) did it primarily in the
form of letters; others (such as John Quincy Adams and James K. Polk)
kept diaries. Jefferson took a stab at an autobiography, and Theodore
Roosevelt published his life story in 1913. Other presidents have shared
their thoughts on national affairs in books written after they left office—Grover Cleveland, Herbert Hoover, and even the taciturn Calvin
Coolidge practiced this form of presidential literature. Although these
books are essentially retrospective, there is a forward-looking element as
well, extending the presidential life story into the future in the new role
of nonpartisan sage, the person above party squabbles.

The presidential memoir as publishing phenomenon is a fairly recent development, launched in a modest way by Harry Truman's memoirs, followed by similar books from Dwight Eisenhower, Lyndon Johnson, Richard Nixon, Gerald Ford, Jimmy Carter, and so forth through the present. A memoir can have many elements and can take different forms. It can be a simple testimony—"This is what happened"; it can be a complaint—"This is what ought to have happened"; or a lesson—"This is how you ought to live your life if you want to be as successful as I have been." It can be a way of settling scores. But the memoir's fundamental and most valuable purpose has been that of bearing witness.

Harry Truman put it well: "I should like to record," he wrote at the start of his memoirs, "before it is too late, as much of the story of my occupancy of the White House as I am able to tell. The events, as I saw them and as I put them down here, I hope may prove helpful in informing some people and in setting others straight on the facts." And because presidents have a level of access to their own stories beyond what anyone else can possibly have, the form gives the ex-president an opportunity to define the story of his own administration with seemingly unrivaled authority. When the ex-president's version of events maps nicely onto the existing master narrative, this is easy; when it contradicts the master narrative, the ex-president must employ all his persuasive powers to rewrite the past to his liking.[1]

Presidential memoirs rarely reach a high level of literary or human interest; a lifetime of guardedness about oneself and one's policies can hardly be expected to evaporate once a book contract is signed, even when one's political life is in the past. Old habits die hard, and presidential memoirs are laden with propaganda, as ex-presidents try to bend history to conform to a flattering life story. Nonetheless, the presidential memoir can be revealing and useful. It is an important part of a president's effort to define not just the political landscape but the historical one. It offers an opportunity for every politician to set the record straight, to say, "Although this is what the press said was going on, it wasn't what was in my mind at all"; or "This is what my enemies accused me of, but nothing could have been further from the truth." In general, the presidential memoir allows the politician to bathe himself in the brightest and warmest possible light.

SETTING THINGS STRAIGHT

Dwight Eisenhower had already been a memoirist before he entered the White House. He had recounted his role as commander of the Allied forces during the D-Day invasion and in the subsequent destruction of the Axis war machine in Europe. His account of that part of his life, entitled *Crusade in Europe,* had been published to considerable success in 1948. After Eisenhower left the Oval Office, he eventually produced two volumes of memoirs, one for each term (*Mandate for Change, 1953–1956* and *Waging Peace, 1956–1961*). Eisenhower had a deep reverence for American history and was certainly conscious of parallels between his own career and that of George Washington. His affection for Washington began early; indeed, as a young student he "conceived almost a violent hatred" (as he later put it) of a group of Revolutionary War officers who once schemed to remove Washington as commander. Ike's postpresidential retirement to Gettysburg, Pennsylvania, the site of Abraham Lincoln's great speech, also expressed the depth of his historical sense. Eisenhower was conscious of history and eager to cement his place in it by connecting himself to iconic figures in American history.[2]

In *Mandate for Change,* he stressed that he had been far from eager to become a candidate for the presidency. Throughout the first chapter, which he calls "Prelude to Politics," he emphasized his reluctance to run for office. He wrote that after the 1945 armistice, riding with Eisenhower and General Omar Bradley in Berlin, President Truman "abruptly said that he would help me get anything I might want, including the Presidency, in 1948." Eisenhower declined the offer. "My prompt reply was that while I thanked him for his flattering thought I had no ambition whatsoever along political lines and would not consider the possibility of seeking a political position." Again, in 1948, he was sought, and again he turned down the offer. Eisenhower wrote proudly of his achievements at Columbia University, where he was president after the war. That civilian interlude ended when President Truman called him back to serve as commander in chief of the new North Atlantic Treaty Organization (NATO). As NATO commander, Eisenhower felt it was inappropriate for him to consider a career in politics. At one point, he drafted a strong statement declaring his lack of interest in any political career, but upon reflection he set it aside. "The statement I had drafted was so unequivocal," he later remarked, "that if I'd carried out my intention of publicizing it, my political life would have ended without ever starting. The paper was destroyed." Beneath all that stoical reluctance, though, ambition had become an itch. But how to scratch it?[3]

In the first volume of his memoirs, Eisenhower professed his concern about a rising spirit of isolationism within the Republican party as the 1952 election approached. Yet he was still reluctant to go after the nomination. He knew that his hard-earned reputation from the Second World War would inevitably be clouded by a political career. But then he received a crucial visit from Jacqueline Cochran, a famous aviator who flew from the United States to NATO headquarters in France in February 1952. Miss Cochran had brought with her a film, made earlier that month, of a midnight rally of Eisenhower supporters at Madison Square Garden. "The entire proceedings were put on film," Eisenhower recalled. Then she persuaded Ike to watch it. "It was a moving experience to witness the obvious unanimity of such a huge crowd—to realize that everyone present was enthusiastically supporting me for the highest office in the land. As the film went on,

Mamie and I were profoundly affected. The incident impressed me more than had all the arguments presented by the individuals who had been plaguing me with political questions for many months. When our guests departed, I think we both suspected, although we did not say so, that our lives were to be once more uprooted." Like Washington, Eisenhower found that to entertain ambition he had first to name it duty. In a letter to President Truman on New Year's Day 1952, Ike said that despite his desire for a quiet retirement, "I've found that fervent desire may sometimes have to give way to a conviction of duty."[4]

In his 1971 memoir, *The Vantage Point*, Lyndon Johnson was similarly eager to address the question of presidential candidacy—in his case, the decision against running for reelection. Shortly after Wisconsin senator Eugene McCarthy's surprisingly strong second-place finish behind Johnson in the 1968 New Hampshire primary, Johnson had announced that he would not be a candidate that year. The press treated his withdrawal as a retreat from the field, a tail-between-the-legs escape from impending defeat at the polls. Probably no part of *The Vantage Point* is more deeply felt and more strenuously argued than Johnson's efforts to prove that long before Eugene McCarthy stepped onto the scene, he himself was planning to step out of it.

"When I took the oath of office in January 1965 to begin my first full term in office," Johnson insisted, "I felt that it would be my last, and this feeling grew stronger with every passing week in the White House." It was important to push his programs through Congress quickly, and he had a history of health problems, including a heart attack back in 1955. Johnson then invoked the legacy of earlier presidents. "I did not fear death so much as I feared disability. Whenever I walked through the Red Room and saw the portrait of Woodrow Wilson hanging there, I thought of him stretched out upstairs in the White House, powerless to move, with the machinery of the American government in disarray around him." Johnson strived to portray himself as having made his decision to retire for reasons that had nothing to do with either Eugene McCarthy or the dramatic Tet Offensive that was launched by the Viet Cong and the North Vietnamese on January 30, 1968.[5]

Many historians have since seen the Tet Offensive as the point at which domestic support for the war, from citizens and particularly the press, began to decline dramatically. After Tet, and after McCarthy's strong showing in New Hampshire, Johnson scheduled an address to the nation concerning a new peace initiative. "I wanted to put the enemy's Tet Offensive in proper perspective," Johnson later wrote, "and now that the offensive had been blunted and there was a chance that the enemy might respond favorably, I wanted to announce our new initiative for peace. If we were going to take the risk of a bombing pause, I felt I should make it clear that my decision had been made without political considerations." Then Johnson, laboring to impress the reader with how disinterested he was about his own career, wrote of telling Texas governor John Connally early in 1967 that he had decided not to run for reelection. Johnson recalled a meeting he had with his secretaries of state and defense, Dean Rusk and Robert McNamara, in July 1967, during which he repeated to them what he'd told Connally. While Eisenhower presented himself as entirely responsive to the will of the people, Johnson tried to present himself as independent of the will of the people or of anyone else, a man who made his own decisions.[6]

In *An American Life,* perhaps the most unrevealing of presidential autobiographies, Ronald Reagan presents his decision to run as, like Ike's, the product of a kind of Washingtonian reluctance. "A candidate doesn't make the decision whether to run for President," Reagan writes. "The people make it for him." But he also provides himself with a plausible reason to run, a personal motivation to go along with the nation's call to duty. In an account devoid of any admission of ambition, Reagan gives his take on Washington in the late 1970s. "With each passing month of the Carter administration, I became more concerned about the things that were happening—and not happening—in Washington. Jimmy Carter had run for the Presidency on a platform calling for cuts in defense spending and implementation of what the Democrats called 'national economic planning.' That meant one thing to me: The Democrats wanted to borrow some of the principles of the Soviets' failed five-year plans, with Washington setting national production goals, deciding where people worked, what they would do, where they would live, what they would produce." Reagan's overinterpretation of a plank in the Democratic platform is meant to show himself as roused to action to defend the republic against the forces of socialism. In other words, he felt a call to duty, the patriot's burden.[7]

Each of these memoirs provides idealistic self-justification for a course of action. But the desire to set the record straight—which is to say, to make oneself look good—can sometimes lead to surprising insights, some of which are found in the unfinished autobiography of a thrice unsuccessful presidential candidate, William Jennings Bryan. In the section of his memoirs Bryan managed to complete before his death, he speaks of his political passions and career. He had managed in the course of his career to manufacture for himself a political persona that involved equal parts orator, idealist, and dreamer. Yet he takes pains in his autobiography to work against existing notions of him, and to portray himself as a canny, detail-oriented politician whose passion for politics was formed in his early youth. He paints himself as a man with a longtime interest in Democratic politics, telling of going to the 1876 Democratic National Convention in St. Louis, when he was sixteen. He goes on to recount that he'd been to all of the Democratic conventions since the '76 convention, except the Cincinnati convention of 1880, and also excepting the 1900 and 1908 conventions, at which he was nominated for president. (His absence sprang from the tradition of the reluctant candidate.) In developing the story of his acumen at backroom politics, Bryan discusses befriending a doorman at the 1892 Democratic Convention in Chicago and using this connection to dispense a kind of patronage (admission to the convention floor) to other interested Democrats, thus putting "a liberal number of western Democrats under obligation to me."[8]

In 1896 the Democrats again convened in Chicago. Ahead of that gathering, Bryan spent many months traveling around the country organizing the silver forces. "It was through these speeches that I became acquainted with a number of delegates who were present at Chicago," he wrote. He also revealed that he'd used the cross of gold and crown of thorns images in a few speeches before the Chicago convention. He went into great detail about his machinations on the day of the convention speech—how he carefully arranged to get more time for his speech, how he won the advantage of being the last speaker. He recalled that his "voice reached to the uttermost parts of the hall," and that "the audience acted like a trained choir." Once again a man who had set his sights on the White House was setting the record straight, but this time not to show himself to be a disinterested or idealistic person but to portray himself as a hardheaded, crafty political operator. Presidential losers, too, have their vanities.[9]

Most early efforts at presidential autobiography make tedious reading today. Martin Van Buren's autobiography begins, "At the age of seventy one, and in a foreign land, I commence a sketch of the principal events of my life." Van Buren may be obscure today, but he was one of the great innovators of American politics, who made his way to the White House by mastering, and to a significant degree inventing, the art of popular democratic politics. But his memoir, unfortunately, includes very little about his presidential career. There is a vast amount about political maneuvering, first in New York State, where he began his career, and more of the same later in Washington during the administrations of John Quincy Adams and Andrew Jackson. Van Buren's memoirs are highly specific in addressing slights and settling scores concerning issues long forgotten even in his day. But they are often unmoored to specific dates and written in a mid-nineteenth-century style of such strenuous circumlocution as to leave even the dedicated reader absolutely baffled as to what Van Buren is talking about, and why he or she should care.[10]

AFTER THE WHITE HOUSE

Few ex-presidents have had major accomplishments after they left the White House. Eight presidents have been deprived of the opportunity for a postpresidential career through assassination or natural death in office. Others left office so broken in health or spirit as to be unable to pursue much of a career. James K. Polk died three months after leaving office. Woodrow Wilson was an invalid from his stroke in 1919 until his death in 1924. Other retired presidents have understandably felt that they have done enough and want only relief from the pressures of leadership. Gerald Ford, for example, has spent much of his retirement playing golf and serving on corporate boards, apparently seeking the financial security that a life in public service never provided him.

But some have managed notable postpresidential careers. Van Buren himself was nominated a third time for the presidency in 1848, this time as the candidate of the Free Soil party. He also wrote a quite serious manuscript on the subject of party politics, *Inquiry into the Origin and Course of Political Parties in the United States,* which was published in 1867, five years after his death.

Failed presidencies often lead to active writing careers after leaving office. The authors may feel the need to justify—or rehabilitate—themselves. Or perhaps they feel that the more they tell their story, the better chance they will have of changing history's verdict. Certainly, two presidents who suffered painful departures from office in the past half century became prolific authors. Both Richard Nixon and Jimmy Carter published profusely. Nixon, true to his character and to his interest in world history, wrote extensively about world politics and the Cold War. Carter has ventured out more broadly, including not only presidential memoirs and meditations upon the Middle East but also a book of poetry, inspirational volumes, a novel of the Revolutionary War, and a children's book illustrated by his daughter, Amy, entitled *The Little Baby Snoogle Fleejer.*

Thomas Jefferson made a start at an autobiography, but his enthusiasm for the project trailed off long before his account reached the White House years. It was published after his death but while many who knew him and had worked with or against him still lived. The book was the subject of a January 12, 1831, diary entry of John Quincy Adams, which is worth quoting at length because of who wrote it, because of who it's about, and because of the light it casts on presidential autobiographies in general:

I finished the memoir of Jefferson's Life, which terminates on the 21st of March, 1790, when he arrived at New York to take upon him the office of Secretary of State. There it ends; and there, as a work of much interest to the present and future ages, it should have begun. It is much to be regretted that he did not tell his own story from that time until his retirement from the office of President of the United States in 1809. It was then that all the good and all the evil parts of his character were brought into action. His ardent passion for liberty and the rights of man; his patriotism; the depth and compass of his understanding; the extent and variety of his knowledge, and the enviable faculty of applying it to his own purposes; the perpetual watchfulness of public opinion, and the pliability of principle and temper with which he accommodated it to his own designs and opinions;—all these were in ceaseless operation during those twenty years; and with them were combined a rare mixture of infidel philosophy and epicurean morals, of burning ambition and stoical self-control, of deep duplicity and of generous sensibility, between which two qualities, and a treacherous and inventive memory, his conduct towards his rivals and opponents appears one tissue of inconsistency. His treatment of Washington, of Knox, of my father, of Bayard, who made him President of the United States, and, lastly, of me, is marked with features of perfidy worthy of Tiberius Caesar or Louis the Eleventh of France. This double-dealing character was often imputed to him during his life, and was sometimes exposed. His letter to Mazzei, and the agonizing efforts which he afterwards made to explain it away; his most insidious attack upon my father with his never-ceasing professions of respect and affection for his person and his character; and his letter to Giles concerning me, in which there is scarcely a single word of truth—indicate a memory so pandering to the will that in deceiving others he seems to have begun by deceiving himself.[11]

Adams's concluding remark sounds a warning about presidential memory that applies to the other memoirs under consideration here. Both Harry Truman and Lyndon Johnson were worried about the danger of trusting to their memories in writing their accounts of their presidencies. In the preface to the first volume of his presidential memoirs, *Year of Decisions,* Truman admitted that he was so busy in the course of his presidency that he could not "possibly remember every detail of all that happened." He wrote, "For the last two and a half years I have checked my memory against my personal papers, memoranda, and letters and with some of the persons who were present when certain decisions were made, seeking to recapture and record accurately the significant events of my administration." Similarly, Lyndon Johnson wrote that "memory is an unreliable source for any writer," and assured his readers, "I have tried to document every statement made in this book. Only in a few cases have I had to rely entirely on memory. In most instances, I have cut what I could not document." Whether their attention to the documentary record freed Truman and Johnson from the charge that Adams laid against Jefferson is for their readers to judge.[12]

If for some ex-presidents the biggest concern is how reliable their memories are, and others give themselves over to the pursuit of golf, a few former presidents have pursued significant careers after the White House. Jefferson worked to found the University of Virginia. Taft served as Chief Justice of the United States. Jimmy Carter's long post-presidential dedication to promoting diplomatic solutions to world problems, drawing attention to such issues as the housing crisis for poor Americans, and working for peace in various troubled spots of the world has earned him much greater respect than he had on leaving the White House. Carter even received the 2002 Nobel Peace Prize—an honor that was partly based on his post–White House career.

But it was John Quincy Adams who provided perhaps the most impressive example of a postpresidential career. After the presidency Adams, at the urging of his Massachusetts neighbors, embarked upon a congressional career. In the House he championed northern opposition to slavery. He single-handedly managed the effort to end "the gag rule," which automatically tabled any petition to the Congress that came in support of abolitionism or the rights of the slaves more generally. Adams's tireless, selfless, and rigorous attention to this cause is one of the brightest spots in American congressional history and by far the most glorious episode of his career. Adams also argued before the Supreme Court in favor of the slaves in the famous *Amistad* case and managed even to attain one of his presidential goals, the establishment of a national observatory, through his role as a congressman. When the wealthy Englishman James Smithson left a large bequest to the United States to found an institution for the promotion of knowledge, Adams shepherded the gift through Congress, defending it against efforts to seize the money for other, more transient purposes. Adams made sure that money was used to create the Smithsonian Institution and the National Observatory.

This most irascible, aggressive, and undiplomatic of men managed not so much to redeem his presidential career as to transcend it. At the end of his days he was known in the halls of Congress as Old Man Eloquent. John Quincy Adams is the only president to have died in the Capitol; stricken there while performing his duties as a congressman on February 23, 1848, he was taken to the Speaker's chamber, where he breathed his final breath.

CHAPTER TWELVE

THE JUDGMENT OF HISTORY

EATH IS NOT THE END OF THE STORY. IT IS, OF COURSE, THE END OF the president's ability to influence the story himself. But the various stories have their own lives, much more enduring than the life of the man who gave birth to them.

All these presidents and challengers, and all their life stories, are ultimately consigned to the care of historians, who tell and retell the stories, sorting and categorizing them, looking for deeper meanings and bedrock truths. All the stories that were tested in life by adversaries, the press, and the people are disinterred and reexamined, and with the distance of historical study some of the complexities that were jettisoned from the stories in life are inserted back into the mix after death.

But the historians, too, are part of larger narratives, ones that involve changing interpretations of the past, changing tools for studying history, changing concerns in the worlds they inhabit. Ultimately the poor politician cannot hope to safeguard his historical reputation, for he cannot foresee what future generations will deem important. Thomas Jefferson would little have suspected that Americans of the twenty-first century would pay far more attention to his affair with one of his slave women, Sally Hemings, than to his uncompromising advocacy of religious freedom. Franklin Roosevelt could not have known how poor his record in the field of civil rights would look as the decades passed, particularly when compared with his other accomplishments.

The stories that the presidents leave behind are not dead, though their authors may be. They are part of the larger story of the nation and of the many issues being contested at any historical moment. As the civil rights movement grew a half century ago, the history of earlier decades and eras was recast, and the stories retold, in ways that anticipated and furthered the great changes of the 1950s and '60s. New interpretations of Reconstruction helped restore the vote to African Americans in the South at the same time that the winning of those voting rights was helping to change historical interpretations. Such a dialectic is not unusual—it is routine, and it affects every matter of national consequence. The struggle over the stories in history is every bit as much a struggle for power as the collision of stories during a presidential campaign.

A MAN IN FULL

These struggles begin in the newspapers. Obituaries, for all their good intentions, are rather limited attempts to come to grips with the life and career of a president. If a president has died in office, then the tone of such notices is often deeply reverential and likely to be heavily revised over time. And in any case, too much remains concealed for the poor journalist to render a suitable account on the life lived. Even if the death occurs many years after the president has left office, the charitable spirit of remembrance and mourning tends to gild such articles with a kindly glow.

In the years that follow a president's death, new information constantly becomes available. His papers are cataloged and made available to scholars. Government documents of the United States and other nations are declassified and shed new light on diplomatic issues of the day. Memoirs and correspondence of aides and adversaries are published or make their way into archives, and so gradually into the public record. Another reason early assessments fall short is that the values and concerns of American society change over time. Because of this, matters that once loomed large in historical consciousness fade, and other matters long ignored come into the foreground.

The fact that George Washington owned slaves, once simply taken for granted as part of his time, is now viewed by many with a very critical eye. What we see in the career of a presidential contender from the past depends on what our current concerns are.

Consider, for example, William Jennings Bryan's career, the different ways it can be understood, and the different aspects of it that seem most important. It is a matter of which story of Bryan's life you take to be the core.

There is Bryan the Populist, emerging as the voice of agrarian discontent in 1896. (The same Bryan has also been portrayed as the betrayer of that agrarian movement, the faux radical whose oratorical skills helped turn the Populist movement away from true radicalism and back into the corrupt, compromising arms of the Democratic party.)

There is Bryan the opponent of American imperialism, running against William McKinley in 1900 and criticizing the consequences of the United States' easy victory in the Spanish-American War. The Democratic platform on which Bryan ran that year was unusually direct on the subject and included a politically deft paraphrase of the Declaration of Independence: "We declare again that all governments instituted among men derive their just powers from the consent of the governed; that any government not based upon the consent of the

governed is a tyranny; and that to impose upon any people a government of force is to substitute the methods of imperialism for those of
a republic." But Bryan's criticisms of American policy in the Philippines, which in 1900 was the scene of a guerrilla war pitting American
forces against partisans led by the Filipino patriot Emilio Aguinaldo,
proved politically fruitless. Bryan was trounced by McKinley and his
archimperialist running mate, Teddy Roosevelt. For decades that anti-
imperialist strain was largely forgotten. Then, in the 1980s, as the
longtime American-dominated regime of Ferdinand Marcos in the
Philippines was toppling in the face of widespread popular resistance,
Bryan's attitudes again seemed relevant.[1]

Another Bryan was revealed in 1915, the man of principle who resigned as Wilson's secretary of state in opposition to the president's
stern response to German submarine warfare. It is a story that plays
out in different ways to different people at different times, according
to one's own attitude toward war and one's views on principle versus
expediency. When Secretary of State Cyrus Vance resigned in opposition to Jimmy Carter's attempt to find a military solution to the Iran
hostage crisis, the Bryan story was recalled as the only other example
of a secretary of state resigning in public protest ("MOST OFFICIALS IN
PAST QUIT QUIETLY" was the headline the *New York Times* gave the
story).[2]

For others, the image is of Bryan the creationist. The play and film
Inherit the Wind casts Bryan as a bumptious, bloviating champion of
literal Bible truth matched against the witty and cunning Clarence
Darrow in the "Monkey Trial" of 1925. Bryan's closing argument in
the case turned out to be the last speech he wrote; as it happened, the
case went to the jury before closing arguments could be delivered, so
Bryan arranged to have his summation printed. He died just after
making his last changes to the proof. In the speech, Bryan opens by
citing Demosthenes, "the greatest of ancient orators," no doubt in-
tending his audience to confer upon him the modern title. Bryan

lumbers forward, first declaring that the law of Tennessee banning the teaching of Darwin's theory of evolution is properly drafted and just, and then offering his own "indictments" against the "evolutionary hypothesis." (One example—evolution is bad because it "diverts attention from pressing problems.") He concludes that should the Tennessee law be overturned, "there will be rejoicing wherever God is repudiated, the Saviour scoffed at and the Bible ridiculed." But if the law is upheld, "millions of Christians will call you [the jury] blessed."[3]

How Bryan is seen and understood depends to a large extent on what larger story one is trying to fit him into. For diplomatic historians, the Bryan of the Monkey Trial is beside the point, just as the anti-imperialist Bryan of 1900 is of little concern to the student of American religion. Historians, like voters and reporters, select the narratives they prefer.

BIG STORIES

As in Bryan's case, how any individual's life story is understood depends upon the larger design into which one is fitting the pieces. For there are, in history, any number of larger historical master narratives from which to choose.

Consider the history of the United States itself. Some see it as part of a great story of historical progress, part of the march toward greater freedom that Hegel hopefully identified as the fundamental trajectory of human history. This optimistic interpretation has dominated both American historical writing and the popular conception of the nation's story. It is a narrative that has drawn support from many sources, even Bryan's hated Darwinism.

But a very different lesson on the course of American history could be drawn from Christianity. There the story is of a Garden of Eden, from which man was expelled owing to sin. It is a story of declension, with the decline being manifest in various ways. For many Americans, the importation of slaves into the colonies beginning in 1619 can be seen as the fundamental fall from grace of the nation. It is into this narrative structure that the image of Lincoln as a Christ figure fits so readily, with his martyrdom serving as our redemption. And later Martin Luther King Jr. and John F. Kennedy could be added to the list of martyrs, a story line simple and strong enough to be memorialized in a pop song, Dion's 1968 hit "Abraham, Martin and John."

Another view is the more Manichaean one, a contest between opposing forces. The most influential version of this constructs the nation's history as a struggle between the popular, rights-based republic embodied by Thomas Jefferson and the competitive, capitalistic nation represented by Alexander Hamilton. In 1925, the historian Claude G. Bowers published *Jefferson and Hamilton: The Struggle for Democracy in America,* which presented the schism as a straightforward one between democracy and aristocracy, in essence taking Jefferson's point of view.

Most influential works of history take a strong point of view. The Progressive Era historian Charles A. Beard, for example, tried to overturn the filiopietistic treatment of the Founding Fathers in his influential 1913 book, *An Economic Interpretation of the Constitution.* In place of the Olympian, disinterested figures wrestling to form a "more perfect union" that had peopled earlier accounts of the nation's founding, Beard presented the delegates to the Constitutional Convention in Philadelphia as a group of self-interested aristocrats mostly concerned about their own economic well-being. Or, more recently, historians like Bernard Bailyn and J. G. A. Pocock rejected the long-held view that John Locke was the intellectual father of the American Revolution and discovered a strong intellectual tradition they call "classical republicanism," a tradition, incidentally, that saw it as more likely that republics would decline into anarchy or tyranny than that they would rise in a seamless ascent to greater freedom.

There are fads and fashions in historical writing, but there is no simple progression of historical approaches, and examples of each approach can be found at almost any time. Discussions of how historians "rewrote" the history of the Civil War and Reconstruction around the time of the modern civil rights movement have to recognize that W. E. B. Du Bois had already written brilliantly on the subject decades earlier. Similarly, we continue to see both critical and doting biographies of the Founders.

And of course the social historians who have revitalized the study of history and opened whole new areas of study over the past generation viewed the entire obsession with presidents as overplayed and tending to obscure the larger shifts in the economic and social structure of the United States over the past two centuries. Other stories, with other, less distinct characters, attracted their attention. The slimly documented lives of common people were mined for collective stories and general truths. Indeed, for some of these historians, stories themselves came to seem more likely to hide than to reveal the truth. Narrative itself had become suspect.

But common to all these efforts has been a reliance, to a greater or lesser degree, on stories. In recent years, even some of the pioneering social historians of the 1960s and '70s have lost this aversion to storytelling and moved toward more explicitly narrative styles of historical writing, seeking to embed their insights into stories. One of the apostates was Yale's John Demos, whose career began in pursuit of historical writing "in which analysis and interpretation became the main—if not the only—thing." But eventually "a narrative voice crept into" his later work, and he finally resolved, "I wanted to write a *story.*" Demos's book *The Unredeemed Captive,* about an Indian raid in western Massachusetts in 1704, simultaneously embraced and reflected upon storytelling, and was itself part of a larger return to narrative writing by academic historians.[4]

THE AMERICAN NARRATIVE TRADITION

The return to narrative history was a natural enough step. From Herodotus to the present, storytelling has been central to the work of historians. American historical writing was launched in earnest in the nineteenth century, and the leading lights of the field were three products of Harvard College, George Bancroft, Francis Parkman, and Henry Adams. All three were storytellers, although the stories they wanted to tell were vastly different. Bancroft's subject was the founding of the nation, from colonial times through the end of the Revolutionary War; Parkman strove to write the "history of the American forest," which was published as *France and England in North America;* and Adams narrowed his focus to a *History of the United States of America During the Administrations of Thomas Jefferson and James Madison.* Yet each was setting forth what he saw as the essential story of the nation's founding. Their attitudes and anecdotes greatly shaped the notions of the historians who came after them.[5]

Bancroft was both a politician and a historian. His early enthusiasm for Jacksonian democracy in Whig Massachusetts helped him to land patronage appointments as collector of the Port of Boston and later as secretary of the navy and ambassador to Britain. The sectional crisis finally drew him to the Republican party, and he later served as minister to Prussia and then to the German Empire. But the same democratic enthusiasm that drew him to Jackson animated his historical writing. His ten-volume *History of the United States* concluded with the end of the Revolution, but what he saw in the period he covered was the essential story of American life taking shape. That story was about the highest realization of human freedom ever achieved in the world. It was a story he saw in global, and also spiritual, terms. "Freedom is of all races and all nationalities, it is in them all older than bondage and ever rises again . . . for the rights of man spring from eternal law . . . and by their own indestructibility prove their own lineage as the children of omnipotence." When the last volume of the history was published, in 1874, the United States was in the midst of a serious depression, and the tensions between labor and capital were beginning to supplant the lingering wounds of the Civil War at the center of national consciousness. Bancroft told his readers that in a land of such freedom, the real issue had become that "the liberty of the individual must know how to set itself bounds."[6]

Parkman, who of the three had the greatest pure gift as a writer, wrote about the same period as Bancroft, but stopped short of the era of the American Revolution, ending his volumes on the struggle between England and France with the British victory in the French and Indian War, concluded by the Treaty of Paris in 1763. The final volume of his work, *Montcalm and Wolfe,* was published ten years after the last volume of Bancroft's optimistic account. Parkman was concerned that the country, which had survived a civil war that worked to "compact and consolidate" the nation's fundamental values and unity, needed to "resist the mob and the demagogue as she resisted Parliament and King," and that she should resist as well the "delirium of prosperity" to work for higher goals than mere wealth and "the game of party politics." The United States, now strong, must prove "if she can, that the rule of the masses is consistent with the highest growth of the individual; that democracy can give the world a civilization as mature and pregnant, ideas as energetic and vitalizing, and types of manhood as lofty and strong, as any of the systems which it boasts to supplant."[7]

Henry Adams, too, thought he was dealing with a defining period of the nation's history. He opens the final chapter of his multivolume history with these words: "Until 1815 nothing in the future of the American Union was regarded as settled. As late as January, 1815, division into several nationalities was still thought to be possible." But the choice had then been made, and a vast and united nation had resulted. At the end of his book, Adams asks, "What interests were to vivify a society so vast and uniform? What ideals were to ennoble it? What object, besides physical content, must a democratic continent aspire to attain? For the treatment of such questions, history required another century of experience." The last volume of his *History* was published in 1891, but his judgment on the modern world was not fully exposed to the public until the posthumous publication of *The Education of Henry Adams* in 1918. In that book, Adams made clear his own profound worries about the shape modern America had taken. In place of the optimistic democratic vision of Bancroft, Adams offered a deeply pessimistic view of the modern world, where human intelligence and feeling was subject to the awful power of the mechanistic domain of what he called the "dynamo." Man's technological power was creating wealth, yes, but also hurtling civilization toward disaster.[8]

Each of these historians was a storyteller. Each identified a crucial era in the nation's history and sought to understand the entire nation from that slice of time. Each saw tremendous challenges, and each clearly had a personal point of view, a set of values he sought to get across to the reader. They were not mere fabulists like Parson Weems; they relied on documents, and strove against significant obstacles to secure the source materials they needed for their work. And each small story told was, for these writers, part of a larger narrative scheme, illustrating part of a greater moral lesson.

Professional historians who have followed also dedicate themselves to original sources, to rigorous delineation of fact from fiction, truth from lie. Yet they are also storytellers, both in the simple stories they tell about their subjects and in the larger, more complicated story of what it all means. After all, historians do not write about limited subjects for the sake of limits; they do so in the hope that by really coming to terms with a single moment, a single personality, they can uncover larger truths about human events, human motives, human aspirations.

THE JEFFERSON IMAGE

In 1960 Merrill D. Peterson published *The Jefferson Image in the American Mind*, a study, as he wrote, not of "the history Thomas Jefferson made" but of "what history made of Thomas Jefferson." He did so, he explained, because attitudes toward Jefferson proved to be a "sensitive reflector, through several generations, of America's troubled search for the image of itself."[9]

Jefferson himself was somewhat troubled by the iconic status his career had won him. He tried to keep his birth date a secret so that enthusiastic partisans would not turn it into a day of riotous demonstrations as Federalists had done with Washington's birthday. Nevertheless, he was quite concerned with his place in history, taking pains to let people know what he wanted to be known for. Around 1800 he wrote "A Memorandum (Services to My Country)" in which he set forth what he had done that he thought worth remembering. He opened with a meditation, "I have sometimes asked myself whether my country is the better for my having lived at all?" Among the items he put on the positive side of the ledger for himself were the Declaration of Independence and various laws, including one "prohibiting the importation of slaves." He also took note of the role he had played trying to promote the cultivation of "heavy upland rice" to replace, or at least supplement, the lowland rice grown in coastal South Carolina and Georgia, and he recorded a shipment of olive plants he had sent from Marseilles to Charleston. "The greatest service which can be rendered in any country is, to add a useful plant to its culture; especially, a bread grain; next in value to bread is oil." In 1826, as his death was approaching, Jefferson pared his principal achievements down to three for his headstone: "Author of the Declaration of American Independence[,] of the [Virginia] Statute for religious freedom & Father of the University of Virginia."[10]

In life Jefferson was never casual about his own image. In death his image, and the stories attached to the various representations of him, were employed in various causes. But so varied was his career, and so extensive his writings, that adherents of many, and often opposing, causes could invoke his name in furtherance of their claims. The accomplishments he cited on his tombstone were expressive of Jefferson the freethinker, the champion of equality, the patron of education. But there was also Jefferson the pragmatic exerciser of executive power (as in the Louisiana Purchase); Jefferson the champion of states' rights (in the Virginia and Kentucky resolutions in opposition to the Alien and Sedition Acts of 1798); Jefferson the critic of slavery and Jefferson the slaveholder.

As Peterson carefully delineates, Jefferson's legacy has lived on throughout American history in many forms. His posthumous endorsement has been as eagerly sought as the corpse of Hector.

The beatification of Jefferson began auspiciously, with the coincidence of his death on the same day as his old colleague and opponent, John Adams—July 4, 1826, the fiftieth anniversary of the Declaration of Independence. President John Quincy Adams proclaimed the concurrence of events "Heaven directed," and commentators across the growing nation marveled at the divine hand that seemed so clearly to put its mark on the two men, and on the nation they had served.[11]

The Jacksonian era saw both Jacksonians and Whigs claim the mantle of Jefferson. Democrats said they were true to the popular enthusiasms of the Virginian, who had scandalized European visitors to the White House with his casual dress and lack of respect for hierarchy. Whigs were drawn to Jefferson's educational enthusiasms and appropriated some of his attacks on monarchical power to lambaste the imperious Jackson and his ways.

When North-South tension boiled over in the South Carolina nullification crisis of the early 1830s, Carolinians like John C. Calhoun invoked Jefferson's own explicit mention of the doctrine of nullification in some unpublished notes of the late 1790s, while James Madison himself called out from retirement that the South Carolinians were correct in their interpretation of Jefferson's views.

The fundamental line of division in the Jeffersonian legacy was drawn: on one side was the author of the ringing statement that "all men are created equal"; on the other was the champion of small government and states' rights. And for each of these main positions there were many supporting stories—and many opposing ones. A story about Jefferson's simple notions of etiquette could be balanced with one about his aristocratic tastes (in French wines, for example); his reluctance to empower a strong national government could be instanced by his opposition to Hamilton's ambitious economic schemes under Washington, but could also be undercut by reference to the Louisiana Purchase or to his enforcement of the unpopular embargo policy of 1807–1809. Almost any partisan could find a quotation from or characteristic of Jefferson to cite in support of his position.

Not everyone, however, wanted to fly Jefferson's flag. George Fitzhugh, the fiery tribune of proslavery thought in the 1850s, discarded Jefferson's legacy as one harmful to the South. Republican politicians of the Gilded Age denounced the Virginian as the "American Robespierre." And Teddy Roosevelt found him weak—as a naval historian, Teddy had a well-founded contempt for Jefferson's laughable policy of trying to use gunboats against the might of the Royal Navy in the early 1800s.

But most politicians found the Jefferson legacy attractive. Even the New Deal, the crucial step of the United States into the era of big government, invoked Jefferson as a patron saint. In 1925 Franklin Roosevelt himself reviewed Bowers's hagiographic *Jefferson and Hamilton*. At the end of the review, FDR mused that perhaps "the same contending forces" of the Jefferson-Hamilton rivalry—the people versus the propertied—might be "again mobilizing." And he asked: "Is a Jefferson on the horizon?" To many, FDR himself proved to be that figure, although the incongruity between Jefferson's opposition to big government and Roosevelt's embrace of it troubled some. The philosopher John Dewey resolved the matter in his own mind by stating that the great truth of Jefferson's political thought was his faith in the ability of people to govern themselves. That truth, for Dewey, outweighed any particular policy Jefferson may have favored in his own time.[12]

Almost any dispute in American politics could be referred to Jefferson for arbitration—and he could be found presenting cogent arguments for either side. When the debate on imperialism ignited following the Spanish-American War, expansionists cited the Louisiana Purchase, while those who opposed American dominion over Cuba and the Philippines quoted Jefferson on the fundamental right of people to choose their own governments.

BLACK SAL

In recent years, a different story about Thomas Jefferson has emerged to unprecedented prominence—the story, first given publicity by the scandalmonger James Callender, that Jefferson had sired a family with one of his slaves.

Merrill D. Peterson noted that the abolitionists made use of this story in the 1850s and during the Civil War, but indicated his own view on the matter with the statement: "The legend survives, although no serious student of Jefferson has ever declared his belief in it." Jefferson's fastidious biographer Dumas Malone looked into Jefferson's whereabouts nine months before the birth of each of Sally's children, and discovered that Jefferson was on the scene each time; nevertheless, he ruled that such an affair was "virtually unthinkable in a man of Jefferson's moral standards and habitual conduct." Of this defense, Callender's biographer Michael Durey observed, "It is a clear tautology; Jefferson's high moral standards and habitual conduct depend on the presumption of his innocence of miscegenation." Jefferson's defenders frequently defend him from the accusation by pointing out Callender's base motives for attacking the president, but Durey wrote, "What is surprising is not Callender's penchant for falsification, but his ability to uncover facts that have later been found to be true."[13]

The Sally Hemings story was thrust back into public notice by Fawn Brodie's 1974 book, *Thomas Jefferson: An Intimate History*. At the time of its publication, the credence Brodie gave to the Hemings story was treated dismissively by "serious" historians, an attitude that remained prevalent into the late 1990s. In his widely praised Jefferson biography, *American Sphinx* (1997), Joseph Ellis reviewed the history of the controversy, and reached the conclusion that the likelihood that the affair had happened was "remote." Ellis decided that Jefferson lacked a vigorous sex drive, and following his wife's death in 1782, he most likely sublimated what sexual urges he had "to safer and more sentimental regions."[14]

In November 1998, not long after the publication of Ellis's work, a DNA analysis of African Americans claiming (on the basis of a family oral tradition) to be descended from Jefferson provided very strong, albeit inconclusive, evidence that they were right, and that what Peterson had dismissed as "the memories of a few Negroes" appears to have been more sound than the learned speculations of the historians.

Not all historians, however, had been so dismissive of that African American oral tradition. Fawn Brodie, after all, had led the charge. And in 1997 a professor of law named Annette Gordon-Reed published *Thomas Jefferson and Sally Hemings: An American Controversy*. Her book was not intended so much to prove that the affair had taken place as to demonstrate how, in their efforts to disprove the allegation, "historians, journalists, and other Jefferson enthusiasts have in the past (and continue to do so today) shamelessly employed every stereotype of black people and distortion of life in the Old South to support their positions." As epigraph to her work, Gordon-Reed quoted a passage from W. E. B. Du Bois on the history of African Americans in which he laments that he stands "at the end of this writing, literally aghast at what American historians have done to this field."[15]

HISTORY, STORIES, AND THEIR USES

Jefferson's many stories remind us of the fact that people of each era construct their own version of the nation's past, one that fits their outlooks, concerns, and prejudices. Just as the abolitionists circulated the Jefferson-Hemings story, so it is hardly surprising that Fawn Brodie's book appeared during a time of ferment in both racial relations and sexual politics. And the swift progress of the story from discounted legend to widely accepted fact after the DNA results were published is a testimony to more than our faith in modern science; it represents the nation's continuing effort to deal with its racial past, an ever more important project as the nation moves into an increasingly multiracial future.

But the concerns of a particular era are not the only elements conducive to wider acceptance of the story. It is also part of an ongoing process of the debunking of heroes, and of the incorporation of political figures' private lives into their public reputations. Now that the sexual escapades, actual and rumored, of so many presidents are the matter of common conjecture, the leveling instinct that Jefferson himself encouraged has included him in the exercise.

Emerson said, "Every hero becomes a bore at last," and perhaps the key to Jefferson's enduring fascination is that he is not really a hero; he is too much a bundle of contradictions for that, a Hamlet, not a Laertes. Washington, after all, was vastly more admired by his contemporaries than Jefferson, and was a greater president, but his shortage of human frailties makes him a more distant, hence less compelling, figure. Even Washington, though, is subject to changing values in America. In October 1997, an elementary school in a black neighborhood of New Orleans removed Washington's name from the school because he had owned slaves. (Washington, unlike Jefferson, manumitted his slaves in his will.) The school was renamed for Dr. Charles Richard Drew, an African American surgeon who helped develop ways of preserving blood plasma. One story replaces another.[16]

The story of fluctuating presidential reputations is a familiar one. John Kennedy's reputation today is far lower than it was in the wake of his assassination; his foreign policy moves considered sometimes inept, his support for civil rights grudging and opportunistic. By contrast, Harry Truman, who left office almost in disgrace, has become an adored figure, and the conclusion of the Cold War has seemingly vindicated the thrust of many of the policies he improvised in the wake of the Second World War.

America's Cold War triumph even led the diplomatic strategist Francis Fukuyama to proclaim "The End of History?" in an influential 1989 essay in *The National Interest*. But for the stories of presidents, there is no end. They go on, being lost and recovered, recycled and transformed. They help us understand our present by helping us understand our past. As Merrill Peterson showed, how Jefferson's life is viewed tells us much about the society that is viewing him. And as Annette Gordon-Reed's book demonstrates, historians stand inside, not outside, this process.

ROUGH JUSTICE

Just as different eras take the stories they need from the past, they also take the stories they need from the present. By choosing presidents, Americans are writing their own story as they go along. They choose the elements they feel they need at a given moment. This is not to say that the choices that voters make are the "right" ones, simply that the stories the voters endorse are a useful gauge of their hopes and fears. For all the racism and misrepresentation involved in the "Willie Horton" ad campaign of the 1988 race, it did reflect widespread fear of crime at a time when the epidemic of crack cocaine was lifting murder rates to astounding heights. The lack of such a bogeyman figure in the 2000 race is not evidence of rising ethical standards in politics but rather of the drastic fall in violent crime during the 1990s.

George Washington did not cut down the cherry tree. William Henry Harrison did not grow up in a log cabin. Sometimes campaigns are fought in a realm that seems largely detached from reality. But Harrison's opponent in 1840, Martin Van Buren, had presided over a major recession that began in 1837 and was still being felt as the campaign progressed. Perhaps the real subtext of the 1840 race was not "Tippecanoe and Tyler, too" but "It's the economy, stupid." The faux-plebeian Harrison versus the faux-patrician Van Buren is hardly a model of elevated political discourse, but the story it told did have resonance for voters enduring an economic crisis that was at least partly Van Buren's fault.

Stories are the vessels of history, but they are also the vessels of the present. In a world of boundless complexity, we grasp meaning through stories, as humans have always done. Stories are told to inform, instruct, inspire. Symbols and stereotypes are concentrated essences of stories, interpreted by a sophisticated public with lightning speed. A photo of Bill Clinton hugging Monica Lewinsky at a White House event; Michael Dukakis looking foolish in the turret of a tank; George W. Bush in pilot's garb aboard an aircraft carrier: all these images remind us that stories have power.

Is this, in the end, a good or a bad thing? It is both, of course. Stories simplify a complex world, and allow us to make quick decisions. There is an undeniable explanatory power in analogies—comparing

Saddam Hussein to Hitler, or Ferdinand Marcos to Fulgencio Batista, helps us to understand them. Yet the power of such stories often obscures the specific facts of a historical situation. The story of Munich tends to brand all attempts to secure "peace in our time" as appeasement; but surely peace is preferable to war, and sometimes negotiation can prevent armed conflict without becoming capitulation.

The point is not to judge whether the power of stories is good or bad; the point is to recognize that such power exists, and to allow that realization to deepen one's understanding of specific people and events. Stories shape how presidents and other leaders act, the way journalists write about their actions, and how citizens interpret them. For good and for ill, stories are the currency of our public life.

CHAPTER THIRTEEN

A STORY IN PROGRESS: GEORGE W. BUSH

GEORGE W. BUSH CAME TO THE WHITE HOUSE with a reputation that rested most of its weight on his father. With his hard-partying past and general lack of gravitas, Bush was a Texas Prince Hal yearning to become Henry V. Why was unclear: Bush never managed to explain what compelled him to run for president, other than that he stood a good chance of winning and, possibly, wished to redeem his father's presidency. When the tragedy of the 9/11 attacks took place, Bush had an occasion to rise to, an opportunity to prove himself worthy of his office. September 11 pushed a new master narrative to the foreground, and Bush and his team adroitly seized this new story line and made it theirs, just as in 2000 they had managed to construct a winning campaign around his modest life story.

The theme of suffering and redemption was central in both instances. In Bush's personal life, the tale of his struggles with—and victory over—alcohol rendered sympathetic a figure who might easily have been perceived as a spoiled rich kid. Rather conveniently, this story line also relegated the first forty years of his life to the bin of irrelevancy, which meant less focus on Bush's ambling road to a life of public service. His turn away from alcohol was accompanied by a turn toward a deepening engagement with Christianity, which helped connect him to Christian conservatives, the most active Republican constituency.

And just as his problems with alcohol allowed his life story to be crafted into one of triumph over adversity, the real adversity of the 9/11 attacks permitted Bush to recast a large set of political issues in a new light. The complexities of the situation in the Middle East and many of the causes of resentment of American power abroad were left out of the new master narrative, which set forth a Manichaean struggle between good and evil in which the righteousness of America's cause justifies its government's harsh actions and rhetoric. Controversial measures—"preemptive" war, civilian casualties, the denial of fundamental legal rights to those accused of attacking the United States, and unsupported or exaggerated claims about Iraqi weaponry—all could be portrayed merely as actions necessary to defeat the "evildoers." At the same time, heightened threats to American citizens demanded stricter attention to national security and closer control over "classified" information, which fit nicely with the Bush administration's dedication to tightly managed public relations, "message discipline," and restricted access to government information. Even before the 9/11 attacks, for example, Attorney General John Ashcroft had moved to weaken significantly the Freedom of Information Act, one of journalists' most vital tools for securing government documents.

To understand the power of this new narrative, consider where Bush's presidency might have been in mid-2003 without 9/11—with high unemployment, a stagnant economy, and a string of corporate scandals, the president might have seen the Democrats retake the Senate (and maybe even the House) in 2002. Bush might have been seen as faithfully, and disastrously, re-creating his father's story.

September 11, of course, really happened, and the change of attitudes that ensued cannot all be credited to (or blamed upon) George W.

Bush. But alert to the political power of stories, the Bush administration has made skillful use of every story it could get its hands on to advance its cause. Even when a story turns out to be flawed (Iraq's weapons of mass destruction, Jessica Lynch as Rambo), the power of the master narrative can prove stronger than truth.

THE MEDIA ENVIRONMENT

Although crafted presidential narratives have been important throughout American history, their power has increased over time, and that growth has accelerated markedly in the past half century. Changing technologies, the changing structure of media businesses, and changing cultural mores have all played a role in increasing the importance of stories in politics and broadening the boundaries of public disclosure. Television and the Internet have accelerated the news cycle, requiring that news judgments be made in minutes rather than hours, and tilting the balance in favor of being first with a story, regardless of its importance or propriety. Changing mores and the accumulated history of past misdeeds have opened up the private lives of public figures to withering media scrutiny.

The increasing consolidation of the news media, with an ever larger proportion of American newspapers, magazines, and broadcast outlets being held by an ever smaller number of media conglomerates, has reduced the number of gatekeepers in the news business and encouraged a lowest-common-denominator standard, where celebrity news, violence, and scandal take precedence over less popular (and more expensive) international reporting and investigative series. The presence of Internet bloggers and others who hurry to circulate the most scurrilous material they can find can dramatically influences the content of reports from more responsible news organizations. The old journalistic saw that "good news is no news" is truer than ever. And so campaigns turn to negative stories, and negative ads, because they know that the press will focus on the bad news. The bad press candidates get for "going negative" is a price worth paying for the media firestorms those negative ads inflict on opponents.

This is why the Bush administration wisely dedicates itself to maintaining strict discipline over what messages come from the White House and the agencies of the executive branch. Without containing the bad stories, no administration can find room for the good ones. And careful management of the good stories can pay dividends far out of proportion to the intrinsic importance of the stories. The press may complain about the tight-lipped message discipline of the Bush White House, but they also respect it.

President Bush's own life story has been fashioned over the years into a powerful tool for his own political purposes. And his success in this realm belies the image of Bush as a dim-witted man. It's true that he has talented aides to help him in this sphere, but he deserves credit for hiring and trusting them. Every president is besieged with conflicting advice; a vital element of success is knowing which advice to accept and which to reject. Bush's performance shows a keen understanding of the rules of the narrative game.

ROOTS

One cannot discuss the life story of George W. Bush without also considering the achievements of his father. The career of George H. W. Bush—as naval aviator, Texas oilman, Republican functionary, CIA director, vice president and then president—made it possible for George W. Bush (and his brother Jeb, the governor of Florida) to succeed in politics. George H. W. Bush's success established a family narrative from which his sons have profited. But there are both assets and liabilities in the Bush family saga. By all accounts George W. Bush was not, for most of his life, a source of pride to his parents—he himself owned to being the black sheep in the family, and his life well into his forties was marked more by the scantness than by the distinction of his achievements. But Bush has managed to construct a narrative that has capitalized on the useful parts of his family past and overwritten or omitted those parts that detract from his story. Others, of course, offer counternarratives, and these stories will continue to contend for the balance of his presidency and far beyond. But Bush has displayed remarkable discipline in promulgating his version of the story, and remarkable success in getting it accepted.

The story of Texas is instructive. The elder Bush (henceforth Bush 41—he was the forty-first president) never seemed truly comfortable in Texas regalia. He wore a cowboy hat with the same unease that Coolidge brought to Indian headdress, and his professed love for pork rinds came across as pandering, even if the affection was genuine. He was by origin and inclination a New Englander, the son of a U.S. senator from Connecticut. His seashore retreat in Kennebunkport, Maine, always seemed to fit him better than the plains of Texas.

His son, though born in Connecticut, was raised in Texas and adopted Texas attitudes and accent. But there is more than one Texas. Lyndon Johnson was part of the Texas Populist tradition. Bush, by contrast, embodies a more conservative Texas tradition rooted in its Confederate past. (The Texas of African Americans and Latino Texas are two other stories.) The Populist and Confederate Texases could coexist within the old Democratic party of the first half of the twentieth century, but once the national party committed itself to support the civil rights movement under Kennedy and Johnson, the state party fragmented and "Texas Republican" became a political reality rather than an oxymoron. Bush successfully tied this nostalgic Confederate strain to the energies of a more modern, business-friendly Texas, where cowboy boots and hat are identity politics, not work clothes.[1]

It is part of Texas's success, and of its burden, that its larger-than-life self-image has become part of the international reputation of the United States. Texas bluster and bravado and the tradition of frontier justice play out very differently on the Hollywood screen and the world stage. The image of America as a Texas Ranger (Bush's baseball team was the Rangers) or a lone cowboy has become one stereotype of America's view of its role in the world, and leaders as diverse as Lyndon Johnson and Henry Kissinger have been pictured in this role. (Indeed Kissinger relished the role, likening himself, in a famous interview with the Italian journalist Oriana Fallaci, to "the cowboy who leads the wagon train by riding ahead alone on his horse, the cowboy who rides all alone into the town, the village, with his horse and nothing else.") George W. Bush's statement that Osama bin Laden was "Wanted: Dead or Alive" fit neatly into this pattern, and was seen very differently abroad and at home. Later Vice President Dick Cheney explicitly endorsed the cowboy narrative, saying on *Meet the Press* that "the notion that the President is a cowboy . . . that's not necessarily a bad idea." Bush, Cheney said, "cuts to the chase."[2]

Bush and his team are clearly alert to the resonances of his Texas upbringing. In his autobiography, *A Charge to Keep,* written with (and largely by) Karen Hughes, his communications director, Bush describes his Texas boyhood, recalling his fondness for pickup games of baseball in Midland, Texas: "We were always organizing a game, in the schoolyard, or in the buffalo wallow behind my house on Sentinel Street." He remembered the plains environment vividly: "Tumbleweeds blew in our yard. Once it rained and frogs came out everywhere, like the biblical plague, covering the fields and front porches." The image mixed Hollywood iconography—the tumbleweeds—with a religious reference; Ronald Reagan himself couldn't have said it better. Tragedy found him in the death of his young sister, Robin, when he was seven. Soon after, at a football game, he told his father he wished he was Robin: his father asked why, and the boy explained, "Because she can probably see better from up there than we can from down here." Later the family moved to the greener and busier city of Houston, and then George was sent off to Phillips Academy, Andover, to be prepared for college.[3]

Bush 41 had attended Andover as well, and had suffered from it politically—the private-school credential cemented his reputation as a preppy and a son of privilege. In fact, Bush 41 was both of those things, as is his son. But the younger Bush's identity never became indelibly linked to the privileged eastern education he received, including not just Andover but undergraduate studies at Yale and then a business degree from Harvard.

In Bush's first campaign, for a Texas congressional seat in 1978, this educational background (and supposed northeastern perspective) was successfully used against him. His rival in the Republican primary attacked him for having "Rockefeller-type Republicans such as Karl Rove" on his side, and in the general election his Democratic opponent, Kent Hance, derided Bush's time at Andover and Yale while highlighting his own all-Texas education. Hance also raised an issue that would reverberate with evangelical voters—drinking; Bush's campaign had announced a "beer bash" rally in a Texas Tech student paper, and Bush was portrayed as having tried to buy votes with alcohol. Bush was labeled a rich kid and a corrupter of youth, and he lost the race. He learned his lesson. The next time Bush ran for office, he made certain he would not have to fear attacks from the right.[4]

ASCENT

Bush 41 was a pilot, and George W. Bush became one as well. Yet the difference in their stories is more meaningful than the similarities. Bush 41 flew combat missions and was shot down in the Second World War; his son flew in the Texas Air National Guard. Bush's own account of how he came to enlist in the guard is cursory: he heard "from contemporaries" that there were available slots for pilots in the Texas Air National Guard; "I met the qualifications and was accepted," he writes. The actual story is more complicated and not as politically beneficial. Such guard slots were eagerly sought by those wishing to avoid service in Vietnam, and children of the rich and powerful were uncannily successful at securing them: Bush's guard unit had also found slots for the sons of other politically prominent Texans, including Lloyd Bentsen and John Connally. But the actual story of how Bush made it in is too complex and obscure to prove politically damaging, in spite of the efforts of journalists and political opponents. There's a story there, but not a simple story, and there's no "smoking gun," no clear piece of evidence to show that strings were pulled, however likely that seems based on circumstantial evidence. Moreover, eight years earlier the press had raked Bill Clinton over the coals for his efforts at draft dodging. The public just didn't seem to care that Bush had done something similar; and after all, he had served in the guard, which was something. His guard service gave Bush training as a jet pilot, but even more valuable was the political cover it provided, allowing him to claim military experience while avoiding the dangers other pilots faced in Vietnam.[5]

After his guard service, Bush worked briefly for an antipoverty organization in Houston and then went to Harvard Business School. He was encouraged to do so, Bush recounts, by the head of the organization, who told him to "go and learn more and then you can really help" the poor. Bush got his MBA and returned to Texas, but not to help the poor. He entered the oil business. His timing, however, was bad—he arrived during an oil downturn. Critical accounts of his career in the oil business focus on the intersection of his father's influence and the investors who several times bailed Bush out of difficult situations. These stories follow the pattern of his acceptance into the National Guard—family influence and privilege loom large, but the stories are murky enough and the relationships diffuse enough

THE POWER AND THE STORY

that the efforts of Bush's critics to construct a coherent, damaging account have fallen short. Perhaps if the press had not exhausted itself
with its investigation of Whitewater, the Clintons' failed investment
in Arkansas real estate, it would have investigated Bush's business
dealings more closely. But once again Bill Clinton had felt pain so that
George W. Bush would not have to.[6]

Bush's next business effort, ownership of the Texas Rangers baseball team, proved a better move. In addition to being a business success, the ownership stake provided a high-profile stage from which
George W. could endear himself to other Texans. And association
with the "national pastime" added another note to the patriotic med-
ley of careers Bush was composing.

Throughout this period, though, there was another George W.
Bush in evidence—a hard-partying businessman. And it was this
thread of his narrative—and the overcoming of his drinking problem—that came to form the central story of Bush's personal narrative.
Bush devoted a chapter of his autobiography to this change, which
happened just after his fortieth birthday. He and some friends had
gathered to celebrate in Colorado Springs, and "had a big time at a
dinner at the Broadmoor Hotel." The next morning he awoke hung
over, and decided then and there to quit drinking. Bush claims that he
was a disciplined drinker and only drank after work. His friends think
his image "as a party animal" is "vastly overblown," he says, adding
that he probably helped create that impression by telling reporters,
"When I was young and irresponsible, I sometimes behaved young
and irresponsibly." Bush claims that the rumors started because of this
remark, and that it was because he refused to "itemize a laundry list of
things I wish I hadn't done."[7]

Bush takes care not to refer to himself as an alcoholic, wisely fear-
ing the label. (Bill Clinton had similarly worked hard to avoid the label "adulterer.") But Bush still succeeded in making the story of his

drinking a powerful positive element in his own master narrative. In his 2000 campaign it worked beautifully. Rather than clinging to categorical and implausible denials of past misdeeds involving alcohol, and possibly cocaine, Bush and his aides crafted a narrative of suffering and redemption. Yes, the story went, in his younger days Bush had been a bit of a hellion but now he's a teetotaling family man. End of story. Not only had he quit, he'd found God. On the footsteps of his renunciation of booze Bush encountered the Reverend Billy Graham, who was spending a weekend with the elder Bushes in Kennebunkport. There Bush and Graham talked, and the reverend "planted a mustard seed in my soul," writes Bush, that developed into a deeper engagement with Christianity and Bible study. "It was the beginning of a new walk where I would recommit my heart to Jesus Christ."[8]

With his life story composed—son of a president, Texan, former jet pilot, oilman, baseball entrepreneur, clean-living Christian—Bush was prepared to launch his political career in earnest. Bush's campaign for governor of Texas in 1994, against the popular incumbent Ann Richards, was well timed. Richards, who had famously mocked Bush 41 as "born with a silver foot in his mouth," was at first a heavy favorite. But it was the year of Newt Gingrich's "Contract with America," and Republicans ran strong across the nation. In Texas, Bush and his campaign, directed by the strategist Karl Rove, attacked Richards for vetoing a bill that would have loosened restrictions on carrying concealed weapons in the state—an attack reinforced by a concurrent anti-Richards effort by the National Rifle Association. Richards also came under fire for appointing gays and lesbians to a handful of state offices. Bush beat her in a fairly close race, then won reelection in 1998 by a two-to-one margin against an underfunded Democratic opponent who never had much hope. The lopsided win and Bush's surprisingly good showing among Texas Hispanic voters positioned him well for a run for the White House in 2000.

CAMPAIGN

Bush entered the 2000 campaign with a host of established stories buzzing around him: positive stories he and his staff had watered and pruned, and negative stories his opponents had carefully cultivated. That year it was hard to tell what the best forum was for getting one's stories into circulation. The line between serious news operations and entertainment shows had blurred, and a clever joke made at a candidate's expense by Jay Leno or David Letterman could be far more worrisome than a carefully reported exposé of a past misdeed unearthed by an enterprising reporter. Though a variety of stories contended, few of them had much bearing on the problems the nation faced or the solutions either candidate was proposing. What mattered was not the dignity of the program on which the campaign was discussed but the size of its audience and the power of the stories told.

Many of these stories are hardy perennials, having little to do with any particular candidate in any particular year—stories about liberals versus conservatives, outsiders versus insiders, blue states versus red ones; stories about campaign consultants and media buys, ad strategies and organizational wrangling; stories about black voters and white ones, suburban voters and urban ones, NASCAR dads and soccer moms. Such recurring narratives form the white noise of all presidential races. Even the specific issues of a particular race provoke a sense of déjà vu—stories about bad schools, factory closings, underfunded Social Security benefits, and foreign trouble spots. While the details of these stories change, the underlying issues remain more or less constant—Korea is replaced by Vietnam, then Nicaragua, then Iraq, and perhaps Korea again; inflation bows to deflation, the Japanese economic threat to one from China; and Social Security is always in danger. Such issues are more important in some races than others, but presidential life stories are central to the outcome of every race.

One story that established itself early in the 2000 campaign was that Bush was stupid, a man whose impressive educational background was the result of family pull and whose undistinguished post-college career did not bode well for the White House. The many verbal gaffes that Bush committed didn't help; he generated a rich enough lode that several collections of his malapropisms ("I know how hard it is for you to put food on your family") have since been published. His occasional forays into unscripted public discourse would often come a cropper, as when he failed (in a 1999 interview with a Boston TV reporter named Andrew Hiller) to identify the president of Pakistan or the prime minister of India.

This line of detraction was very hard to counter. After all, Bush could not exactly proclaim his intelligence. And his problems with the English language resurfaced often enough to keep the story alive, no matter how scripted his campaign appearances were—especially as the campaign neared its finish and he was frequently exhausted. Bush's side did respond that he could hardly be as thick as he was portrayed or he would not have won reelection in Texas with nearly 70 percent of the vote. Bush's adversaries, though, pointed to his huge campaign war chest in the 1998 race as the best explanation for his overwhelming victory.

It was Texas oil money that inspired the first big story of Bush's presidential campaign. In the summer and fall of 1999, Bush was raising prodigious sums of money, building up a war chest so intimidating that some Republican hopefuls quit the race before it had formally begun. Part of the story was the success of the big-money strategy and the aura of inevitability it bestowed upon Bush's candidacy. But another part of the story was the links it revealed between Bush and wealthy funders, particularly those in the Texas oil industry. Back in 1940, as was mentioned earlier, young Lyndon Johnson turned down funds he very badly wanted because he felt his national political career would be harmed by too close an association with Texas oil interests.

But 1940 had very different values than 2000, and Bush rightly calculated that having the money was a bigger help than the stories
about the contributors would be a hindrance. With his virtually un-
limited funding, Bush held off an early challenge from Arizona senator John McCain and easily took the Republican nomination.

He was fortunate in his Democratic opponent, Al Gore. Gore was
every bit as much a son of privilege as Bush, with a similar educational
background and a politically prominent father (a well-respected senator from Tennessee). Gore had the mixed blessing of having been vice
president for eight years under Bill Clinton. He hoped to associate
himself with the strong economic performance turned in under Clinton while distancing himself from the president who had carried on
with a White House intern. Most fortunate for Bush was the fact that
Gore had his own unflattering character story. In the place of Bush's
apparent stupidity there was Gore's bloodless wonkiness, his droning
well-briefed-ness. The simplest version of the campaign was that it
pitted a genial dolt against a tedious know-it-all. However rankling
Bush may have found it to be deemed a lightweight, this simple anti-
nomy of the frat boy against the wonk worked very well for Bush
when it mattered, in the debates. Handicappers had expected Gore to
do very well against Bush—the *Atlantic Monthly* had run a cover piece
on Gore as a fearsome debater, the cover depicting the candidate with
vampire fangs—and expectations of Bush were so low that when he
actually managed to stay in the ring with Gore it was treated as a huge
victory and the image of Bush as dummy began to dissipate.

In the final week of the campaign, a controversial story broke that revived an embarrassing aspect of Bush's past. A Fox TV station in Maine
discovered that Bush had been arrested there in the summer of 1976
and charged with driving under the influence of alcohol. What turned
an embarrassing incident from twenty-four years earlier into major
news was that Bush had earlier told a Texas political reporter that he had
not been arrested since 1968, when he and some frat brothers stole—or

as Bush put it in his autobiography, "liberated"—a large Christmas wreath from a hotel to "dress up the DKE house for an upcoming party." Bush's campaign first tried denying that Bush had ever denied the post-1968 arrest, and then Karen Hughes put forth a new line: "He made a decision as a father that he did not want to set that bad example for his daughters." Here the dutiful-father story was pushed forward to replace the drunk-driver story, with some success. The timing of the disclosure raised questions as to whether the story had been planted by the Democrats, and most voters seemed to conclude that the arrest was far enough in the past to be forgiven and forgotten.[9]

Indeed, the entire subject was forgotten the following week in the epochal story of the disputed 2000 election. Because much of that dispute took place in the courts, the power of master narratives had to give way somewhat before the power of statute and legal interpretation. But the Florida dispute generated—and revived—many narratives. One particular historical story—that of the 1876 election, with its disputed votes, extra-electoral final decision, and key role for the state of Florida—proved much too enticing an analog to the 2000 situation to be ignored. Thoughtful and complicated analyses of the Florida vote mess were offered in the press, but in the face of a fait accompli most Americans eventually moved on to other matters and hoped for the best from the new president.

THE NEW PRESIDENT

Bush's first challenge as president was to establish his legitimacy in office. The questionable outcome in Florida, and the fact that Al Gore had received a half million more popular votes than Bush had, left many voters dissatisfied. The new president gave a conciliatory inaugural address, paying tribute to the contributions of his predecessor and the character of his vanquished opponent.

In his first months in office, Bush was surely the beneficiary of issue fatigue in the press. After the many investigations of President
Clinton, and then the whirligig dramatics of the electoral outcome,
weary reporters, editors, and readers were disposed to give the new
guy a chance, the traditional presidential honeymoon. Bush moved
quickly to secure his political base by pushing aggressively for a tax cut
and with the Republicans controlling both houses of Congress he succeeded. But in May, Bush suffered a major setback when the narrow
Republican control of the Senate was overturned by the defection of
Senator Jim Jeffords of Vermont, whose decision to leave the GOP
gave control to the Democrats.

The summer of 2001 was a time of slow news weeks, with shark attacks and the disappearance of Chandra Levy, a Washington intern,
dominating. Karen Hughes advised Bush to take the month of August
off and return to Texas, saying, "I don't want to see the President in a
jacket and tie until Labor Day." Hughes hoped to remind voters of
Bush's Texas roots and to maintain the image of the new president as a
Washington outsider. Bush was to be shown clearing brush on his
ranch, meeting with his advisers from time to time (to deflect accusations of laziness), and making occasional trips whose photo opportunities stressed the outside-the-Beltway bona fides of the new president.[10]

SEPTEMBER 11

The attacks of September 11, 2001, transformed every aspect of the
Bush presidency. Shock, grief, and anger galvanized the United States,
and prior issues of legitimacy were thrust aside by the manifest need
and desire for national unity. Despite some initial stumbles, Bush's response was sufficiently resolute to lift him to opinion-poll ratings that
indicated that nine out of ten Americans approved of the job he was
doing. He had left Prince Hal behind.

But it did not happen immediately—the first day was a problem. The president wore a strangely blank look as his chief of staff, Andrew Card, told him, "America is under attack." Bush was meeting with schoolchildren in a classroom at the time, so he may simply have wanted to avoid alarming them. Still, he looked oddly detached. And that was the principal image of the president most people saw that day. He left the school, was whisked aboard Air Force One and took off. For hours, confusion seemed to reign as aides tried to determine where it was safe to land and what were the chances of an attack on the plane—at 10:30 that morning Vice President Cheney told the president that a credible threat to the presidential plane had been received. Bush aides later insisted that the president had wanted to get back to Washington as soon as possible, but the image of that day's hectic progress across the country—from the school in Sarasota, Florida, where Bush heard of the attacks, to an air base in Louisiana, to Strategic Command headquarters in Nebraska before finally returning to the capital—gave many the impression of a leader who was putting his own safety above the nation's troubles. This impression, however widely held, was unfair; the president's safety was clearly an issue of legitimate national concern.[11]

That night, before turning in, Bush noted for his diary, "The Pearl Harbor of the 21st Century took place today." And this old story would help form attitudes and responses in the new century. Bush and his aides soon began preparing the way for America's response. They began by defining the terms of the debate. By September 12, Bush had decided that the attacks were an act of war, not a crime, and that the nation's response would be military. Almost no debate on this momentous decision took place at the time, and little has occurred since, at least in American domestic politics. (The notion that treating terrorism as a crime might have proved a better strategy did not make it into the discussion.) Bush combined this decision with a unilateral challenge to the other nations of the world, as expressed in a speech to a joint session of Congress on September 20. "Either you are with us, or you are with the terrorists," the president declared. "From this day forward, any nation that continues to harbor or support terrorism will be regarded by the United States as a hostile regime."[12]

Politically, all of these moves worked to Bush's advantage. By declaring terrorism an act of war he transformed himself into a wartime leader who was therefore entitled to greater support than a president can expect in peacetime. The conditions of war justified even greater efforts to control government information and to narrow the boundaries of acceptable criticism, whether in the press or outside it. In a country that had given the world the Bill of Rights, the White House and Congress designated a new set of restrictions on immigration, limits on foreign students studying in the United States, and a host of other measures as the "Patriot Act." Opposition to the measures became, by definition, unpatriotic.

The fall of 2001 was a terrible time. The remains of the Twin Towers still smoldered in lower Manhattan, the Pentagon itself was wounded, and in a Pennsylvania cornfield the bodies of passengers who had fought to take their plane back from terrorists lay obliterated. Then came a series of mysterious anthrax attacks against journalists and government officials. Sympathy for the United States around the world was high— even *Le Monde* declared after 9/11 that "We are all Americans now." Surely the French were recalling the words of their admirer Thomas Jefferson two centuries earlier: "We are all Republicans, we are all Federalists." Unity was the order of the day. When victory came to American-led forces in Afghanistan, it was welcomed in much of the world.

IRAQ

When Bush named his running mate, and later his cabinet, he had included many men who had served in his father's administration—

Dick Cheney, Defense Secretary Donald Rumsfeld, and Secretary of State Colin Powell were only the most prominent veterans of the Bush 41 team. Some of these men had unfinished business: the removal of Saddam Hussein from power in Iraq. With the Taliban routed in Afghanistan, the administration's attention turned to an old nemesis.

As early as September 17, 2001, Bush was persuaded that Hussein had had a role in the attacks six days earlier: "I believe Iraq was involved, but I'm not going to strike them now. I don't have the evidence at this point." What he did have, though, was conviction that he was right, and he turned the struggle into one of good versus an "axis of evil." The phrase cleverly incorporated the old enemy faced by the Greatest Generation—the Axis of the Second World War—into the modern adversaries of Iraq, Iran, and North Korea. It would also justify some of the administration's efforts to curtail civil liberties at home.[13]

In time, the Bush administration did construct a case for war based on the charge that Iraq had weapons of mass destruction that could, and probably would, be used against the United States. This was laid on top of the new doctrine of "preemptive war"—that is, that the United States proclaimed a right to attack another nation if it felt that there was reason to fear an attack on "the homeland."

That argument found significant support in a nation still recovering from 9/11. But the Bush case for war on Iraq met with skepticism and hostility outside America's borders, and the "coalition of the willing" that lined up with the United States was dominated by a single major ally, Britain. The Iraq war was won quickly, but the peace proved more elusive. On May 1, 2003, the former Texas Air National Guard pilot landed on the aircraft carrier *Abraham Lincoln* sitting in the copilot's seat of an S-3B Viking jet. The words "George W. Bush Commander-in-Chief" were painted just below the cockpit window. The beaming president changed out of his flight suit and into a dark suit and a red tie and, in front of a banner saying "Mission Accomplished," proclaimed major combat in Iraq over.

Soon, rather than declaring a glorious victory the press was raising the old Vietnam specter of a "quagmire"—a truly toxic story line—and the Bush administration was working hard to shore up its position. As the postwar chaos in Iraq claimed more American lives than the war itself had, the Bush White House distanced itself even from the carrier's banner, claiming it was "put there by the sailors" and ignoring the obvious fact that the entire shot was framed by his press staff for maximum effect. When a diplomat questioned evidence that the Bush administration put forward to support its claim that Iraq was seeking "yellowcake" uranium from Africa for an atom-bomb program, his wife was exposed in the press as a CIA agent, and evidence that the leak may have come from high up in the White House was strong enough to result in a special investigation of the matter. The master narrative of liberating the Iraqi people was complicated by evidence that many Iraqis felt ill will toward the United States in spite of their loathing of Saddam Hussein. Late in 2003, two masterstrokes of public relations helped Bush reclaim the Iraq story when it seemed to be getting away from him. A carefully choreographed, secretly organized visit to American troops in Iraq provided vivid images of a daring and caring president for all Americans to ponder over their Thanksgiving holidays. White House reporters complained about the way the event had been managed, but the public gave little weight to their concerns. And on December 13 Saddam Hussein was captured, his bearded and unkempt figure broadcast to the world as he was checked for head lice. "President Bush sends his regards" were reportedly the Americans' first words to Hussein. True or not, it made a hell of a story.

The capture of Saddam brought closure to an element of the Bush family story. Once President Bush began to prepare to make war on Saddam Hussein, the narrative that seemed most obvious was that Bush was seeking to finish what his father had started, to topple the despot who had once plotted to have Bush 41 assassinated. Once the major ground war was over, a new story line emerged in the summer of 2003, one suggesting that having won an ultimately inconclusive war in the Persian Gulf, Bush might fall victim to the weakness of the American economy, as his father had in the 1992 race. The possible parallelism of two presidential life stories was too attractive to resist. But as the economy showed signs of reviving, and with Saddam in custody, George W. Bush appeared to be writing a different ending for himself.

Yet the central character in the 9/11 drama, Osama bin Laden, was seemingly lost in all the attention directed toward Iraq. The Bush administration was largely successful in persuading Americans that there was a link between Al Qaeda and Iraq (various polls showed a majority of Americans accepted this claim), although evidence of such a tie remained tenuous at best.

The issue of terrorism and the Iraq war—in particular, the issue of how closely the two are related—would be central to the 2004 race. President Bush had Iraq in his sights from the first days of his presidency, according to Paul O'Neill, his former treasury secretary, and he quickly drew a link between the 9/11 attacks and Saddam Hussein— first privately, as Richard A. Clarke, the president's former top counterterrorism adviser, testified, then publicly.

There are several reasons that this link might have been stressed by Bush—a sincere belief that it really existed, a desire to finish the family's unfinished Iraq business, or the fact that Iraq was a much less shadowy enemy than Al Qaeda and therefore provided a ready outlet for America's post-9/11 need for revenge. President Bush justified the war on Iraq in terms of Saddam Hussein's possession of weapons of mass destruction, and said that the United States was obliged to take preemptive action to terminate such a threat. Speaking to the nation on October 8, 2002, he had said: "America must not ignore the threat gathering against us. Facing clear evidence of peril, we cannot wait for the final proof—the smoking gun—that could come in the form of a mushroom cloud."[14]

One of the arguments deployed by the Bush team was an analogy

between the Iraq situation and the Franco-British attempt to negotiate peace with Adolf Hitler at Munich in 1938. Defense Secretary
Donald Rumsfeld was one of those making this connection. The
charge that those favoring a continued reliance on the United Nations
and its weapons inspectors (who had left Iraq in 1998 after complain-
ing of obstructionist tactics by the government of Saddam Hussein)
were practicing "appeasement" was part of the story line the administration put forth in order to win support for its more aggressive course.

To defeat Bush, the Democrats in 2004 would have to succeed in
determining which stories would dominate the discussion. Would the
dangers of another Munich or those of a second Vietnam loom larger?
Would the "message discipline" of the White House withstand the as-
saults of the Democrats and the enterprise of the press? The success
Bush had in shifting the focus away from Osama bin Laden toward
Iraq was remarkable, and the perils of questioning this became clear in
December 2003 when Democratic challenger Howard Dean said that
"the capture of Saddam has not made America safer" and was blasted
by critics in both parties, including his rivals for the nomination.

It is unfortunate, for both the Democrats and the nation, that the
only way of really proving the truth of Dean's statement would be for
the United States to be hit by another major terrorist attack. The fact
that the war in Iraq drained intelligence efforts away from the fight
against Al Qaeda was mentioned by some of Bush's opponents and
chronicled in a *New Yorker* story by the investigative reporter Seymour Hersh. But the issue did not take off until a suitably strong
story caught the imagination of reporters and the public. Richard A.
Clarke's *Against All Enemies* told of an administration insufficiently
alert to the danger of terrorist attacks on American soil and obsessed
with the goal of toppling Saddam Hussein. The result of these stories
was that the president had to contend with the suspicion that greater
vigilance by his administration might have detected the 9/11 plot in
time to prevent it.[15]

President Bush had significant advantages to prevent the issue from doing serious harm to his reelection effort. First there was his administration's proven ability to manage its public image effectively. Then there were the powers of incumbency and the national tendency to line up behind a president in time of war. And beyond all these there was the long-standing story of the Democratic party as militarily weak and lacking in geopolitical resolve. In revisionist accounts of the Vietnam conflict, it is liberal Democrats who are blamed (along with student protesters) for sapping the nation's will to fight and delivering South Vietnam to the Communists. Other stories and images—Jimmy Carter's response to the Iranian hostage crisis, symbolized by the ruined American aircraft at "Desert One" in the Iranian desert, and the photo of Michael Dukakis looking foolish in the turret of a tank—have helped secure for the Democrats a reputation for ineptitude and lack of spine in international affairs. A leading counterstory—that the Bush administration has jettisoned two generations' worth of multilateral cooperation, particularly with America's NATO allies—will be tested in the 2004 race.

The debate would not be confined to foreign affairs. In domestic policy, too, stories would collide in the 2004 campaign. Here, again, long-present story lines demarcated the field of battle. The tax cuts the Bush administration championed would be much discussed, as would the resulting budget deficits. The lines of this debate are old and familiar, and with the exception of Bill Clinton, no Democratic candidate in the past quarter century has managed to control the terms of this discussion. He won election at a time when what he called the "Reagan-Bush recession" was still being felt in the country, and in a race in which the third-party candidate, Ross Perot, was making budget deficits a central part of the debate. That made Clinton's story easier to sell, and his campaign never lost its focus on "the economy, stupid."

Beyond the issues, the Democratic candidates labored to construct appealing life stories. Their campaign books hit the shelves, with var-

THE POWER AND THE STORY

ied approaches. There were casual ones, like *An Amazing Adventure* by Joe and Hadassah Lieberman, or *Al on America* by Al Sharpton; there were dutiful ones, like John Kerry's *A Call to Service* and Dennis Kucinich's *A Prayer for America;* and there were upbeat, hortatory ones, like Howard Dean's *Winning Back America* and Wesley Clark's *Winning Modern Wars.* Humble origins were played up (by John Edwards and Dick Gephardt) and privileged ones played down (by John Kerry and Howard Dean). The candidate's spouse was made central to his life story by the candidate, in the case of Joe Lieberman, and by the candidate's opponents, as in the story of John Kerry and his wealthy wife, Teresa Heinz Kerry. And, in a true rarity, one candidate's wife remained apart from the race, as Howard Dean's wife, Dr. Judith Steinberg Dean, stayed in Vermont to look after their children and attend to her medical practice.

The power of stories was amply demonstrated in the early months of the Democratic primary struggle. John Kerry, whose campaign had been stalled through much of the second half of 2003, finally began to make progress when he relied more heavily on the story of his Vietnam service and built emotional tributes to his fellow veterans into his public appearances. Kerry's narrative was strong enough to prevail in the Democratic primaries. And Howard Dean learned the perils of becoming too fully the character he was portraying. The self-proclaimed tribune of the "Democratic wing of the Democratic party" rose swiftly during the fall of 2003 by proving himself the most effective avatar of the party's anger against George W. Bush; he fell after that story line lapsed into farce with his "I have a scream" speech following his poor showing in the Iowa caucuses.

How these candidates' stories worked on their own and in conjunction with the major issues of the year would determine both the outcome of the race for the Democratic nomination and November's election.

Some of the old stories about George W. Bush were likely to prove ineffective after a term in office—it is hard to label a man stupid whose performance in office was, at one point, approved by 90 percent of the American people. And the story of his age-forty reformation continued to offer some protection against damage from the discovery of any further youthful indiscretions. His privileged upbringing, though, could prove harmful if carefully linked to aspects of his economic policy, although not if the attack could be portrayed as demagogic. And unforeseen events could scramble careful plans and raise new stories to the forefront.

WHATEVER THE SPECIFICS of the stories that emerge, the 2004 race, like all the presidential elections that have come before it, would be defined by the power of stories. This power, like any other, can be used for good purposes or bad ones, responsibly or irresponsibly, honestly or corruptly. Stories have power in politics because they have power everywhere in our lives, and it is no good wishing that weren't so. Indeed, without stories we would be unable to find order in the world around us, or to remember what that order consists of. Stories simplify, even oversimplify, but without that winnowing out of excessive detail we would never be able to boil issues down to their essences or to make decisions. Stories will remain fundamental to the way American politics is conducted and will become only more important in the coming decades, as the means of disseminating stories become ever more widespread and sophisticated.

The point is not to bewail this, but to understand it. Citizens will be less easily misled by stories if they are aware of the way stories are marshaled to serve political ends. Such awareness will lead to questions about how true the stories are, and how relevant the issues embedded in the stories are to the fundamental problems the nation faces. And perhaps this awareness will make us all more alert to our hunger for heroes and more skeptical of our need to sort public figures into winners and losers, good guys and villains.

Yet we must also recognize that the power of stories is an important part of the nation's strength. A successful presidential narrative creates a bond between the president and the nation, just as the stories of American history create a bond between citizens from many different backgrounds and the nation. These bonds help to hold the nation together, to strengthen it and give it a sense of common purpose. The future of the nation, and the world, depends upon the abilities of American citizens to choose the right stories.

ACKNOWLEDGMENTS

FROM THE FIRST GLIMMER OF THE IDEA FOR THIS BOOK THROUGH ITS completion I have been aided, prodded, encouraged, and guided by Ann Godoff, my editor and publisher. She has helped me immeasurably with detailed editorial suggestions and wise, sometimes stern, advice.

Melanie Jackson, my agent, has also been with me for each stage of the process, providing a welcome sounding board. I am grateful for her keen judgment and her sympathetic ear.

Editorial help of various kinds has been provided by friends old and new. Anne Hemmett Stern provided editorial support early on, helping me think through approaches and assisting in laying out the structure. Richard Blow read the completed manuscript and helped me say what I wanted to say more clearly and directly. Hope Glassberg fact-checked the manuscript against a tight deadline, catching errors and providing a comforting safety net. Other research help was provided by Ariel Hart and James Laughlin. Editorial suggestions, ideas, and encouragement were offered by John Bennet, Diane McWhorter, Sarah Rose, and Ron Taffel. At the Penguin Press, Meredith Blum,

Bruce Giffords, Trent Duffy, Darren Haggar, and Stephanie Hunt-work all contributed to making this book better.

My wife, Lauren McCollester, read numerous versions and provided invaluable help in getting my arguments focused and my direction clear. Now she will get to learn what our lives will be like without "the book" devouring every weekend moment.

NOTES

INTRODUCTION
1. *New York Times,* October 25, 1952.

CHAPTER I. AMERICAN HEROES, AMERICAN MYTHS
1. Robert J. Donovan, *PT-109: John F. Kennedy in World War II* (New York: McGraw-Hill, 1961), 163–65.
2. Ibid., 144–62.
3. Ibid., 203.
4. John Hersey, "A Reporter at Large: Survival," *The New Yorker,* June 17, 1944.
5. Fred Anderson, *Crucible of War: The Seven Years' War and the Fate of Empire in British North America, 1754–1766* (New York: Alfred A. Knopf, 2000), 55–59.
6. Ibid., 59.
7. Francis Parkman, *France and England in North America* (New York: Library of America, 1983), 2:954.
8. John William Ward, *Andrew Jackson: Symbol for an Age* (New York: Oxford University Press, 1955), 4–10; Robert Remini, *Andrew Jackson and the Course of American Empire, 1767–1821* (New York: Harper & Row, 1977), 276–90.
9. Remini, *Andrew Jackson and the Course of American Empire,* 290–97.
10. Ward, *Andrew Jackson,* 14.
11. Pauline Maier, *American Scripture: Making the Declaration of Independence* (New York: Alfred A. Knopf, 1997), 98.
12. Abraham Lincoln, *Speeches and Writings, 1832–1858* (New York: Library of America, 1989), 426.

13. William H. Herndon and Jesse W. Weik, *Abraham Lincoln: The True Story of a Great Life* (New York: D. Appleton, 1901), 2:69.

14. Allan Nevins, *The Emergence of Lincoln* (New York: Charles Scribner's Sons, 1950), 1:381. Hitt was Robert R. Hitt, later a member of Congress.

15. Herbert Mitgang, *Abraham Lincoln: A Press Portrait* (Chicago: Quadrangle Books, 1971), 118–21.

CHAPTER 2. FAMILIES MATTER

1. Mason L. Weems, *The Life of Washington* (repr., Cambridge, Mass.: Harvard University Press, Belknap Press, 1962), 12, 9, xxxiii.

2. Ibid., 12.

3. Robert Remini, *Daniel Webster: The Man and His Time* (New York: W. W. Norton, 1997), 36; Brooks D. Simpson, *Ulysses S. Grant: Triumph over Adversity, 1822–1865* (Boston: Houghton Mifflin, 2000), 3.

4. William M. Thayer, *The Pioneer Boy and How He Became President* (Boston: Walker, Wise, 1863), 176–84; Merrill D. Peterson, *Lincoln in American Memory* (New York: Oxford University Press, 1994), 33.

5. *New York Times,* June 9, 1860, June 12, 1860.

6. Benjamin Franklin, *Autobiography* (New York: Library of America, 1990), 15–16.

7. John Reid and John Henry Eaton, *The Life of Andrew Jackson* (repr., Tuscaloosa, Ala.: University of Alabama Press, 1974), 12.

8. Alexis de Tocqueville, *Democracy in America,* trans. George Lawrence, ed. J. P. Mayer (Garden City, N.Y.: Doubleday, 1969), 179.

9. Carl Sandburg, *Abraham Lincoln: The Prairie Years* (New York: Harcourt, Brace, 1929), 9–10.

10. Edmund Morris, *The Rise of Theodore Roosevelt* (New York: Coward, McCann & Geoghegan, 1979), 34, 60.

11. See James MacGregor Burns, *Roosevelt: The Lion and the Fox* (New York: Harcourt Brace Jovanovich, 1956), 6.

12. For an excellent discussion of the film, see Thomas Rosteck, "The Intertextuality of *The Man from Hope,*" in Stephen A. Smith, ed., *Bill Clinton on Stump, State, and Stage: The Rhetorical Road to the White House* (Fayetteville, Ark.: University of Arkansas Press, 1994), quote on 223.

13. Ibid., 232, 224.

14. *St. Louis Post-Dispatch,* July 12, 1992; *Boston Globe,* July 17, 1992.

15. Arthur M. Schlesinger Jr., ed., *History of American Presidential Elections* (New York: Chelsea House, 1971), 1:450.

16. Hillary Rodham Clinton, *Living History* (New York: Simon & Schuster, 2003), 52; Rosteck, "The Intertextuality of *The Man from Hope,*" 233.

17. Evan Cornog and Richard Whelan, *Hats in the Ring: An Illustrated History of American Presidential Campaigns* (New York: Random House, 2000), 260.

CHAPTER 3. FINDING A STORY, CHOOSING A CHARACTER

1. *New York Times,* August 9, 1896.

2. Edmund Morris, *The Rise of Theodore Roosevelt* (New York: Coward, McCann & Geoghegan, 1979), 613; Theodore Roosevelt, *The Autobiography of Theodore Roosevelt,* ed. Wayne Andrews (New York: Octagon Books, 1975), 125.

3. *New York Times,* September 20, September 21, 1992.

4. Ulysses S. Grant, *Personal Memoirs of U. S. Grant* (New York: Library of America, 1990), 141–42.

5. *New York Times,* July 25, 1948.

6. Keynes quoted in Richard Hofstadter, *The American Political Tradition* (New York: Alfred A. Knopf, 1948), 389.

7. Jimmy Carter, *Why Not the Best?* (Nashville, Tenn.: Broadman Press, 1975), 9–10.

8. *Lexington* (Ky.) *Gazette,* May 15, 1810, quoted in *Dictionary of American Biography,* "Henry Clay."

9. John Quincy Adams, *The Diary of John Quincy Adams,* ed. Allan Nevins (New York: Charles Scribner's Sons, 1951), 239.

10. The anecdote forms the opening scene of the first volume of Robert Caro's biography of Johnson, *The Years of Lyndon Johnson: The Path to Power* (New York: Alfred A. Knopf, 1982), xii–xvi.

11. James Moore and Wayne Slater, *Bush's Brain: How Karl Rove Made George W. Bush Presidential* (New York: John Wiley & Sons, 2003), 8.

12. George Bush with Victor Gold, *Looking Forward* (New York: Doubleday, 1987), 207; *New York Times,* April 27, 1980.

13. William Allen White, *A Puritan in Babylon: The Story of Calvin Coolidge* (New York: Macmillan, 1938), 166; H. R. Haldeman, *Haldeman Diaries: Inside the Nixon White House* (New York: Putnam, 1994), 138.

CHAPTER 4. FASHIONING THE STORY

1. Nathaniel Hawthorne, *The Life of Franklin Pierce,* in Thomas Woodson, Claude M. Simpson, and L. Neal Smith, eds., *The Centenary Edition of the Works of Nathaniel Hawthorne* (Columbus, Ohio: Ohio State University Press, 1994), 23:274.

2. Ibid., 275, 279, 337, 340.

3. Ibid., 290, 364.

4. Evan Cornog and Richard Whelan, *Hats in the Ring: An Illustrated History of American Presidential Campaigns* (New York: Random House, 2000), 70.

5. William Dean Howells, *Sketch of the Life and Character of Rutherford B. Hayes* (New York: Hurd & Houghton, 1876), 4–5, 35, 38–43, 97.

6. Norman Hapgood and Henry Moskowitz, *Up from the City Streets: A Life of Alfred E. Smith* (New York: Grosset & Dunlap, 1927), 3, 12, 9, 339.

7. Frederick Palmer, *This Man Landon* (New York: Dodd, Mead, 1936), 3, 223.

8. Thomas E. Dewey, *The Case Against the New Deal* (New York: Harper & Brothers, 1940), 157–58.

9. Richard M. Nixon, *Six Crises* (Garden City, N.Y.: Doubleday, 1962), xi–xii.

10. Ibid., 295.

11. Ibid., 296, 299.

12. Arthur M. Schlesinger Jr., ed., *History of American Presidential Elections* (New York: Chelsea House, 1971), 1:138.

13. Ibid., 151.

14. Ibid., 451.

15. J. G. Randall and David Herbert Donald, *The Civil War and Reconstruction,* 2nd ed. (Lexington, Mass.: D. C. Heath, 1969), 48.

16. James M. McPherson, *Battle Cry of Freedom* (New York: Oxford University Press, 1988), 90.

17. Ibid., 196.

18. *New York Times,* December 26, 1999.

19. Kempton quoted in David Oshinsky, *A Conspiracy So Immense: The World of Joe Mc-Carthy* (New York: Free Press, 1983), 235–36.

CHAPTER 5. WHEN STORIES COLLIDE: CAMPAIGNING FOR PRESIDENT

1. Lou Cannon, *President Reagan: The Role of a Lifetime* (New York: Simon & Schuster, 1991), 68; Arthur M. Schlesinger Jr., ed., *History of American Presidential Elections, Supplemental Volume, 1972–1984* (New York: Chelsea House, 1986), 208–9.

2. Arthur M. Schlesinger Jr., ed., *History of American Presidential Elections* (New York: Chelsea House, 1971), 2:1397–98; http://www.infidels.org/library/historical/robert_ingersoll/nomination_of_blaine.html; *New York Times,* July 22, 1899.

3. Evan Cornog and Richard Whelan, *Hats in the Ring: An Illustrated History of American Presidential Campaigns* (New York: Random House, 2000), 158.

4. Schlesinger, *Presidential Elections,* Supplemental Volume, 1972–1984, 294–95.

5. Ibid., 295.

6. Jonathan Schell, *The Time of Illusion* (New York: Alfred A. Knopf, 1976), 219–20.

7. H. Wayne Morgan, *From Hayes to McKinley: National Party Politics, 1877–1896* (Syracuse, N.Y.: Syracuse University Press, 1969), 118–19; Schlesinger, *Presidential Elections,* 2:1513.

8. Alan Schroeder, *Presidential Debates: Forty Years of High-Risk TV* (New York: Columbia University Press, 2000), 190–93; Schlesinger, *Presidential Elections,* Supplemental Volume, 1972–1984, 102.

9. Schlesinger, *Presidential Elections,* Supplemental Volume, 1972–1984, 304.

10. Cornog and Whelan, *Hats in the Ring,* 299.

11. Peter Goldman et al., *Quest for the Presidency: 1992* (College Station, Tex.: Texas A&M University Press, 1994), 558.

12. Robert Dallek, "The Medical Ordeals of JFK," *The Atlantic Monthly,* December 2002, 49.

13. Greta R. Marlow, "Dodging Charges and Charges of Dodging: Bill Clinton's Defense on the Character Issue," in Stephen A. Smith, ed., *Bill Clinton on Stump, State, and*

Stage: The Rhetorical Road to the White House (Fayetteville, Ark.: University of Arkansas Press, 1994), 152–54.

14. Merle Miller, *Plain Speaking: An Oral Biography of Harry S. Truman* (New York: Berkley, 1973), 340; Kay Summersby, *Past Forgetting: My Love Affair with Dwight D. Eisenhower* (New York: Simon & Schuster, 1976); *New York Times*, January 21, 1975.

15. Stephen E. Ambrose, *Nixon: The Education of a Politician, 1913–1962* (New York: Simon & Schuster, 1987), 276–89; Kathleen Hall Jamieson, *Packaging the Presidency: A History and Criticism of Presidential Campaign Advertising*, 2nd ed. (New York: Oxford University Press, 1992), 71–75.

16. Ambrose, *Nixon*, 289.

17. Cannon, *President Reagan*, 544–50.

18. http://usinfo.state.gov/usa/infousa/facts/democrac/73.htm.

19. Cornog and Whelan, *Hats in the Ring*, 296–300; Jamieson, *Packaging the Presidency*, 476.

CHAPTER 6. A BRAND-NEW STORY: ELECTION AND INAUGURATION

1. Harry S. Truman, *Memoirs by Harry S. Truman: Years of Trial and Hope, 1946–1952* (Garden City, N.Y.: Doubleday, 1955), 220–22.

2. Stephen E. Ambrose, *Eisenhower: The President* (New York: Simon & Schuster, 1984), 370; *New York Times*, December 14, 2000.

3. Francis Russell, *The Shadow of Blooming Grove: Warren G. Harding and His Times* (New York: McGraw-Hill, 1968), 421.

4. James Thomas Flexner, *George Washington and the New Nation, 1783–1793* (New York: Little, Brown, 1970), 174–81.

5. Hillary Rodham Clinton, *Living History* (New York: Simon & Schuster, 2003), 121.

6. George Templeton Strong, *The Diary of George Templeton Strong*, ed. Allan Nevins and Milton Halsey Thomas (New York: Macmillan, 1952), 3:102.

7. http://www.yale.edu/lawweb/avalon/presiden/inaug/wash1.htm.

8. Ibid.

9. Thomas Jefferson, *Writings* (New York: Library of America, 1984), 493.

10. Abraham Lincoln, *Speeches and Writings, 1859–1865* (New York: Library of America, 1989), 221.

11. Ibid., 224.

12. http://www.yale.edu/lawweb/avalon/presiden/inaug/froos1.htm.

13. http://www.yale.edu/lawweb/avalon/presiden/inaug/hoover.htm.

14. http://www.yale.edu/lawweb/avalon/presiden/inaug/kennedy.htm.

15. Ibid.

16. Arthur M. Schlesinger Jr., ed., *History of American Presidential Elections*, Supplemental Volume, 1972–1984 (New York: Chelsea House, 1986), 110; http://www.yale.edu/lawweb/avalon/presiden/inaug/carter.htm.

17. Thomas Hobbes, *Leviathan*, Part 1, Chapter 4.

18. Edmund Morris, *Dutch: A Memoir of Ronald Reagan* (New York: Random House,

1999), 451; Lou Cannon, *President Reagan: The Role of a Lifetime* (New York: Simon & Schuster, 1991), 497.

19. *New York Times,* September 9, 1974.
20. Harry S. Truman, *Memoirs by Harry S. Truman: Year of Decisions* (Garden City, N.Y.: Doubleday, 1955), 19; Robert J. Donovan, *Conflict and Crisis: The Presidency of Harry S. Truman, 1945–1948* (New York: W. W. Norton, 1977), 20.
21. *New York Times,* December 13, 1952.
22. Ibid., December 15, 1952.

CHAPTER 7. THE WHITE HOUSE AS MOVIE SET

1. Stanley Elkins and Eric McKitrick, *The Age of Federalism: The Early American Republic, 1788–1800* (New York: Oxford University Press, 1993), 48.
2. Henry Adams, *History of the United States of America During the Administrations of Thomas Jefferson* (New York: Library of America, 1986), 548.
3. Ibid., 550.
4. Ibid., 551–53.
5. A fine summary of the development of Washington reporting may be found in Donald Ritchie, *High-Placed Sources: A History of the Washington Press Corps* (New York: Oxford University Press, forthcoming).
6. Ibid.; Arthur M. Schlesinger Jr., *The Age of Roosevelt: The Crisis of the Old Order* (Boston: Houghton Mifflin, 1957), 259–65.
7. Phyllis Lee Levin, *Edith and Woodrow: The Wilson White House* (New York: Scribner, 2001), 165.
8. *The New Yorker,* June 3, 1933, 15.
9. Evan Cornog and Richard Whelan, *Hats in the Ring: An Illustrated History of American Presidential Campaigns* (New York: Random House, 2000), 217; Joseph P. Lash, *Eleanor and Franklin* (New York: W. W. Norton, 1971), 445–46.
10. Ickes quoted in Ted Morgan, *FDR: A Biography* (New York: Simon & Schuster, 1985), 450; Lash, *Eleanor and Franklin,* 446.
11. Lash, *Eleanor and Franklin,* 516.
12. Ibid., 525–27.
13. Robert J. Donovan, *Conflict and Crisis: The Presidency of Harry S Truman, 1945–1948* (New York: W. W. Norton, 1977), 147–48.
14. Stephen E. Ambrose, *Eisenhower: Soldier, General, President-Elect, 1890–1952* (New York: Simon & Schuster, 1983), 532.
15. Lou Cannon, *President Reagan: The Role of a Lifetime* (New York: Simon & Schuster, 1991), 585–87; Haynes Johnson, *Sleepwalking Through History: America in the Reagan Years* (New York: W. W. Norton, 1991), 453–54.
16. *New York Times,* May 18, 1992.
17. Peggy Noonan, *The Case Against Hillary Clinton* (New York: Regan Books, 2000), xix.
18. David McCullough, *John Adams* (New York: Simon & Schuster, 2001), 637.

19. *New York Times,* January 9, 1892; Henry F. Graff, *Grover Cleveland* (New York: Times Books, 2002), 99–100, 133.

CHAPTER 8. WINNERS AND LOSERS

1. Arthur M. Schlesinger Jr., *The Age of Jackson* (Boston: Little, Brown, 1946), 89–90.
2. Ibid., 92; Robert Remini, *Daniel Webster: The Man and His Time* (New York: W. W. Norton, 1997), 365–67.
3. Arthur M. Schlesinger Jr., *A Thousand Days: John F. Kennedy in the White House* (Boston: Houghton Mifflin, 1965), 1027.
4. Robert A. Caro, *The Years of Lyndon Johnson: Master of the Senate* (New York: Alfred A. Knopf, 2002), 111.
5. Mark White, *The Cuban Missile Crisis* (London: Macmillan, 1996), 139, 166–69, 176–77; *New York Times,* December 4, 1962; Arthur M. Schlesinger Jr., ed., *History of American Presidential Elections* (New York: Chelsea House, 1985), 8:3246.
6. Stephen E. Ambrose, *Nixon: The Education of a Politician, 1913–1962* (New York: Simon & Schuster, 1987), 671.
7. H. Wayne Morgan, *From Hayes to McKinley: National Party Politics, 1877–1896* (Syracuse, N.Y.: Syracuse University Press, 1969), 138–41; Henry F. Graff, *Grover Cleveland* (New York: Times Books, 2002), 115–16.
8. Jonathan Schell's *The Time of Illusion* (New York: Alfred A. Knopf, 1976) develops this aspect of Nixon's thought and character in fascinating and precise detail.

CHAPTER 9. GOOD AND EVIL

1. Stanley Elkins and Eric McKitrick, *The Age of Federalism: The Early American Republic, 1788–1800* (New York: Oxford University Press, 1993), 293–94; Michael Durey, *"With the Hammer of Truth": James Thomson Callender and America's Early National Heroes* (Charlottesville, Va.: University Press of Virginia, 1990), 97–102.
2. Durey, *Hammer of Truth,* 100–102.
3. Ibid., 157–60; Joseph J. Ellis, *American Sphinx: The Character of Thomas Jefferson* (New York: Alfred A. Knopf, 1997), 302–7.
4. Evan Cornog and Richard Whelan, *Hats in the Ring: An Illustrated History of American Presidential Campaigns* (New York: Random House, 2000), 58.
5. Marquis James, *The Life of Andrew Jackson* (New York: Bobbs-Merrill, 1938), 63–68.
6. Henry F. Graff, *Grover Cleveland* (New York: Times Books, 2002), 60–62; Cornog and Whelan, *Hats in the Ring,* 139–44.
7. H. Wayne Morgan, *From Hayes to McKinley: National Party Politics, 1877–1896* (Syracuse, N.Y.: Syracuse University Press, 1969), 215.
8. Francis Russell, *The Shadow of Blooming Grove: Warren G. Harding and His Times* (New York: McGraw-Hill, 1968), 168–71, 289–93, 319.
9. Peter Goldman, *Quest for the Presidency: 1992* (College Station, Tex.: Texas A&M University Press, 1994), 92–99, 126–46.

10. http://www.lib.ohio-state.edu/cgaweb/nast/bio.htm.
11. *New York Times,* April 21, 1962.
12. Lou Cannon, *President Reagan: The Role of a Lifetime* (New York: Simon & Schuster, 1991), 737–38.
13. Thomas Jefferson, *Writings* (New York: Library of America, 1984), 169–81.
14. Thomas Paine, *Common Sense* (repr., New York: Penguin Books, 1976), 83.
15. Marshall Smelser, *The Democratic Republic, 1801–1815* (New York: Harper & Row, 1968), 175; Washington Irving, *History, Tales, and Sketches* (New York: Library of America, 1983), 517.
16. One historian who has explored this aspect of Jefferson is Leonard Levy, in *Jefferson and Civil Liberties: The Darker Side* (Cambridge, Mass.: Harvard University Press, Belknap Press, 1963).
17. Samuel Flagg Bemis, *John Quincy Adams and the Foundations of American Foreign Policy* (New York: Alfred A. Knopf, 1956), 393.
18. Ibid., 389.
19. Ibid., 403.
20. Arthur M. Schlesinger Jr., ed., *History of American Presidential Elections* (New York: Chelsea House, 1971), 3:1947.

CHAPTER 10. EXITS

1. James M. McPherson, *Battle Cry of Freedom* (New York: Oxford University Press, 1988), 853; William Shakespeare, *Julius Caesar,* III, i.
2. William Shakespeare, *King Lear,* V, ii.
3. Herbert Mitgang, *Abraham Lincoln: A Press Portrait* (Chicago: Quadrangle Books, 1971), 463–64.
4. Kati Marton, *Hidden Power: Presidential Marriages That Shaped Our Recent History* (New York: Pantheon, 2001), 135.
5. *New York Times,* April 19, 1945; James MacGregor Burns, *Roosevelt: The Soldier of Freedom, 1940–1945* (New York: Harcourt Brace Jovanovich, 1970), 604.
6. Phyllis Lee Levin, *Edith and Woodrow: The Wilson White House* (New York: Scribner, 2001), 341–49.
7. Edmund Morris, *Dutch: A Memoir of Ronald Reagan* (New York: Random House, 1999), 620–22.
8. David McCullough, *John Adams* (New York: Simon & Schuster, 2001), 562–64.
9. John Quincy Adams, *The Diary of John Quincy Adams,* ed. Allan Nevins (New York: Charles Scribner's Sons, 1951), 390–91.
10. Robert Remini, *Daniel Webster: The Man and His Time* (New York: W. W. Norton, 1997), 304.
11. http://www.yale.edu/lawweb/avalon/washing.htm; Stanley Elkins and Eric McKitrick, *The Age of Federalism: The Early American Republic, 1788–1800* (New York: Oxford University Press, 1993), 492–97.
12. Elkins and McKitrick, *The Age of Federalism,* 492–97.

13. Ibid.
14. http://www.yale.edu/lawweb/avalon/presiden/speeches/eisenhower001.htm.
15. http://www.presidency.ucsb.edu/site/docs/sou.php.
16. http://www.presidency.ucsb.edu/site/docs/doc_sou.php?admin=36&doc=6.
17. http://www.presidency.ucsb.edu/site/docs/doc_sou.php?admin=38&doc=3.
18. http://www.presidency.ucsb.edu/site/docs/doc_sou.php?admin=39&doc=4.
19. http://www.ku.edu/carrie/docs/texts/nixon081974.html.
20. Dwight D. Eisenhower, *The White House Years: Waging Peace, 1956–1961* (New York: Doubleday, 1965), 617.
21. Harry S. Truman, *Memoirs by Harry S. Truman: Year of Decisions* (Garden City, N.Y.: Doubleday, 1955), x.
22. Morris, *Dutch,* 643.
23. Ibid., 649–52.
24. Ibid., 653.

CHAPTER II. MEMOIRS AND SECOND ACTS

1. Harry S. Truman, *Memoirs by Harry S. Truman: Year of Decisions* (Garden City, N.Y.: Doubleday, 1955), ix.
2. Dwight D. Eisenhower, *At Ease: Stories I Tell to Friends* (Garden City, N.Y.: Doubleday, 1967), 32.
3. Dwight D. Eisenhower, *The White House Years: Mandate for Change, 1953–1956* (Garden City, N.Y.: Doubleday, 1963), 5, 14.
4. Ibid., 19–20.
5. Lyndon B. Johnson, *The Vantage Point* (New York: Holt, Rinehart & Winston, 1971), 425.
6. Ibid., 426–28.
7. Ronald Reagan, *An American Life* (New York: Simon & Schuster, 1990), 205.
8. William Jennings Bryan and Mary Baird Bryan, *The Memoirs of William Jennings Bryan* (Philadelphia: John C. Winston, 1925), 97–99.
9. Ibid., 102–15.
10. Martin Van Buren, *The Autobiography of Martin Van Buren* (repr., New York: Chelsea House, 1983), 7.
11. John Quincy Adams, *The Diary of John Quincy Adams,* ed. Allan Nevins (New York: Charles Scribner's Sons, 1951), 409.
12. Truman, *Year of Decisions,* x; Johnson, *Vantage Point,* x.

CHAPTER 12. THE JUDGMENT OF HISTORY

1. Arthur M. Schlesinger Jr., ed., *History of American Presidential Elections* (New York: Chelsea House, 1971), 3:1919; David Haward Bain, *Sitting in Darkness: Americans in the Philippines* (Boston: Houghton Mifflin, 1984), 202, 384.
2. *New York Times,* April 29, 1980.

3. William Jennings Bryan and Mary Baird Bryan, *The Memoirs of William Jennings Bryan* (Philadelphia: John C. Winston, 1925), 529–56.
4. John Demos, *The Unredeemed Captive* (New York: Alfred A. Knopf, 1994), xi.
5. Francis Parkman, *Montcalm and Wolfe* (repr., New York: Atheneum, 1984), xxv.
6. Lilian Handlin, *George Bancroft: The Intellectual as Democrat* (New York: Harper & Row, 1984), 325.
7. Parkman, *Montcalm and Wolfe*, 547.
8. Henry Adams, *History of the United States of America During the Administrations of James Madison* (New York: Library of America, 1986), 1331, 1345.
9. Merrill D. Peterson, *The Jefferson Image in the American Mind* (New York: Oxford University Press, 1960), vii.
10. Thomas Jefferson, *Writings* (New York: Library of America, 1984), 702–3, 705.
11. Peterson, *Jefferson Image*, 3–5.
12. Ibid., 352–53, 358.
13. Ibid., 186; Joseph Ellis, *American Sphinx: The Character of Thomas Jefferson* (New York: Alfred A. Knopf, 1997), 304; Michael Durey, *"With the Hammer of Truth": James Thomson Callender and America's Early National Heroes* (Charlottesville, Va.: University Press of Virginia, 1990), 158, 160.
14. Ellis, *American Sphinx*, 305–6.
15. Annette Gordon-Reed, *Thomas Jefferson and Sally Hemings: An American Controversy* (Charlottesville, Va.: University Press of Virginia, 1997), ii.
16. *New York Times*, November 12, 1997.

CHAPTER 13. A STORY IN PROGRESS: GEORGE W. BUSH

1. A fuller discussion of the various strains of Texas politics can be found in Michael Lind, *Made in Texas: George W. Bush and the Southern Takeover of American Politics* (New York: Basic Books, 2003), 3–24.
2. Oriana Fallaci, *Interview with History* (Boston: Houghton Mifflin, 1976), 41; Dick Cheney, *Meet the Press,* interview with Tim Russert on NBC, March 16, 2003.
3. George W. Bush, *A Charge to Keep* (New York: William Morrow, 1999), 15–16.
4. Molly Ivins and Lou Dubose, *Shrub: The Short but Happy Political Life of George W. Bush* (New York: Random House, 2000), 15–17.
5. Bush, *A Charge to Keep*, 51; Ivins and Dubose, *Shrub*, 3–11.
6. Bush, *A Charge to Keep*, 59; Ivins and Dubose, *Shrub*, 19–33; Lind, *Made in Texas*, 105–7.
7. Bush, *A Charge to Keep*, 132–33.
8. Ibid., 136.
9. Ibid., 47; Dana Milbank, *Smashmouth: Two Years in the Gutter with Al Gore and George W. Bush—Notes from the 2000 Campaign Trail* (New York: Basic Books, 2001), 368.
10. David Frum, *The Right Man: The Surprise Presidency of George W. Bush* (New York: Random House, 2003), 105–6.

11. Bob Woodward, *Bush at War* (New York: Simon & Schuster, 2002), 15–17.
12. Ibid., 37–41; Frum, *Right Man,* 142; http://www.cnn.com/2001/US/09/20/gen. bush.transcript.
13. Woodward, *Bush at War,* 99.
14. http://www.cnn.com/2002/ALLPOLITICS/10/07/bush.transcript/.
15. Seymour M. Hersh, "Annals of National Security: The Stovepipe," *The New Yorker,* October 27, 2003, 80; Richard A. Clark, *Against All Enemies; Inside America's War on Terror* (New York; Free Press, 2004), 32.

INDEX

Johnson, Lyndon B. (*cont.*)
   in 1968 New Hampshire primary, 94, 95
   as permanent candidate, 62
   as politician, 60
   Vietnam War and, 176–77
   withdrawal of, 92, 212, 222–23
   World War III's start feared by, 216
Joint Chiefs of Staff, U.S., 134
Jones, Paula, 186
Jordan, Hamilton, 95–96
Journal of Major George Washington, The
   (Washington), 14
Jumonville, Joseph Coulon de Villiers de, 15–16
Jumonville, Louis Coulon de Villiers de, 16

Kaltenborn, H. V., 119
Kelley, Virginia, 157
Kempton, Murray, 89
Kennedy, Jacqueline, 45, 156, 160, 206
Kennedy, John, Jr., 158
Kennedy, John F., 12, 17, 19, 27, 61, 77–78,
   113, 157, 172, 216
   affairs of, 107, 185–86
   assassination of, 123, 141, 164, 166, 205–6
   Bay of Pigs disaster and, 136, 168
   Camelot and, 141, 158, 206
   as Catholic, 38, 63
   civil rights issues and, 164–65, 247, 254
   Cuban Missile Crisis and, 166–68
   health problems kept secret by, 105–6, 108,
      174
   inaugural address of, 130–31
   marriage of, 45
   as martyr, 236
   Nixon's 1960 debates with, 103
   political career of, 49
   posthumous reputation of, 247
   privileged background of, 10–11, 63
   Pulitzer Prize awarded to, 78
   Vietnam War and, 167
   as war hero, 9–11, 20, 25–26, 131
Kennedy, Joseph P., 10–11
Kennedy, Robert F., 157, 167
Kennedy family, 43, 46, 131, 157
Kerry, John, 272
Kerry, Teresa Heinz, 272
Keynes, John Maynard, 56–57
Khrushchev, Nikita S., 167–68
King, Martin Luther, Jr., 236

King, Rufus, 143
King Lear (Shakespeare), 3, 174, 203
Kissinger, Henry A., 102, 255
Kline, Kevin, 159
Korea, People's Democratic Republic of
   (North Korea), 267
Korean War, 1, 89, 134, 140
Kroft, Steve, 106, 187
Kucinich, Dennis, 272
Kuwait, 168

Lafayette, Marquis de, 157, 196
Lambrecht, Bill, 39
Lance, Bert, 189
Landon, Alfred M., 76–77, 172
Latin America, 196
Lawn, Victor H., 207
League of Nations, 200
leaks, to media, 94
Levy, Chandra, 264
Lewinsky, Monica, 5, 186, 189, 248
Lexington Gazette, 59
liberalism, U.S. move to conservatism from,
   68
Liberal Republican movement, 71–72
liberals, 151
   first election contest of conservatives and, 83
Lieberman, Hadassah, 272
Lieberman, Joseph, 38, 272
lies, stories and, 2, 4
Life of Franklin Pierce, The (Hawthorne), 73–74
Life of Martin Van Buren, The (Crockett or
   Clayton), 75
Lincoln, Abraham, 12, 25, 27, 34, 45, 48, 71,
   76, 113, 120, 127, 129, 130, 165, 207
   assassination of, 141, 162, 203, 205–6
   background stories of, 31–33, 35, 36
   as Christ figure, 236
   contrasting roles of, 112
   Douglas's debates with, 22–24
   first inaugural address of, 127–28, 129, 131
   Gettysburg Address of, 79, 220
   impoverished background of, 5
   Stowe's meeting with, 86
   as war president, 162
   Washington journey of, 123
Lincoln, Mary Todd, 45, 149
Lincoln Memorial, 152, 206
literacy campaign, of Laura Bush, 153

ABOUT THE AUTHOR

EVAN CORNOG is the associate dean for planning and policy at Columbia Graduate School of Journalism and publisher of the *Columbia Journalism Review*. He was educated at Harvard and Columbia and has taught American history at Columbia, CUNY, and Lafayette College. He also worked as press secretary for former mayor Edward I. Koch of New York City. Cornog is the author of *The Birth of Empire: DeWitt Clinton and the American Experience, 1769–1828* and coauthor of *Hats in the Ring: An Illustrated History of American Presidential Campaigns*. He lives in New York City.